## OTHER BOOI

*How Highly Effective People Speak*

*Eloquence*

*How Legendary Leaders Speak*

*Influential Leadership*

*Public Speaking Mastery*

*The 7 Keys to Confidence*

*Trust is Power*

*Influence*

*Decoding Human Nature*

*The Psychology of Persuasion*

*How Visionaries Speak*

*The Eloquent Leader*

*The Language of Leadership*

*The Psychology of Communication*

*The Charisma Code*

Available on Amazon

Claim These Free Resources that Will Help You Unleash the Power of Your Words and Speak with Confidence. Visit **www.speakforsuccesshub.com/toolkit** for Access.

### 18 Free PDF Resources

### 30 Free Video Lessons

### 2 Free Workbooks

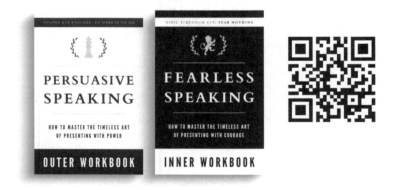

## Claim These Free Resources that Will Help You Unleash the Power of Your Words and Speak with Confidence. Visit www.speakforsuccesshub.com/toolkit for Access.

### 18 Free PDF Resources

*12 Iron Rules for Captivating Story, 21 Speeches that Changed the World, 341-Point Influence Checklist, 143 Persuasive Cognitive Biases, 17 Ways to Think On Your Feet, 18 Lies About Speaking Well, 137 Deadly Logical Fallacies, 12 Iron Rules For Captivating Slides, 371 Words that Persuade, 63 Truths of Speaking Well, 27 Laws of Empathy, 21 Secrets of Legendary Speeches, 19 Scripts that Persuade, 12 Iron Rules For Captivating Speech, 33 Laws of Charisma, 11 Influence Formulas, 219-Point Speech-Writing Checklist, 21 Eloquence Formulas*

### 30 Free Video Lessons

We'll send you one free video lesson every day for 30 days, written and recorded by Peter D. Andrei. Days 1-10 cover authenticity, the prerequisite to confidence and persuasive power. Days 11-20 cover building self-belief and defeating communication anxiety. Days 21-30 cover how to speak with impact and influence, ensuring your words change minds instead of falling flat. Authenticity, self-belief, and impact – this course helps you master three components of confidence, turning even the most high-stakes presentations from obstacles into opportunities.

### 2 Free Workbooks

We'll send you two free workbooks, including long-lost excerpts by Dale Carnegie, the mega-bestselling author of *How to Win Friends and Influence People* (5,000,000 copies sold). *Fearless Speaking* guides you in the proven principles of mastering your inner game as a speaker. *Persuasive Speaking* guides you in the time-tested tactics of mastering your outer game by maximizing the power of your words. All of these resources complement the Speak for Success collection.

# HOW LEGENDARY
# LEADERS
# SPEAK

## 451 PROVEN COMMUNICATION SECRETS OF THE WORLD'S TOP LEADERS

_Peter Andrei_

# HOW LEGENDARY
# LEADERS
# SPEAK

## SPEAK FOR SUCCESS COLLECTION BOOK

# III

SPEAK
TRUTH
WELL
**PRESS**

A SUBSIDIARY OF SPEAK TRUTH WELL LLC
800 Boylston Street
Boston, MA 02199

**SPEAK
TRUTH
WELL LLC**

SPEAK FOR SUCCESS COLLECTION

Printed in the United States of America
40 39 38 37 36 35 34 33 32 31

While the author has made every effort to provide accurate internet addresses at the time of publication, neither the publisher nor the author assumes any responsibility for errors, or for changes that occur after publication. Further, the publisher does not have any control over and does not assume any responsibility for author or third-party websites or their content.

www.speakforsuccesshub.com/toolkit

# FREE RESOURCES FOR OUR READERS

We believe in using the power of the internet to go above and beyond for our readers. That's why we created the free communication toolkit: 18 free PDF resources, 30 free video lessons, and even 2 free workbooks, including long-lost excerpts by Dale Carnegie, the mega-bestselling author of *How to Win Friends and Influence People*. (The workbooks help you put the most powerful strategies into action).

**We know you're busy. That's why we designed these resources to be accessible, easy, and quick. Each PDF resource takes just 5 minutes to read or use. Each video lesson is only 5 minutes long. And in the workbooks, we bolded the key ideas throughout, so skimming them takes only 10 minutes each.**

Why give so much away? For three reasons: we're grateful for you, it's useful content, and we want to go above and beyond. Questions? Feel free to email Peter directly at pandreibusiness@gmail.com.

www.speakforsuccesshub.com/toolkit

# WHY DOES THIS HELP YOU?

### I

The PDF resources cover topics like storytelling, logic, cognitive biases, empathy, charisma, and more. You can dig deeper into the specific topics that interest you most.

### II

Many of the PDF resources are checklists, scripts, example-compilations, and formula-books. With these practical, step-by-step tools, you can quickly create messages that work.

### III

With these free resources, you can supplement your reading of this book. You can find more specific guidance on the areas of communication you need to improve the most.

### IV

The two workbooks offer practical and actionable guidance for speaking with complete confidence (*Fearless Speaking*) and irresistible persuasive power (*Persuasive Speaking*).

### V

You can even learn from your phone with the free PDFs and the free video lessons, to develop your skills faster. The 30-lesson course reveals the secrets of building confidence.

### VI

You are reading this because you want to improve your communication. These resources take you to the next level, helping you learn how to speak with power, impact, and confidence. We hope these resources make a difference. They are available here:

## www.speakforsuccesshub.com/toolkit

From the desk of Peter Andrei
Speak Truth Well LLC
800 Boylston Street
Boston, MA 02199
pandreibusiness@gmail.com

May 15, 2021

## What is Our Mission?

To whom it may concern:

The Wall Street Journal reports that public speaking is the world's biggest fear – bigger than being hit by a car. According to Columbia University, this pervasive, powerful, common phobia can reduce someone's salary by 10% or more. It can reduce someone's chances of graduating college by 10% and cut their chances of attaining a managerial or leadership position at work by 15%.

If weak presentation kills your good ideas, it kills your career. If weak communication turns every negotiation, meeting, pitch, speech, presentation, discussion, and interview into an obstacle (instead of an opportunity), it slows your progress. And if weak communication slows your progress, it tears a gaping hole in your confidence – which halts your progress.

Words can change the world. They can improve your station in life, lifting you forward and upward to higher and higher successes. But they have to be strong words spoken well: rarities in a world where most people fail to connect, engage, and persuade; fail to answer the question "why should we care about this?"; fail to impact, inspire, and influence; and, in doing so, fail to be all they could be.

Now zoom out. Multiply this dynamic by one thousand; one million; one billion. The individual struggle morphs into a problem for our communities, our countries, our world. Imagine the many millions of paradigm-shattering, life-changing, life-saving ideas that never saw the light of day. Imagine how many brilliant convictions were sunk in the shipyard. Imagine all that could have been that failed to be.

Speak Truth Well LLC solves this problem by teaching ambitious professionals how to turn communication from an obstacle into an engine: a tool for converting "what could be" into "what is." There is no upper limit: inexperienced speakers can become self-assured and impactful; veteran speakers can master the skill by learning advanced strategies; masters can learn how to outperform their former selves.

We achieve our mission by producing the best publications, articles, books, video courses, and coaching programs available on public speaking and communication, and at non-prohibitive prices. This combination of quality and accessibility has allowed Speak Truth Well to serve over 70,000 customers in its year of launch alone (2021). Grateful as we are, we hope to one day serve millions.

Dedicated to your success,

Peter Andrei
President of Speak Truth Well LLC
pandreibusiness@gmail.com

# PROLOGUE:

*This three-part prologue reveals my story, my work, and the practical and ethical principles of communication. It is not a mere introduction. It will help you get more out of the book. It is a preface to the entire 15-book Speak for Success collection. It will show you how to use the information with ease, confidence, and fluency, and how to get better results faster. If you want to skip this, flip to page 42, or read only the parts of interest.*

## I

*page XIII*

**MY STORY AND THE STORY OF THIS COLLECTION**

*how I discovered the hidden key to successful communication, public speaking, influence, and persuasion*

## II

*page XXI*

**THE 15-BOOK SPEAK FOR SUCCESS COLLECTION**

*confidence, leadership, charisma, influence, public speaking, eloquence, human nature, credibility - it's all here*

## III

*page XXIV*

**THE PRACTICAL TACTICS AND ETHICAL PRINCIPLES**

*how to easily put complex strategies into action and how to use the power of words to improve the world*

# I

## MY STORY AND THE STORY OF THIS COLLECTION

*how I discovered the hidden key to successful communication, public speaking, influence, and persuasion (by reflecting on a painful failure)*

## HOW TO GAIN AN UNFAIR ADVANTAGE IN YOUR CAREER, BUSINESS, AND LIFE BY MASTERING THE POWER OF YOUR WORDS

I WAS SITTING IN MY OFFICE, TAPPING A PEN against my small wooden desk. My breaths were jagged, shallow, and rapid. My hands were shaking. I glanced at the clock: 11:31 PM. "I'm not ready." Have you ever had that thought?

I had to speak in front of 200 people the next morning. I had to convince them to put faith in my idea. But I was terrified, attacked by nameless, unreasoning, and unjustified terror which killed my ability to think straight, believe in myself, and get the job done.

Do you know the feeling?

After a sleepless night, the day came. I rose, wobbling on my tired legs. My head felt like it was filled with cotton candy. I couldn't direct my train of thoughts. A rushing waterfall of unhinged, self-destructive, and meaningless musings filled my head with an uncompromising cacophony of anxious, ricocheting nonsense.

"Call in sick."

"You're going to embarrass yourself."

"You're not ready."

I put on my favorite blue suit – my "lucky suit" – and my oversized blue-gold wristwatch; my "lucky" wristwatch.

"You're definitely not ready."

"That tie is ugly."

"You can't do this."

The rest went how you would expect. I drank coffee. Got in my car. Drove. Arrived. Waited. Waited. Waited. Spoke. Did poorly. Rushed back to my seat. Waited. Waited.

Waited. Got in my car. Drove. Arrived home. Sat back in my wooden seat where I accurately predicted "I'm not ready" the night before.

Relieved it was over but disappointed with my performance, I placed a sheet of paper on the desk. I wrote "MY PROBLEMS" at the top, and under that, my prompt for the evening: "What did I do so badly? Why did everything feel so off? Why did the speech fail?"

"You stood in front of 200 people and looked at... a piece of paper, not unlike this one. What the hell were you thinking? You're not fooling anyone by reading a sentence and then looking up at them as you say it out loud. They know you're reading a manuscript, and they know what that means. You are unsure of yourself. You are unsure of your message. You are unprepared. Next: Why did you speak in that odd, low, monotone voice? That sounded like nails on a chalkboard. And it was inauthentic. Next: Why did you open by talking about yourself? Also, you're not particularly funny. No more jokes. And what was the structure of the speech? It had no structure. That, I feel, is probably a pretty big problem."

I believed in my idea, and I wanted to get it across. Of course, I wanted the tangible markers of a successful speech. I wanted action. I wanted the speech to change something in the real world. But my motivations were deeper than that. I wanted to see people "click" and come on board my way of thinking. I wanted to captivate the audience. I wanted to speak with an engaging, impactful voice, drawing the audience in, not repelling them. I wanted them to remember my message and to remember me. I wanted to feel, for just a moment, the thrill of power. But not the petty, forceful power of tyrants and dictators; the justified power – the earned power – of having a good idea and conveying it well; the power of Martin Luther King and John F. Kennedy; a power harnessed in service of a valuable idea, not the personal privilege of the speaker. And I wanted confidence: the quiet strength that comes from knowing your words don't stand in your way, but propel you and the ideas you care about to glorious new mountaintops.

Instead, I stood before the audience, essentially powerless. I spoke for 20 painful minutes – painful for them and for me – and then sat down. I barely made a dent in anyone's consciousness. I generated no excitement. Self-doubt draped its cold embrace over me. Anxiety built a wall between "what I am" and "what I could be."

I had tried so many different solutions. I read countless books on effective communication, asked countless effective communicators for their advice, and consumed countless courses on powerful public speaking. Nothing worked. All the "solutions" that didn't really solve my problem had one thing in common: they treated communication as an abstract art form. They were filled with vague, abstract pieces of advice like "think positive thoughts" and "be yourself." They confused me more than anything else. Instead of illuminating the secrets I had been looking for, they shrouded the elusive but indispensable skill of powerful speaking in uncertainty.

I knew I had to master communication. I knew that the world's most successful people are all great communicators. I knew that effective communication is the bridge between "what I have" and "what I want," or at least an essential part of that bridge. I knew that without effective communication – without the ability to influence, inspire, captivate, and move – I would be all but powerless.

I knew that the person who can speak up but doesn't is no better off than the person who can't speak at all. I heard a wise man say "If you can think and speak and write, you are absolutely deadly. Nothing can get in your way." I heard another wise man say "Speech is power: speech is to persuade, to convert, to compel. It is to bring another out of his bad sense into your good sense." I heard a renowned psychologist say "If you look at people who are remarkably successful across life, there's various reasons. But one of them is that they're unbelievably good at articulating what they're aiming at and strategizing and negotiating and enticing people with a vision forward. Get your words together... that makes you unstoppable. If you are an effective writer and speaker and communicator, you have all the authority and competence that there is."

When I worked in the Massachusetts State House for the Department of Public Safety and Homeland Security, I had the opportunity to speak with countless senators, state representatives, CEOs, and other successful people. In our conversations, however brief, I always asked the same question: "What are the ingredients of your success? What got you where you are?" 100% of them said effective communication. There was not one who said anything else. No matter their field – whether they were entrepreneurs, FBI agents, political leaders, business leaders, or multimillionaire donors – they all pointed to one skill: the ability to convey powerful words in powerful ways. Zero exceptions.

Can you believe it? It still astonishes me.

My problem, and I bet this may be your obstacle as well, was that most of the advice I consumed on this critical skill barely scratched the surface. Sure, it didn't make matters worse, and it certainly offered some improvement, but only in inches when I needed progress in miles. If I stuck with the mainstream public speaking advice, I knew I wouldn't unleash the power of my words. And if I didn't do that, I knew I would always accomplish much less than I could. I knew I would suffocate my own potential. I knew I would feel a rush of crippling anxiety every time I was asked to give a presentation. I knew I would live a life of less fulfillment, less success, less achievement, more frustration, more difficulty, and more anxiety. I knew my words would never become all they could be, which means that I would never become all I could be.

To make matters worse, the mainstream advice – which is not wrong, but simply not deep enough – is everywhere. Almost every article, book, or course published on this subject falls into the mainstream category. And to make matters worse, it's almost impossible to know that until you've spent your hard-earned money and scarce time with the resource. And even then, you might just shrug, and assume that shallow, abstract advice is all there is to the "art" of public speaking. As far as I'm concerned, this is a travesty.

I kept writing. "It felt like there was no real motive; no real impulse to action. Why did they need to act? You didn't tell them. What would happen if they didn't? You didn't tell them that either. Also, you tried too hard to put on a formal façade; you spoke in strange, twisted ways. It didn't sound sophisticated. And your mental game was totally off. You let your mind fill with destructive, doubtful, self-defeating thoughts. And your preparation was totally backward. It did more to set bad habits in stone than it did to set you up for success. And you tried to build suspense at one point but revealed the final point way too early, ruining the effect."

I went on and on until I had a stack of papers filled with problems. "That's no good," I thought. I needed solutions. Everything else I tried failed. But I had one more idea: "I remember reading a great speech. What was it? Oh yeah, that's right: JFK's inaugural address. Let me go pull it up and see why it was so powerful." And that's when everything changed.

I grabbed another sheet of paper. I opened JFK's inaugural address on my laptop. I started reading. Observing. Analyzing. Reverse-engineering. I started writing down what I saw. Why did it work? Why was it powerful? I was like an archaeologist, digging through his speech for the secrets of powerful communication. I got more and more excited as I kept going. It was late at night, but the shocking and invaluable discoveries I was making gave me a burst of energy. It felt like JFK – one of the most powerful and effective speakers of all time – was coaching me in his rhetorical secrets, showing me how to influence an audience, draw them into my narrative, and find words that get results.

"Oh, so that's how you grab attention."

"Aha! So, if I tell them this, they will see why it matters."

"Fascinating – I can apply this same structure to my speech."

Around 3:00 in the morning, an epiphany hit me like a ton of bricks. That night, a new paradigm was born. A new opportunity emerged for all those who want to unleash the unstoppable power of their words. This new opportunity changed everything for me and eventually, tens of thousands of others. It is now my mission to bring it to millions, so that good people know what they need to know to use their words to achieve their dreams and improve the world.

Want to hear the epiphany?

**The mainstream approach:** Communication is an art form. It is unlike those dry, boring, "academic" subjects. There are no formulas. There are no patterns. It's all about thinking positive thoughts, faking confidence, and making eye contact. Some people are naturally gifted speakers. For others, the highest skill level they can attain is "not horrible."

**The consequences of the mainstream approach:** Advice that barely scratches the surface of the power of words. Advice that touches only the tip of the tip of the iceberg. A limited body of knowledge that blinds itself to thousands of hidden, little-known communication strategies that carry immense power; that blinds itself to 95% of what great communication really is. Self-limiting dogmas about who can do what, and how great communicators become great. Half the progress in twice the time, and everything that entails: missed opportunities, unnecessary and preventable frustration and anxiety, and confusion about what to say and how to say it. How do I know? Because I've been there. It's not pretty.

**My epiphany, the new Speak for Success paradigm:** Communication is as much a science as it is an art. You can study words that changed the world, uncover the hidden secrets of their power, and apply these proven principles to your own message. You can discover precisely what made great communicators great and adopt the same strategies. You can do this without being untrue to yourself or flatly imitating others. In fact, you can do this while being truer to yourself and more original than you ever have been before. Communication is not unpredictable, wishy-washy, or abstract. You can apply predictable processes and principles to reach your goals and get results. You can pick and choose from thousands of little-known speaking strategies, combining your favorite to create a unique communication approach that suits you perfectly. You can effortlessly use the same tactics of the world's most transformational leaders and speakers, and do so automatically, by default, without even thinking about it, as a matter of effortless habit. That's power.

The benefits of the Speak for Success paradigm: Less confusion. More confidence. Less frustration. More clarity. Less anxiety. More courage. You understand the whole iceberg of effective communication. As a result, your words captivate others. You draw them into a persuasive narrative, effortlessly linking your desires and their motives. You know exactly what to say. You know exactly how to say it. You know exactly how to keep your head clear; you are a master of the mental game. Your words can move mountains. Your words are the most powerful tools in your arsenal, and you use them to seize opportunities, move your mission forward, and make the world a better place. Simply put, you speak for success.

Fast forward a few years.

I was sitting in my office at my small wooden desk. My breaths were deep, slow, and steady. My entire being – mind, body, soul – was poised and focused. I set my speech manuscript to the side. I glanced at the clock: 12:01 AM. "Let's go. I'm ready."

I had to speak in front of 200 people the next morning. I had to convince them to put faith in my idea. And I was thrilled, filled with genuine gratitude at the opportunity to do what I love: get up in front of a crowd, think clearly, speak well, and get the job done.

I slept deeply. I dreamt vividly. I saw myself giving the speech. I saw myself victorious, in every sense of the word. I heard applause. I saw their facial expressions. I rose. My head was clear. My mental game was pristine. My mind was an ally, not an obstacle.

"This is going to be fun."

"I'll do my best, and whatever happens, happens."

"I'm so lucky that I get to do this again."

I put on my lucky outfit: the blue suit and the blue-gold watch.

"Remember the principles. They work."

"You developed a great plan last night. It's a winner."

"I can't wait."

The rest went how you would expect. I ate breakfast. Got in my car. Drove. Arrived. Waited. Waited. Waited. Spoke. Succeeded. Walked back to my seat. Waited. Waited. Waited. Got in my car. Drove. Arrived home. Sat back in my wooden seat where I accurately predicted "I'm ready" the night before.

I got my idea across perfectly. My message succeeded: it motivated action and created real-world change. I saw people "click" when I hit the rhetorical peak of my speech. I saw them leaning forward, totally hushed, completely absorbed. I applied the proven principles of engaging and impactful vocal modulation. I knew they would remember me and my message; I engineered my words to be memorable. I felt the thrilling power of giving a great speech. I felt the quiet confidence of knowing that my words carried weight; that they could win hearts, change minds, and help me reach the heights of my potential. I tore off the cold embrace of self-doubt. I defeated communication anxiety and broke down the wall between "what I am" and "what I could be."

Disappointed it was over but pleased with my performance, I placed a sheet of paper on the desk. I wrote "Speak Truth Well" and started planning what would become my business.

To date, we have helped tens of thousands of people gain an unfair advantage in their career, business, and life by unleashing the power of their words. And they experienced the exact same transformation I experienced when they applied the system.

If you tried to master communication before but haven't gotten the results you wanted, it's because of the mainstream approach; an approach that tells you "smiling at the audience" and "making eye contact" is all you need to know to speak well. That's not exactly a malicious lie – they don't know any better – but it is completely incorrect and severely harmful.

If you've been concerned that you won't be able to become a vastly more effective and confident communicator, I want to put those fears to rest. I felt the same way. The people I work with felt the same way. We just needed the right system. One public speaking book written by the director of a popular public speaking forum – I won't name names – wants you to believe that there are "nine public speaking secrets of the world's top minds." Wrong: There are many more than nine. If you feel that anyone who would boil down communication to just nine secrets is either missing something or holding it back, you're right. And the alternative is a much more comprehensive and powerful system. It's a system that gave me and everyone I worked with the transformation we were looking for.

Want to Talk? Email Me:

**PANDREIBUSINESS@GMAIL.COM**

This is My Personal Email.
I Read Every Message and
Respond in Under 12 Hours.

Visit Our Digital Headquarters:

**WWW.SPEAKFORSUCCESSHUB.COM**

See All Our Free Resources, Books, Courses, and Services.

# THE 15-BOOK SPEAK FOR SUCCESS COLLECTION

*confidence, leadership, charisma, influence, public speaking, eloquence, human nature, credibility – it's all here, in a unified collection*

.................................................A Brief Overview.................................................

- I wrote *How Highly Effective People Speak* to reveal the hidden patterns in the words of the world's most successful and powerful communicators, so that you can adopt the same tactics and speak with the same impact and influence.

- I wrote *Eloquence* to uncover the formulas of beautiful, moving, captivating, and powerful words, so that you can use these exact same step-by-step structures to quickly make your language electrifying, charismatic, and eloquent.

- I wrote *How Legendary Leaders Speak* to illuminate the little-known five-step communication process the top leaders of the past 500 years all used to spread their message, so that you can use it to empower your ideas and get results.

- I wrote *Influential Leadership* to expose the differences between force and power and to show how great leaders use the secrets of irresistible influence to develop gentle power, so that you can move forward and lead with ease.

- I wrote *Public Speaking Mastery* to shatter the myths and expose the harmful advice about public speaking, and to offer a proven, step-by-step framework for speaking well, so that you can always speak with certainty and confidence.

- I wrote *The 7 Keys to Confidence* to bring to light the ancient 4,000-year-old secrets I used to master the mental game and speak in front of hundreds without a second of self-doubt or anxiety, so that you can feel the same freedom.

- I wrote *Trust is Power* to divulge how popular leaders and career communicators earn our trust, speak with credibility, and use this to rise to new heights of power, so that you can do the same thing to advance your purpose and mission.

- I wrote *Decoding Human Nature* to answer the critical question "what do people want?" and reveal how to use this knowledge to develop unparalleled influence, so that people adopt your idea, agree with your position, and support you.

- I wrote *Influence* to unearth another little-known five-step process for winning hearts and changing minds, so that you can know with certainty that your message will persuade people, draw support, and motivate enthusiastic action.

- I wrote *The Psychology of Persuasion* to completely and fully unveil everything about the psychology behind "Yes, I love it! What's the next step?" so that you can use easy step-by-step speaking formulas that get people to say exactly that.

- I wrote *How Visionaries Speak* to debunk common lies about effective communication that hold you back and weaken your words, so that you can boldly share your ideas without accidentally sabotaging your own message.

- I wrote *The Eloquent Leader* to disclose the ten steps to communicating with power and persuasion, so that you don't miss any of the steps and fail to connect, captivate, influence, and inspire in a crucial high-stakes moment.

- I wrote *The Language of Leadership* to unpack the unique, hidden-in-plain-sight secrets of how presidents and world-leaders build movements with the laws of powerful language, so that you use them to propel yourself forward.

- I wrote *The Psychology of Communication* to break the news that most presentations succeed or fail in the first thirty seconds and to reveal proven, step-by-step formulas that grab, hold, and direct attention, so that yours succeeds.

- I wrote *The Charisma Code* to shatter the myths and lies about charisma and reveal its nature as a concrete skill you can master with proven strategies, so that people remember you, your message, and how you electrified the room.

# You Can Learn More Here:
# www.speakforsuccesshub.com/series

Ψ

HOW HIGHLY
EFFECTIVE PEOPLE
**SPEAK**

HOW HIGH PERFORMERS USE
PSYCHOLOGY TO INFLUENCE WITH EASE

**PETER D. ANDREI**

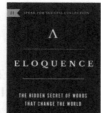

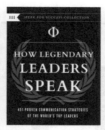

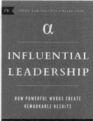

λ

PUBLIC
SPEAKING
MASTERY

HOW TO SPEAK WITH CONFIDENCE,
IMPACT, AND INFLUENCE

**PETER D. ANDREI**

Δ

INFLUENCE

THE PSYCHOLOGY OF WORDS THAT
WIN HEARTS AND CHANGE MINDS

**PETER D. ANDREI**

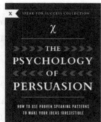

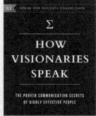

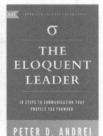

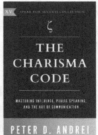

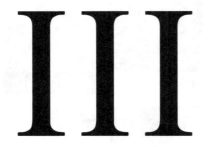

## PRACTICAL TACTICS AND ETHICAL PRINCIPLES

*how to easily put complex strategies into action and how to use the power of words to improve the world in an ethical and effective way*

## MOST COMMUNICATION BOOKS

HAVE YOU READ ANOTHER BOOK ON COMMUNICATION? If you have, let me remind you what you probably learned. And if you haven't, let me briefly spoil 95% of them. "Prepare. Smile. Dress to impress. Keep it simple. Overcome your fears. Speak from the heart. Be authentic. Show them why you care. Speak in terms of their interests. To defeat anxiety, know your stuff. Emotion persuades, not logic. Speak with confidence. Truth sells. And respect is returned."

There you have it. That is most of what you learn in most communication books. None of it is wrong. None of it is misleading. Those ideas are true and valuable. But they are not enough. They are only the absolute basics. And my job is to offer you much more.

Einstein said that "if you can't explain it in a sentence, you don't know it well enough." He also told us to "make it as simple as possible, but no simpler." You, as a communicator, must satisfy both of these maxims, one warning against the dangers of excess complexity, and one warning against the dangers of excess simplicity. And I, as someone who communicates about communication in my books, courses, and coaching, must do the same.

## THE SPEAK FOR SUCCESS SYSTEM

The Speak for Success system makes communication as simple as possible. Other communication paradigms make it even simpler. Naturally, this means our system is more complex. This is an unavoidable consequence of treating communication as a deep and concrete science instead of a shallow and abstract art. If you don't dive into learning communication at all, you miss out. I'm sure you agree with that. But if you don't dive *deep*, you still miss out.

## THE FOUR QUADRANTS OF COMMUNICATION

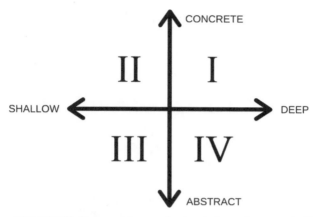

FIGURE VIII: There are four predominant views of communication (whether it takes the form of public speaking, negotiation, writing, or debating is irrelevant). The first view is that communication is concrete and deep. The second view is that communication is concrete and shallow. The third view is that communication is shallow and abstract. The fourth view is that communication is deep and abstract.

## WHAT IS COMMUNICATION?

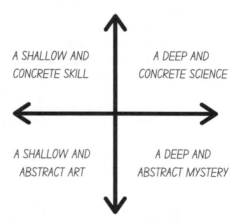

FIGURE VII: The first view treats communication as a science: "There are concrete formulas, rules, principles, and strategies, and they go very deep." The second view treats it as a skill: "Yes, there are concrete formulas, rules, and strategies, but they don't go very deep." The third view treats it as an art: "Rules? Formulas? It's not that complicated. Just smile and think positive thoughts." The fourth view treats it as a mystery: "How are some people such effective communicators? I will never know…"

## WHERE WE STAND ON THE QUESTION

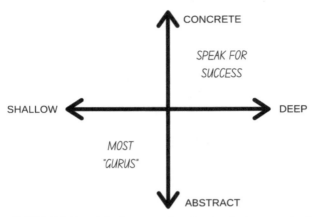

FIGURE VI: Speak for Success takes the view that communication is a deep and concrete science. (And by "takes the view," I mean "has discovered.") Most other writers, thought-leaders, public speaking coaches, and individuals and organizations in this niche treat communication as a shallow and abstract art.

This doesn't mean the Speak for Success system neglects the basics. It only means it goes far beyond the basics, and that it doesn't turn simple ideas into 200 pages of filler. It also doesn't mean that the Speak for Success system is unnecessarily complex. It is as simple as it can possibly be. In this book, and in the other books of the Speak for Success collection, you'll find simple pieces of advice, easy formulas, and straightforward rules. You'll find theories, strategies, tactics, mental models, and principles. None of this should pose a challenge. But you'll also find advanced, complicated tactics. These might.

What is the purpose of the guide on the top of the next page? To reveal the methods that make advanced strategies easy. When you use the tactics revealed in this guide, the difficulty of using the advanced strategies drops dramatically. If the 15-book Speak for Success collection is a complete encyclopedia of communication, to be used like a handbook, then this guide is a handbook for the handbook.

## A SAMPLING OF EASY AND HARD STRATEGIES

| Easy and Simple | Hard and Complicated |
|---|---|
| Use Four-Corner Eye Contact | The Fluency-Magnitude Matrix |
| Appeal to Their Values | The VPB Triad |
| Describe the Problem You Solve | The Illusory Truth Effect |
| Use Open Body Language | Percussive Rhythm |
| Tell a Quick Story | Alliterative Flow |
| Appeal to Emotion | Stacking and Layering Structures |
| Project Your Voice | The Declaratory Cascade |
| Keep it as Simple as Possible | Alternating Semantic Sentiments |

# THE PRACTICAL TACTICS

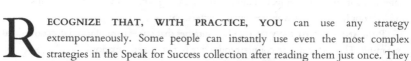

**R**ECOGNIZE THAT, WITH PRACTICE, YOU can use any strategy extemporaneously. Some people can instantly use even the most complex strategies in the Speak for Success collection after reading them just once. They are usually experienced communicators, often with competitive experience. This is not an expectation, but a possibility, and with practice, a probability.

CREATE A COMMUNICATION PLAN. Professional communication often follows a strategic plan. Put these techniques into your plan. Following an effective plan is not harder than following an ineffective one. Marshall your arguments. Marshall your rhetoric. Stack the deck. Know what you know, and how to say it.

DESIGN AN MVP. If you are speaking on short notice, you can create a "minimum viable plan." This can be a few sentences on a notecard jotted down five minutes before speaking. The same principle of formal communication plans applies: While advanced strategies may overburden you if you attempt them in an impromptu setting, putting them into a plan makes them easy.

MASTER YOUR RHETORICAL STACK. Master one difficult strategy. Master another one. Combine them. Master a third. Build out a "rhetorical stack" of ten strategies you can use fluently, in impromptu or extemporaneous communication. Pick strategies that come fluently to you and that complement each other.

PRACTICE THEM TO FLUENCY. I coach a client who approached me and said he wants to master every strategy I ever compiled. That's a lot. As of this writing, we're 90 one-hour sessions in. To warm up for one of our sessions, I gave him a challenge: "Give an impromptu speech on the state of the American economy, and after you stumble, hesitate, or falter four times, I'll cut you off. The challenge is to see how long you can go." He spoke for 20 minutes without a single mistake. After 20 minutes, he brought the impromptu speech to a perfect, persuasive, forceful, and eloquent conclusion. And he naturally and fluently used advanced strategies throughout his impromptu speech. After he closed the speech (which he did because he wanted to get on with the session), I asked him if he thought deeply about the strategies he used. He said no. He used them thoughtlessly. Why? Because he practiced them. You can too. You can practice them on your own. You don't need an audience. You don't need a coach. You don't even need to speak. Practice in your head. Practice ones that resonate with you. Practice with topics you care about.

KNOW TEN TIMES MORE THAN YOU INTEND TO SAY. And know what you do intend to say about ten times more fluently than you need to. This gives your mind room to relax, and frees up cognitive bandwidth to devote to strategy and rhetoric in real-time. Need to speak for five minutes? Be able to speak for 50. Need to read it three times to be able to deliver it smoothly? Read it 30 times.

**INCORPORATE THEM IN SLIDES.** You can use your slides or visual aids to help you ace complicated strategies. If you can't remember the five steps of a strategy, your slides can still follow them. Good slides aren't harder to use than bad slides.

**USE THEM IN WRITTEN COMMUNICATION.** You can read your speech. In some situations, this is more appropriate than impromptu or extemporaneous speaking. And if a strategy is difficult to remember in impromptu speaking, you can write it into your speech. And let's not forget about websites, emails, letters, etc.

**PICK AND CHOOSE EASY ONES.** Use strategies that come naturally and don't overload your mind. Those that do are counterproductive in fast-paced situations.

**TAKE SMALL STEPS TO MASTERY.** Practice one strategy. Practice it again. Keep going until you master it. Little by little, add to your base of strategies. But never take steps that overwhelm you. Pick a tactic. Practice it. Master it. Repeat.

**MEMORIZE AN ENTIRE MESSAGE.** Sometimes this is the right move. Is it a high-stakes message? Do you have the time? Do you have the energy? Given the situation, would a memorized delivery beat an impromptu, in-the-moment, spontaneous delivery? If you opt for memorizing, using advanced strategies is easy.

**USE ONE AT A TIME.** Pick an advanced strategy. Deliver it. Now what? Pick another advanced strategy. Deliver it. Now another. Have you been speaking for a while? Want to bring it to a close? Pick a closing strategy. For some people, using advanced strategies extemporaneously is easy, but only if they focus on one at a time.

**MEMORIZE A KEY PHRASE.** Deliver your impromptu message as planned, but add a few short, memorized key phrases throughout that include advanced strategies.

**CREATE TALKING POINTS.** Speak from a list of pre-written bullet-points; big-picture ideas you seek to convey. This is halfway between fully impromptu speaking and using a script. It's not harder to speak from a strategic and persuasively-advanced list of talking points than it is to speak from a persuasively weak list. You can either memorize your talking points, or have them in front of you as a guide.

**TREAT IT LIKE A SCIENCE.** At some point, you struggled with a skill that you now perform effortlessly. You mastered it. It's a habit. You do it easily, fluently, and thoughtlessly. You can do it while you daydream. Communication is the same. These tactics, methods, and strategies are not supposed to be stuck in the back of your mind as you speak. They are supposed to be ingrained in your habits.

**RELY ON FLOW.** In fast-paced and high-stakes situations, you usually don't plan every word, sentence, and idea consciously and deliberately. Rather, you let your subconscious mind take over. You speak from a flow state. In flow, you may flawlessly execute strategies that would have overwhelmed your conscious mind.

**LISTEN TO THE PROMPTS.** You read a strategy and found it difficult to use extemporaneously. But as you speak, your subconscious mind gives you a prompt: "this strategy would work great here." Your subconscious mind saw the opportunity and surfaced the prompt. You execute it, and you do so fluently and effortlessly.

**FOLLOW THE FIVE-STEP CYCLE.** First, find truth. Research. Prepare. Learn. Second, define your message. Figure out what you believe about what you learned. Third, polish your message with rhetorical strategies, without distorting the precision with which it conveys the truth. Fourth, practice the polished ideas. Fifth, deliver them. The endeavor of finding truth comes before the rhetorical endeavor. First, find the right message. Then, find the best way to convey it.

**CREATE YOUR OWN STRATEGY.** As you learn new theories, mental models, and principles of psychology and communication, you may think of a new strategy built around the theories, models, and principles. Practice it, test it, and codify it.

**STACK GOOD HABITS.** An effective communicator is the product of his habits. If you want to be an effective communicator, stack good communication habits (and break bad ones). This is a gradual process. It doesn't happen overnight.

**DON'T TRY TO USE THEM.** Don't force it. If a strategy seems too difficult, don't try to use it. You might find yourself using it anyway when the time is right.

**KNOW ONLY ONE.** If you master one compelling communication strategy, like one of the many powerful three-part structures that map out a persuasive speech, that can often be enough to drastically and dramatically improve your impact.

**REMEMBER THE SHORTCOMING OF MODELS.** All models are wrong, but some are useful. Many of these complex strategies and theories are models. They represent reality, but they are not reality. They help you navigate the territory, but they are not the territory. They are a map, to be used if it helps you navigate, and to be discarded the moment it prevents you from navigating.

**DON'T LET THEM INHIBIT YOU.** Language flows from thought. You've got to have something to say. And *then* you make it as compelling as possible. And *then* you shape it into something poised and precise; persuasive and powerful; compelling and convincing. Meaning and message come first. Rhetoric comes second. Don't take all this discussion of "advanced communication strategies," "complex communication tactics," and "the deep and concrete science of communication" to suggest that the basics don't matter. They do. Tell the truth as precisely and boldly as you can. Know your subject-matter like the back of your hand. Clear your mind and focus on precisely articulating exactly what you believe to be true. Be authentic. The advanced strategies are not supposed to stand between you and your audience. They are not supposed to stand between you and your authentic and spontaneous self – they are supposed to be integrated with it. They are not an end in themselves, but a means to the end of persuading the maximum number of people to adopt truth. Trust your instinct. Trust your intuition. It won't fail you.

## MASTERING ONE COMMUNICATION SKILL

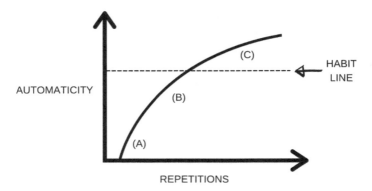

FIGURE V: Automaticity is the extent to which you do something automatically, without thinking about it. At the start of building a communication habit, it has low automaticity. You need to think about it consciously (A). After more repetitions, it gets easier and more automatic (B). Eventually, the behavior becomes more automatic than deliberate. At this point, it becomes a habit (C).

## MASTERING COMMUNICATION

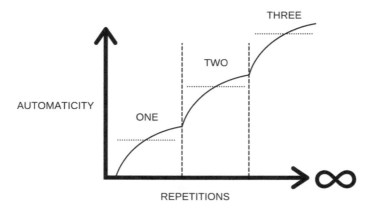

FIGURE IV: Layer good communication habits on top of each other. Go through the learning curve over and over again. When you master the first good habit, jump to the second. This pattern will take you to mastery.

## THE FOUR LEVELS OF KNOWING

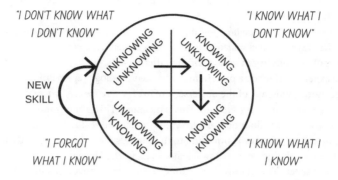

FIGURE III: First, you don't know you don't know it. Then, you discover it and know you don't know it. Then, you practice it and know you know it. Then, it becomes a habit. You forget you know it. It's ingrained in your habits.

## REVISITING THE LEARNING CURVE

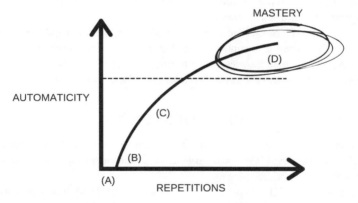

FIGURE II: Note the stages of knowing on the learning curve: unknowing unknowing (A), knowing unknowing (B), knowing knowing (C), unknowing knowing (D).

## WHAT'S REALLY HAPPENING?

Have you ever thought deeply about what happens when you communicate? Let's run through the mile-high view.

At some point in your life, you bumped into an experience. You observed. You learned. The experience changed you. Your neural networks connected in new ways. New rivers of neurons began to flow through them.

The experience etched a pattern into your neurobiology representing information about the moral landscape of the universe; a map of *where we are, where we should go, and how we should make the journey.* This is meaning. This is your message.

Now, you take the floor before a crowd. Whether you realize it or not, you want to copy the neural pattern from your mind to their minds. You want to show them where we are, where we should go, and how we should make the journey.

So, you speak. You gesture. You intone. Your words convey meaning. Your body language conveys meaning. Your voice conveys meaning. You flood them with a thousand different inputs, some as subtle as the contraction of a single facial muscle, some as obvious as your opening line. Your character, your intentions, and your goals seep into your speech. Everyone can see them. Everyone can see you.

Let's step into the mind of one of your audience members. Based on all of this, based on a thousand different inputs, based on complex interactions between their conscious and nonconscious minds, the ghost in the machine steps in, and by a dint of free will, acts as the final arbiter and makes a choice. A mind is changed. You changed it. And changing it changed you. You became more confident, more articulate, and deeper; more capable, more impactful, and stronger.

Communication is connection. One mind, with a consciousness at its base, seeks to use ink or pixels or airwaves to connect to another. Through this connection, it seeks to copy neural patterns about the present, the future, and the moral landscape. Whatever your message is, the underlying connection is identical. How could it not be?

## IS IT ETHICAL?

By "it," I mean deliberately using language to get someone to do or think something. Let's call this rhetoric. We could just as well call it persuasion, influence, communication, or even leadership itself.

The answer is yes. The answer is no. Rhetoric is a helping hand. It is an iron fist. It is Martin Luther King's dream. It is Stalin's nightmare. It is the "shining city on the hill." It is the iron curtain. It is "the pursuit of happiness." It is the trail of tears. It is "liberty, equality, and brotherhood." It is the reign of terror. Rhetoric is a tool. It is neither good nor evil. It is a reflection of our nature.

Rhetoric can motivate love, peace, charity, strength, patience, progress, prosperity, common sense, common purpose, courage, hope, generosity, and unity. It can also sow the seeds of division, fan the flames of tribalism, and beat back the better angels of our nature.

Rhetoric is the best of us and the worst of us. It is as good as you are. It is as evil as you are. It is as peace-loving as you are. It is as hate-mongering as you are. And I know what you are. I know my readers are generous, hardworking people who want to build a better future for themselves, for their families, and for all humankind. I know that if you have these tools in your hands, you will use them to achieve a moral mission. That's why putting them in your hands is my mission.

Joseph Chatfield said "[rhetoric] is the power to talk people out of their sober and natural opinions." I agree. But it is also the power to talk people out of their wrong and harmful opinions. And if you're using rhetoric to talk people out of their sober opinions, the problem isn't rhetoric, it's you.

In the *Institutes of Rhetoric*, Roman rhetorician Quintilian wrote the following: "The orator then, whom I am concerned to form, shall be the orator as defined by Marcus Cato, a good man, skilled in speaking. But above all he must possess the quality which Cato places first and which is in the very nature of things the greatest and most important, that is, he must be a good man. This is essential not merely on account of the fact that, if the powers of eloquence serve only to lend arms to crime, there can be nothing more pernicious than eloquence to public and private welfare alike, while I myself, who have labored to the best of my ability to contribute something of the value to oratory, shall have rendered the worst of services to mankind, if I forge these weapons not for a soldier, but for a robber."

Saint Augustine, who was trained in the classical schools of rhetoric in the 3rd century, summed it up well: "Rhetoric, after all, being the art of persuading people to accept something, whether it is true or false, would anyone dare to maintain that truth should stand there without any weapons in the hands of its defenders against falsehood; that those speakers, that is to say, who are trying to convince their hearers of what is untrue, should know how to get them on their side, to gain their attention and have them eating out of their hands by their opening remarks, while these who are defending the truth should not? That those should utter their lies briefly, clearly, plausibly, and these should state their truths in a manner too boring to listen to, too obscure to understand, and finally too repellent to believe? That those should attack the truth with specious arguments, and assert falsehoods, while these should be incapable of either defending the truth or refuting falsehood? That those, to move and force the minds of their hearers into error, should be able by their style to terrify them, move them to tears, make them laugh, give them rousing encouragement, while these on behalf of truth stumble along slow, cold and half asleep?"

# THE ETHICS OF PERSUASION

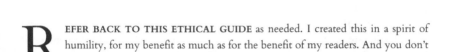

EFER BACK TO THIS ETHICAL GUIDE as needed. I created this in a spirit of humility, for my benefit as much as for the benefit of my readers. And you don't have to choose between efficacy and ethics. When I followed these principles, my words became more ethical *and* more powerful.

FOLLOW THESE TWELVE RULES. Do not use false, fabricated, misrepresented, distorted, or irrelevant evidence to support claims. Do not intentionally use specious, unsupported, or illogical reasoning. Do not represent yourself as informed or as an "expert" on a subject when you are not. Do not use irrelevant appeals to divert attention from the issue at hand. Do not cause intense but unreflective emotional reactions. Do not link your idea to emotion-laden values, motives, or goals to which it is not related. Do not hide your real purpose or self-interest, the group you represent, or your position as an advocate of a viewpoint. Do not distort, hide, or misrepresent the number, scope, or intensity of bad effects. Do not use emotional appeals that lack a basis of evidence or reasoning or that would fail if the audience examined the subject themselves. Do not oversimplify complex, gradation-laden situations into simplistic two-valued, either/or, polar views or choices. Do not pretend certainty where tentativeness and degrees of probability would be more accurate. Do not advocate something you do not believe (Johannesen et al., 2021).

APPLY THIS GOLDEN HEURISTIC. In a 500,000-word book, you might be able to tell your audience everything you know about a subject. In a five-minute persuasive speech, you can only select a small sampling of your knowledge. Would learning your entire body of knowledge result in a significantly different reaction than hearing the small sampling you selected? If the answer is yes, that's a problem.

SWING WITH THE GOOD EDGE. Rhetoric is a double-edged sword. It can express good ideas well. It can also express bad ideas well. Rhetoric makes ideas attractive; tempting; credible; persuasive. Don't use it to turn weakly-worded lies into well-worded lies. Use it to turn weakly-worded truths into well-worded truths.

TREAT TRUTH AS THE HIGHEST GOOD. Use any persuasive strategy, unless using it in your circumstances would distort the truth. The strategies should not come between you and truth, or compromise your honesty and authenticity.

AVOID THE SPIRIT OF DECEIT. Wrong statements are incorrect statements you genuinely believe. Lies are statements you know are wrong but convey anyway. Deceitful statements are not literally wrong, but you convey them with the intent to mislead, obscure, hide, or manipulate. Hiding relevant information is not literally lying (saying you conveyed all the information would be). Cherry-picking facts is not literally lying (saying there are no other facts would be). Using clever innuendo to twist reality without making any concrete claims is not literally lying (knowingly making a false accusation would be). And yet, these are all examples of deceit.

ONLY USE STRATEGIES IF THEY ARE ACCURATE. Motivate unified thinking. Inspire loving thinking. These strategies sound good. Use the victim-perpetrator-benevolence structure. Paint a common enemy. Appeal to tribal psychology. These strategies sound bad. But when reality lines up with the strategies that sound bad, they become good. They are only bad when they are inaccurate or move people down a bad path. *But the same is true for the ones that sound good.* Should Winston Churchill have motivated unified thinking? Not toward his enemy. Should he have avoided appealing to tribal psychology to strengthen the Allied war effort? Should he have avoided painting a common enemy? Should he have avoided portraying the victimization of true victims and the perpetration of a true perpetrator? Should he have avoided calling people to act as the benevolent force for good, protecting the victim and beating back the perpetrator? Don't use the victim-perpetrator-benevolence structure if there aren't clear victims and perpetrators. This is demagoguery. Painting false victims disempowers them. But if there are true victims and perpetrators, stand up for the victims and stand against the perpetrators, calling others to join you as a benevolent force for justice. Don't motivate unified thinking when standing against evil. Don't hold back from portraying a common enemy when there is one. Some strategies might sound morally suspect. Some might sound inherently good. But it depends on the situation. Every time I say "do X to achieve Y," remember the condition: "if it is accurate and moves people up a good path."

APPLY THE TARES TEST: truthfulness of message, authenticity of persuader, respect for audience, equity of persuasive appeal, and social impact (TARES).

REMEMBER THE THREE-PART VENN DIAGRAM: words that are authentic, effective, and true. Donald Miller once said "I'm the kind of person who wants to present my most honest, authentic self to the world, so I hide backstage and rehearse honest and authentic lines until the curtain opens." There's nothing dishonest or inauthentic about choosing your words carefully and making them more effective, as long as they remain just as true. Rhetoric takes a messy marble brick of truth and sculpts it into a poised, precise, and perfect statue. It takes weak truths and makes them strong. Unfortunately, it can do the same for weak lies. But preparing, strategizing, and sculpting is not inauthentic. Unskillfulness is no more authentic than skillfulness. Unpreparedness is no more authentic than preparedness.

APPLY FITZPATRICK AND GAUTHIER'S THREE-QUESTION ANALYSIS. For what purpose is persuasion being employed? Toward what choices and with what consequences for individual lives is it being used? Does the persuasion contribute to or interfere with the audience's decision-making process (Lumen, 2016)?

STRENGTHEN THE TRUTH. Rhetoric makes words strong. Use it to turn truths strong, not falsities strong. There are four categories of language: weak and wrong, strong and wrong, weak and true, strong and true. Turn weak and true language into strong and true language. Don't turn weak and wrong language into strong and wrong language, weak and true language into strong and wrong language, or strong and true language into weak and true language. Research. Question your assumptions. Strive for truth. Ensure your logic is impeccable. Defuse your biases.

**START WITH FINDING TRUTH.** The rhetorical endeavor starts with becoming as knowledgeable on your subject as possible and developing an impeccable logical argument. The more research you do, the more rhetoric you earn the right to use.

**PUT TRUTH BEFORE STYLE.** Rhetorical skill does not make you correct. Truth doesn't care about your rhetoric. If your rhetoric is brilliant, but you realize your arguments are simplistic, flawed, or biased, change course. Let logic lead style. Don't sacrifice logic to style. Don't express bad ideas well. Distinguish effective speaking from effective rational argument. Achieve both, but put reason and logic first.

**AVOID THE POPULARITY VORTEX.** As Plato suggested, avoid "giving the citizens what they want [in speech] with no thought to whether they will be better or worse as a result of what you are saying." Ignore the temptation to gain positive reinforcement and instant gratification from the audience with no merit to your message. Rhetoric is unethical if used solely to appeal rather than to help the world.

**CONSIDER THE CONSEQUENCES.** If you succeed to persuade people, will the world become better or worse? Will your audience benefit? Will you benefit? Moreover, is it the best action they could take? Or would an alternative help more? Is it an objectively worthwhile investment? Is it the best solution? Are you giving them all the facts they need to determine this on their own?

**CONSIDER SECOND- AND THIRD-ORDER IMPACTS.** Consider not only immediate consequences, but consequences across time. Consider the impact of the action you seek to persuade, as well as the tools you use to persuade it. Maybe the action is objectively positive, but in motivating the action, you resorted to instilling beliefs that will cause damage over time. Consider their long-term impact as well.

**APPLY THE FIVE ETHICAL APPROACHES:** seek the greatest good for the greatest number (utilitarian); protect the rights of those affected and treat people not as means but as ends (rights); treat equals equally and nonequals fairly (justice); set the good of humanity as the basis of your moral reasoning (common good); act consistently with the ideals that lead to your self-actualization and the highest potential of your character (virtue). Say and do what is right, not what is expedient, and be willing to suffer the consequences of doing so. Don't place self-gratification, acquisitiveness, social status, and power over the common good of all humanity.

**APPLY THE FOUR ETHICAL DECISION-MAKING CRITERIA:** respect for individual rights to make choices, hold views, and act based on personal beliefs and values (autonomy); the maximization of benefits and the minimization of harms, acting for the benefit of others, helping others further their legitimate interests; taking action to prevent or remove possible harms (beneficence); acting in ways that cause no harm, avoid the risk of harm, and assuring benefits outweigh costs (non-maleficence); treating others according to a defensible standard (justice).

**USE ILLOGICAL PROCESSES TO GET ETHICAL RESULTS.** Using flawed thinking processes to get good outcomes is not unethical. Someone who disagrees should stop speaking with conviction, clarity, authority, and effective paralanguage. All are irrelevant to the truth of their words, but impact the final judgment of the audience. You must use logic and evidence to figure out the truth. But this doesn't mean logic and evidence will persuade others. Humans have two broad categories of cognitive functions: system one is intuitive, emotional, fast, heuristic-driven, and generally illogical; system two is rational, deliberate, evidence-driven, and generally logical. The best-case scenario is to get people to believe right things for right reasons (through system two). The next best case is to get people to believe right things for wrong reasons (through system one). Both are far better than letting people believe wrong things for wrong reasons. If you don't use those processes, they still function, but lead people astray. You can reverse-engineer them. If you know the truth, have an abundance of reasons to be confident you know the truth, and can predict the disasters that will occur if people don't believe the truth, don't you have a responsibility to be as effective as possible in bringing people to the truth? Logic and evidence are essential, of course. They will persuade many. They should have persuaded you. But people can't always follow a long chain of reasoning or a complicated argument. Persuade by eloquence what you learned by reason.

HELP YOUR SELF-INTEREST. (But not at the expense of your audience or without their knowledge). Ethics calls for improving the world, and you are a part of the world – the one you control most. Improving yourself is a service to others.

APPLY THE WINDOWPANE STANDARD. In Aristotle's view, rhetoric reveals how to persuade and how to defeat manipulative persuaders. Thus, top students of rhetoric would be master speakers, trained to anticipate and disarm the rhetorical tactics of their adversaries. According to this tradition, language is only useful to the extent that it does not distort reality, and good writing functions as a "windowpane," helping people peer through the wall of ignorance and view reality. You might think this precludes persuasion. You might think this calls for dry academic language. But what good is a windowpane if nobody cares to look through it? What good is a windowpane to reality if, on the other wall, a stained-glass window distorts reality but draws people to it? The best windowpane reveals as much of reality as possible while drawing as many people to it as possible.

RUN THROUGH THESE INTROSPECTIVE QUESTIONS. Are the means truly unethical or merely distasteful, unpopular, or unwise? Is the end truly good, or does it simply appear good because we desire it? Is it probable that bad means will achieve the good end? Is the same good achievable using more ethical means if we are creative, patient, and skillful? Is the good end clearly and overwhelmingly better than any bad effects of the means used to attain it? Will the use of unethical means to achieve a good end withstand public scrutiny? Could the use of unethical means be justified to those most affected and those most impartial? Can I specify my ethical criteria or standards? What is the grounding of the ethical judgment? Can I justify the reasonableness and relevancy of these standards for this case? Why are these the best criteria? Why do they take priority? How does the communication succeed or fail by these standards? What judgment is justified in this case about the degree of ethicality? Is it a narrowly focused one rather than a broad and generalized one? To whom is ethical responsibility owed – to which individuals, groups, organizations, or professions? In what ways and to what extent? Which take precedence? What is my responsibility to myself and society? How do I feel about myself after this choice? Can I continue to "live with myself?" Would I want my family to know of this choice? Does the choice reflect my ethical character? To what degree is it "out of character?" If called upon in public to justify the ethics of my communication, how adequately could I do so? What generally accepted reasons could I offer? Are there precedents which can guide me? Are there aspects of this case that set it apart from others? How thoroughly have alternatives been explored before settling on this choice? Is it less ethical than some of the workable alternatives? If the goal requires unethical communication, can I abandon the goal (Johannesen et al., 2007)?

VIEW YOURSELF AS A GUIDE. Stories have a hero, a villain who stands in his way, and a guide who helps the hero fulfill his mission. If you speak ineffectively, you are a nonfactor. If you speak deceitfully, you become the villain. But if you convey truth effectively, you become the guide in your audience's story, who leads them, teaches them, inspires them, and helps them overcome adversity and win. Use your words to put people on the best possible path. And if you hide an ugly truth, ask yourself this: "If I found out that *my* guide omitted this, how would I react?"

KNOW THAT THE TRUTH WILL OUT. The truth can either come out in your words, or you can deceive people. You can convince them to live in a fantasy. And that might work. Until. Until truth breaks down the door and storms the building. Until the facade comes crashing down and chaos makes its entry. Slay the dragon in its lair before it comes to your village. Invite truth in through the front door before truth burns the building down. Truth wins in the end, either because a good person spreads, defends, and fights for it, or because untruth reveals itself as such by its consequences, and does so in brutal and painful fashion, hurting innocents and perpetrators alike. Trust and reputation take years to create and seconds to destroy.

MAXIMIZE THE TWO HIERARCHIES OF SUCCESS: honesty *and* effectiveness. You could say "Um, well, uh, I think that um, what we should… should uh… do, is that, well… let me think… er, I think if we are more, you know… fluid, we'll be better at… producing, I mean, progressing, and producing, and just more generally, you know, getting better results, but… I guess my point is, like, that, that if we are more fluid and do things more better, we will get better results than with a bureaucracy and, you know how it is, a silo-based structure, right? I mean… you know what I mean." Or, you could say "Bravery beats bureaucracy, courage beats the status quo, and innovation beats stagnation." Is one of those statements truer? No. Is one of them more effective? Is one of them more likely to get positive action that instantiates the truth into the world? Yes. Language is not reality. It provides signposts to reality. Two different signposts can point at the same truth – they can be equally and maximally true – and yet one can be much more effective. One gets people to follow the road. One doesn't. Maximize honesty. Then, insofar as it doesn't sacrifice honesty, maximize effectiveness. Speak truth. And speak it well.

APPLY THE WISDOM OF THIS QUOTE. Mary Beard, an American historian, author, and activist, captured the essence of ethical rhetoric well: "What politicians do is they never get the rhetoric wrong, and the price they pay is they don't speak the truth as they see it. Now, I will speak truth as I see it, and sometimes I don't get the rhetoric right. I think that's a fair trade-off." It's more than fair. It's necessary.

REMEMBER YOUR RESPONSIBILITY TO SOCIETY. Be a guardian of the truth. Speak out against wrongdoing, and do it well. The solution to evil speech is not less speech, but more (good) speech. Create order with your words, not chaos. Our civilization depends on it. Match the truth, honesty, and vulnerable transparency of your words against the irreducible complexity of the universe. And in this complex universe, remember the omnipresence of nuance, and the dangers of simplistic ideologies. (Inconveniently, simplistic ideologies are persuasive, while nuanced truths are difficult to convey. This is why good people need to be verbally skilled; to pull the extra weight of conveying a realistic worldview). Don't commit your whole mind to an isolated fragment of truth, lacking context, lacking nuance. Be precise in your speech, to ensure you are saying what you mean to say. Memorize the logical fallacies, the cognitive biases, and the rules of logic and correct thinking. (Conveniently, many rhetorical devices are also reasoning devices that focus your inquiry and help you explicate truth). But don't demonize those with good intentions and bad ideas. If they are forthcoming and honest, they are not your enemy. Rather, the two of you are on a shared mission to find the truth, partaking in a shared commitment to reason and dialogue. The malevolent enemy doesn't care about the truth. And in this complex world, remember Voltaire's warning to "cherish those who seek the truth but beware of those who find it," and Aristotle's startling observation that "the least deviation from truth [at the start] is multiplied a thousandfold." Be cautious in determining what to say with conviction. Good speaking is not a substitute for good thinking. The danger zone is being confidently incorrect. What hurts us most is what we know that just isn't so. Remember these tenets and your responsibility, and rhetoric becomes the irreplaceable aid of the good person doing good things in difficult times; the sword of the warrior of the light.

KNOW THAT DECEPTION IS ITS OWN PUNISHMENT. Knowingly uttering a falsehood is a spoken lie of commission. Having something to say but not saying it is a spoken lie of omission. Knowingly behaving inauthentically is an acted-out lie of commission. Knowingly omitting authentic behavior is an acted-out lie of omission. All these deceptions weaken your being. All these deceptions corrupt your own mind, turning your greatest asset into an ever-present companion you can no longer trust. Your conscience operates somewhat autonomously, and it will call you out (unless your repeated neglect desensitizes it). You have a conscious conscience which speaks clearly, and an unconscious conscience, which communicates more subtly. A friend of mine asked: "Why do we feel relieved when we speak truth? Why are we drawn toward it, even if it is not pleasant? Do our brains have something that makes this happen?" Yes, they do: our consciences, our inner lights, our inner north stars. And we feel relieved because living with the knowledge of our own deceit is often an unbearable burden. You live your life before an audience of one: yourself. You cannot escape the observation of your own awareness; you can't hide from yourself. Everywhere you go, there you are. Everything you do, there you are. Some of the greatest heights of wellbeing come from performing well in this one-man theater, and signaling virtue to yourself; being someone you are proud to be (and grateful to observe). Every time you lie, you tell your subconscious mind that your character is too weak to contend with the truth. And this shapes your character accordingly. It becomes true. And then what? Lying carries its own punishment, even if the only person who catches the liar is the liar himself.

BE A MONSTER (THEN LEARN TO CONTROL IT). There is nothing moral about weakness and harmlessness. The world is difficult. There are threats to confront, oppressors to resist, and tyrants to rebuff. (Peterson, 2018). There are psychopaths, sociopaths, and Machiavellian actors with no love for the common good. There is genuine malevolence. If you are incapable of being an effective deceiver, then you are incapable of being an effective advocate for truth: it is the same weapon, pointed in different directions. If you cannot use it in both directions, can you use it at all? Become a monster, become dangerous, and become capable of convincing people to believe in a lie... and then use this ability to convince them to believe in the truth. The capacity for harm is also the capacity for harming harmful entities; that is to say, defending innocent ones. If you can't hurt anyone, you can't help anyone when they need someone to stand up for them. Words are truly weapons, and the most powerful weapons in the world at that. The ability to use them, for good *or* for bad, is the prerequisite to using them for good. There is an archetype in our cultural narratives: the well-intentioned but harmless protagonist who gets roundly defeated by the villain, until he develops his monstrous edge and integrates it, at which point he becomes the triumphant hero. Along similar lines, I watched a film about an existential threat to humanity, in which the protagonist sought to convey the threat to a skeptical public, but failed miserably because he lacked the rhetorical skill to do so. The result? The world ended. Everyone died. The protagonist was of no use to anyone. And this almost became a true story. A historical study showed that in the Cuban Missile Crisis, the arguments that won out in the United States mastermind group were not the best, but those argued with the most conviction. Those with the best arguments lacked the skill to match. The world (could have) ended. The moral? Speak truth... well.

## MASTERING COMMUNICATION, ONE SKILL AT A TIME

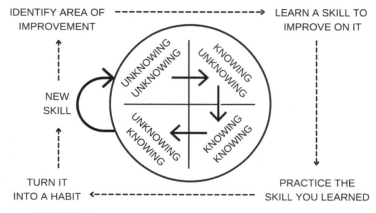

FIGURE I: The proven path to mastery.

**legendary**

.............................................................................

*adjective*

    remarkable enough to be famous; very well known

**leader**

.............................................................................

*noun*

    someone who provides direction and guidance

# CONTENTS

# POLITICAL DISCLAIMER

Throughout this book, and throughout all my books, I draw examples of communication strategies from the political world. I quote from the speeches of many of America's great leaders, like JFK and MLK, as well as from more recent political figures of both major parties. Political communication is ideal for illustrating the concepts revealed in the books. It is the best source of examples of words that work that I have ever found. I don't use anything out of the political mainstream. And it is by extensively studying the inaugural addresses of United States Presidents and the great speeches of history that I have discovered many of the speaking strategies I share with you.

My using the words of any particular figure to illustrate a principle of communication is not necessarily an endorsement of the figure or their message. Separate the speaker from the strategy. After all, the strategy is the only reason the speaker made an appearance in the book at all. Would you rather have a weak example of a strategy you want to learn from a speaker you love, or a perfect example of the strategy from a speaker you detest?

For a time, I didn't think a disclaimer like this was necessary. I thought people would do this on their own. I thought that if people read an example of a strategy drawn from the words of a political figure they disagreed with, they would appreciate the value of the example as an instructive tool and set aside their negative feelings about the speaker. "Yes, I don't agree with this speaker or the message, but I can clearly see the strategy in this example and I now have a better understanding of how it works and how to execute it." Indeed, I suspect 95% of my readers do just that. You probably will, too. But if you are part of the 5% who aren't up for it, don't say I didn't warn you, and please don't leave a negative review because you think I endorse this person or that person. I don't, as this is strictly a book about communication.

# HOW LEGENDARY
# LEADERS
# SPEAK

## 451 PROVEN COMMUNICATION SECRETS OF
## THE WORLD'S TOP LEADERS

**SPEAK FOR SUCCESS COLLECTION BOOK**

# III

**HOW LEGENDARY LEADERS SPEAK CHAPTER**

# I

# A WELL-KEPT SECRET:

## How Great Leaders Use Words to Change the World

## LOOK AROUND YOU – THE FOREWORD

C ONTROLLED HUMAN ATTENTION, centered on a definite purpose, backed by intentional action, supported by correct thinking, and empowered by a deeper motive, is the most powerful resource of humankind. All legendary leaders use it not only within themselves, but within the hearts, minds, and souls of their followers. Napoleon Hill, the author of *Think and Grow Rich*, called it the mastermind principle.

And this mastermind principle is the secret of all the leaders who have changed the world, changed the lives of their followers, or converted an inevitable failure into an incredible success. Effective leadership is simply channeling the controlled attention of those in your charge, centering it on a definite purpose, backing it by their intentional action, helping them think correctly, and giving them a deeper motive that empowers the entire process.

Weak leaders don't understand this. Average leaders intellectually agree, but don't understand the mechanism for manifesting this. The world's legendary leaders understand the gravity of this fundamental truth and have mastered the mechanism for manifesting it: communication.

The leaders who have changed the world have done so by mastering what I call the communication of leadership. Why the fancy name? Because nobody can be a true leader without it.

Every single legendary leader, from Steve Jobs to Bill Gates, to Franklin Delano Roosevelt, to Nelson Mandela, to Mahatma Gandhi, has used the communication of leadership to (1) control the attention of their followers, (2) center the attention of their followers on a definite purpose, (3) back this attention by intentional action, (4) support the action with correct thinking, and (5) empower this entire process with a deep motive.

### THE FIVE-STEP PROCESS OF LEGENDARY LEADERS

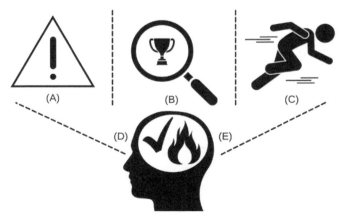

FIGURE 1: First, grab attention (A). Then, direct it to a definite purpose (B). Then, back it with intentional action (C). Back this entire process with correct thinking (D) and a powerful motive (E).

In this book, we will unleash the secrets legendary leaders have used to control the attention of those in their charge (part one). We will unleash the secrets legendary leaders have used to direct that attention in the direction of a definite purpose (part two). We will unleash the secrets legendary leaders have used to back that directed attention with intentional action from those in their charge (part three). We will unleash the secrets legendary leaders have used to support this intentional action with correct thinking from those in their charge (part four). We will unleash the secrets legendary leaders have used to empower this entire force by providing those in their charge with a strong motive (part five)

Every single secret strategy disclosed in this book will be accompanied by an example of its use (if not five or six). You'll read the words of business leaders, world leaders, and spiritual leaders that exemplify the communication of leadership.

But first, let's start with one of the most clear-cut, irrefutable, undeniably obvious examples of the communication of leadership channeling the single most powerful force known to man in the direction of a bold leader's choosing.

## DEPRESSION AND POVERTY

Let's turn back the clock to October 24, 1929. The day America broke. The day the unthinkable happened. The day the seeds were sown for the greatest example of the communication of leadership known to man to manifest itself in plain sight, though nearly nobody then or now would see it.

But most importantly: the day the spirit of the proudest country on Earth was shattered, in the absence of a leader who could use the communication of leadership to repair it. Until Franklin Delano Roosevelt came around, that is. But we'll talk about him after we talk about how bad it was.

One day it was fine. The American dream was real. *Americanism*, the sheer spirit of optimistic, industrious, innovative, and hard-working freedom was alive and well. One of the youngest countries was also one of the strongest. The entire world was surprised – in fact, shocked – by this rags-to-riches story.

The next day that all changed. The country went from riches to rags, and the man who brought it back to riches with the communication of leadership would earn four terms in the White House.

But let me be clear. It was very bad. It was a monumental disaster. It was a tangible mess, but more importantly, America's once-proud people lost their pride. In other words: the tangible disaster was second to the mental disaster that ensued when an entire nation lost touch with the most powerful force known to man.

## OUR ENVIRONMENTS SHAPE US, AND WE SHAPE THEM

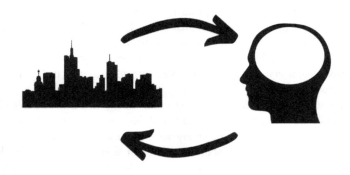

FIGURE 2: Our environment shapes us, and we shape our environment, which shapes us yet further in an ongoing cycle. We are both the architect of our environment and the product of it.

Mind you: the depression sprung from the minds of men. Sixteen million shares lost their value because their owners panicked and lost faith in the economy. What's the story there? Disaster in the human spirit first, and then as a result in the tangible realm. Innovation stagnated because people lost faith in the economy's ability to reward new inventions. Again, disaster in the human spirit first, and then as a result in the tangible realm.

The entire country suffered, struggling under a mountain of economic faithlessness, suffocating under the stifling weight of a deep disbelief in itself, that grew every moment it was left unaddressed. Make no mistake: this started, as all things do, in the minds of human beings, and was brought into existence by the negative actions that negative thoughts inevitably produce.

But let's talk about you. What would your odds during this time have looked like? You have a 25% chance of getting fired. But let's say you're not one of those people. You have a near 100% chance of seeing your wages cut, or your hours shortened. No movies, no fancy food, no new clothes, and for many people, no food, fancy or otherwise. A sense of uselessness; of ennui; of pure anxiety. Dark, dreary dread that penetrates everything sprouts in the cracks of the broken American spirit like a weed, and pervades even those with perfect equanimity.

"Oh, but I'm a professional, like a lawyer, or a doctor, so I would have been fine, right?" "But Peter! I'm a highly valued manager at a successful firm; surely I would be okay, right?" Nope. You can expect a 40% cut in your income. Imagine that today. One day, you're doing okay, maybe making $100,000 a year. Tomorrow? You're making $60,000.

Banks are breaking down. The entire financial system is underwater. People are walking for hundreds of miles to find any employment, and still coming back to their desperate families empty-handed.

Imagine suddenly not being able to provide for your family after decades of financial competence. Imagine financial security instantly turning into financial despair. Imagine this happening not to one person or one handful of people, but to an entire country, and not gradually, but in the blink of an eye.

The United States of America was silently screaming for a leader who could replace the faithlessness at the root of the Great Depression with an unwavering belief. A leader who could control the attention of the country *en masse*, direct it to a definite purpose of economic resurrection, produce intentional action toward that purpose, support that action with correct thinking, and supply a powerful motive to drive the action.

And that's exactly what it took. Now, we turn to Franklin Delano Roosevelt, the man who manifested the greatest economic resurrection known to man with the communication of leadership.

## ELATION AND RICHES

I will tell you exactly how depression and poverty turned to elation and riches. A bold leader, Franklin Delano Roosevelt, used the communication of leadership to channel the most powerful force known to man to the worthy end of resurrecting the United States. So, how did he do it? Let's select one example: fireside chats.

He controlled attention by entering the homes of everyone who would listen with the power of radio, and by *creating a counterfactual simulation*, and *addressing the people's pain* (two strategies you'll learn).

He directed this controlled attention in the direction of the goal of resurrecting the United States with *vision-sharing* and *belief-transfer*.

He created intentional action on a mass-scale with *social-proof-pacing* and *plan-projecting*. Short-sighted historians who do not attribute the economic revival to FDR's communication, and only to his tangible plans, forget that those plans rely on opt-in from confident citizens, which can only be achieved with *communication*.

He supported intentional action with correct thinking by *super-ego-appeals* and *value-invocations*.

He provided a powerful motive to empower the entire process with *benefit-of-benefit statements* and *broken-justice reparations*.

When he repaired the spirit of America, when he reconnected people with the single most powerful force known to man, the whole story changed. It was rags to riches again.

Virtually every single historian agrees on the importance of the mindset shift in producing the economic shift. But you won't find a historian, or anyone, who understands the hidden components of the communication of leadership that created that mindset shift in the first place. Until now.

But why does this matter today? For this reason: in the story of every single organization, in every single voluntary association of human beings, whether it is a fortune-500 company of 100,000 employees or a small, scrappy startup of ten, you will find some element of the story of this country during the depression. In other words: every single "mastermind," whether it is ten people, 100,000, or an entire country, faces problems and looks to leaders to solve them. The legendary leaders that succeed do so by reconnecting the members of the mastermind to the single most powerful force known to man. And they do that by communicating in a certain way.

And here's my question to you: Will you be one of them?

....................................Chapter Summary....................................

- There is a little-known but deeply powerful force available to all, capable of performing the miraculous.
- The legendary leaders of history, like Franklin Delano Roosevelt, Mahatma Gandhi, and John F. Kennedy used it.
- It is human attention centered on a definite purpose backed by action, correct thinking, and a powerful motive.
- Legendary leaders produce legendary results by communicating in such a way that they harness this force.
- Ineffective leaders typically fail to use this force. They produce mediocre results due to this failure.
- This book is broken down into five parts, showing you how to accomplish each of the five steps in sequence.

**KEY INSIGHT:**

Mindset Moves Mountains. A Good Mindset Is a Creative Mindset, Bringing Habitable Order into Being. A Bad Mindset Is a Destructive Mindset, Destroying Habitable Order, Intentionally or Through Ignorance.

**Claim These Free Resources that Will Help You Unleash the Power of Your Words and Speak with Confidence. Visit www.speakforsuccesshub.com/toolkit for Access.**

**18 Free PDF Resources**

*12 Iron Rules for Captivating Story, 21 Speeches that Changed the World, 341-Point Influence Checklist, 143 Persuasive Cognitive Biases, 17 Ways to Think On Your Feet, 18 Lies About Speaking Well, 137 Deadly Logical Fallacies, 12 Iron Rules For Captivating Slides, 371 Words that Persuade, 63 Truths of Speaking Well, 27 Laws of Empathy, 21 Secrets of Legendary Speeches, 19 Scripts that Persuade, 12 Iron Rules For Captivating Speech, 33 Laws of Charisma, 11 Influence Formulas, 219-Point Speech-Writing Checklist, 21 Eloquence Formulas*

**Claim These Free Resources that Will Help You Unleash the Power of Your Words and Speak with Confidence. Visit <u>www.speakforsuccesshub.com/toolkit</u> for Access.**

**30 Free Video Lessons**

We'll send you one free video lesson every day for 30 days, written and recorded by Peter D. Andrei. Days 1-10 cover authenticity, the prerequisite to confidence and persuasive power. Days 11-20 cover building self-belief and defeating communication anxiety. Days 21-30 cover how to speak with impact and influence, ensuring your words change minds instead of falling flat. Authenticity, self-belief, and impact – this course helps you master three components of confidence, turning even the most high-stakes presentations from obstacles into opportunities.

**Claim These Free Resources that Will Help You Unleash the Power of Your Words and Speak with Confidence. Visit www.speakforsuccesshub.com/toolkit for Access.**

**2 Free Workbooks**

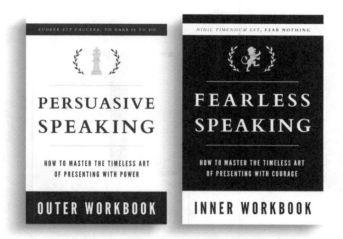

We'll send you two free workbooks, including long-lost excerpts by Dale Carnegie, the mega-bestselling author of *How to Win Friends and Influence People* (5,000,000 copies sold). *Fearless Speaking* guides you in the proven principles of mastering your inner game as a speaker. *Persuasive Speaking* guides you in the time-tested tactics of mastering your outer game by maximizing the power of your words. All of these resources complement the Speak for Success collection.

# SPEAK FOR SUCCESS COLLECTION BOOK

## III

# HOW LEGENDARY LEADERS SPEAK CHAPTER

## II

# STEP ONE:

# 17 Strategies to Control Attention

## PORTRAY EMPATHY

A HANDSOME, CHARISMATIC GOVERNOR WITH A captivating and smooth southern drawl was on the presidential debate stage. Bill Clinton.

One of the most important principles of the communication of leadership was about to be exposed to tens of millions of people on national television. And almost none of them would realize it.

Remember this iron law of leadership: all groups face problems, and look to leaders to help them reconnect to the most powerful force known to man to solve those problems.

And the country was, once again, facing economic destruction. The Great Recession (which sounds only mildly more comforting than the Great Depression) was ravaging America.

Here's what you must understand about the paradigm of a presidential debate. It is a paradigm of leadership selection; it is a competition to become the leader, not to exercise existing leadership.

And who wins? Who portrays themselves as the leader the people want? The person who can control the attention of the audience with the communication of leadership.

Let me show you what happened. You'll never look at communication the same way again.

A lady in a bright red dress asked the candidates a question with a false facade of simplicity, that secretly dived directly to the core of the matter; that directly sought to answer the question "who is the best leader on this stage?"

And the reason it worked was because of its subtlety. It worked because it snuck under the radars of the candidates, and thus precluded them from producing a faux, fabricated response. Let me explain how, embedded in this seemingly direct question, was a hidden inquiry that challenged the candidates to use the communication of leadership.

The words she said were, "how has the national debt personally affected each of your lives, and if it hasn't, how can you honestly find a cure for the economic problems of the common people if you have no experience in what's ailing them?"

But the hidden sentiment embedded in the subtext of those words was invisible to every single person in the room expect Bill Clinton.

Because what she was really asking is this: "who has empathy?" She was asking them to portray the most important quality of a leader. She was asking them to, in that exact moment, in front of the entire nation, decisively settle the question of who belongs in the oval office. And here's the interaction between Bush (Clinton's closest competitor), and the audience member who asked the question:

"Well I think the national debt affects everybody, uh, obviously it has a lot to do with interest rates, it has –"

"She's saying you personally."

"Yes, on a personal basis, how has it affected *you?*"

"Well, I'm sure it has, I love my grandchildren, I want to think that –"

*"How?"*

"I want to think that they're going to be able to afford an education, I think that that's an important part of being a parent - I, if the question, if you're sa - maybe I won't get it wrong, are you suggesting that if somebody has means, that the national debt doesn't affect them?"

"Well what I'm saying is –"

"I – I'm not sure I get it, help me with the question and I'll try to answer."

"Well I have friends that have been laid off from jobs."

"Yeah

"I know people who cannot afford to pay the mortgage on their homes, their car payment, I have personal –"

"Yeah"

"...problems with the national debt, but how has it affected you? And if you have no experience in it, how can you help us? If you don't know what we're feeling?"

"I think she means more the recession, the economic problems today the country faces rather than the national debt "

"Well listen, you oughta, you oughta be in the white house for a day and hear what I hear and see what I see and read the mail I read, and touch the people that I touch from time to ti - I was in the low max, AME church, it's a black church, just outside of Washington D.C., and I read in the bulletin, about teenage pregnancies, about the difficulty that families are having to meet ends - make ends meet, I've talked to parents. I mean, you've gotta care. Everybody cares if people aren't doing well. But I don't think, I don't think it's fair to say you haven't had cancer therefore you don't know what it's like. I don't think it's fair, uhh, you know whatever it is that you haven't been hit by personally, but everybody's affected by the debt, because of the tremendous interest that goes into paying on that debt, everything's more expensive, everything comes out of your pocket and my pocket, so it's, it's set, but I think in terms of the recession, of course you feel it when you're the president of the United States..."

The definition of empathy is the ability to understand and share the feelings of another. Good leaders do that religiously. The communication of leadership is only complete if this critical ingredient, empathy, is there. Now, let me ask you this: did Bush portray an ability to understand and share the feelings of that audience member (and the tens of millions of viewers who felt just like her)?

## KEY INSIGHT:

# The Highest Form of Empathy Is Seeing Oneself in Others; Feeling Another's Common Humanity.

## A LACK OF EMPATHY VISUALIZED

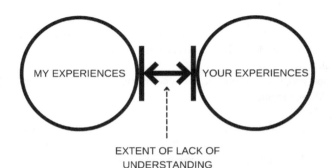

SET OF POSSIBLE EXPERIENCES

MY EXPERIENCES   YOUR EXPERIENCES

EXTENT OF LACK OF
UNDERSTANDING

FIGURE 3: A lack of understanding – or a lack of empathy – is a schism between one set of experiences and another set of experiences. The wider the schism, the less understanding occurs.

I'll let you answer that. Just kidding. The answer is no. Or, rather, not as well as Bill Clinton. Now, let's turn to Mr. Clinton:

"Tell me how it's affected you again?"

"Uhm…"

"You know people who've lost their jobs?"

"Well yeah"

"And lost their homes?"

"Mhm"

"Well, I've been governor of a small state for 12 years. I'll tell you how it's affected me personally. Every year, congress – and the president sign laws that makes us – make us do more things and gives us less money to do it with. I see people in my state, middle class people; their taxes have gone up in Washington and their services have gone down, while the wealthy have gotten tax cuts. I have seen what's happened in this last four years, when – in my state, when people lose their jobs there's a good chance I'll know em' by their names. When a factory closes, I know the people who ran it. When the businesses go bankrupt, I know them. And I've been out here for thirteen months, meeting in meetings just like this ever since October, with people like you all over America; people that have lost their jobs, lost their livelihoods, lost their health insurance…"

I challenge you to show me a more successful example of empathetic communication. Now, let's talk about the empathy embedded in the subtext of Clinton's response.

"I know what you're going through."

"Your problems are my problems."

"I lead a state of people who suffer just like you."

"I am locked in a battle with the forces conspiring against us."

"When people in my state are hit by this, I feel it too."

"I am right there with you, struggling daily with the same problems." All in all, he described ten instances of shared experience. He showed her (and the country at large) that he shared their pain. He positioned himself as a leader because he made the audience member feel understood.

## AN ABUNDANCE OF EMPATHY VISUALIZED

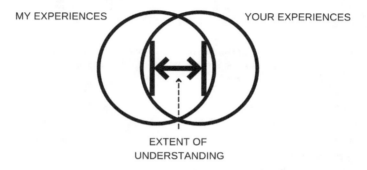

FIGURE 4: Empathy is overlap between "your experiences" and "my experiences." The greater this overlap, the greater the extent of the understanding and the greater the empathy.

He immediately controlled attention with a series of yes-questions (questions that elicit yes responses and build rapport between speaker and audience) that made the person feel understood.

**KEY INSIGHT:**

# Empathetic Questions Send an Unmistakable Signal of Belonging: "You Aren't Alone. I See, Hear, and Feel This Too."

## HOW TO GENTLY SLIDE PEOPLE TO YOUR POINT OF VIEW

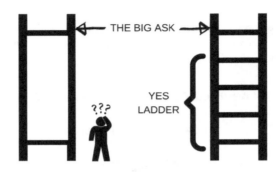

FIGURE 5: If you present people with your big ask immediately, they may feel resistance. A yes-ladder provides a gentle slide to agreement and rapport.

"Tell me how it's affected you again?" Let me listen to you. I want to be there for you and the people of this country, with policy, but also in spirit. Let's talk.

"You know people who've lost their jobs?" Is this what you're going through? Is this the experience we share? Are we together on this? I'm here to listen. Tell me.

"And lost their homes?" No, our shared understanding of this is not superficial. I can keep going on and on about the struggles we share. And is this one of them, yes?

And the individual was shocked by the immediate display of empathy. All she could say was "uhm," with the subtext of "wow, I'm shocked that you immediately connected to me by asking me an empathetic question that seeks to uncover the pain I feel."

"Well yeah," with the subtext of "yes, absolutely... finally, someone who can describe my pain so clearly that I immediately feel understood."

And finally, "mhm," with the subtext of "alright... you get me, man, you clearly understand what I – no, we – are going through."

Clinton's empathy of sentiment was matched by a charming empathy of delivery. He moved away from his stool and closer to the audience member, made eye contact, made gentle outward gestures, spoke with passion, conveyed emotion in his voice, and had a genuine facial expression of pain.

But not just any pain.

Shared pain.

Bush stayed close to his podium, checked his watch as if he had better places to be, made poor eye contact, made no emphatic gestures, spoke with little passion and an oddly paternalistic tone, conveyed no emotion, and had a facial expression of confusion.

The facial expressions tell the whole story. Clinton had a facial expression of pain; his face told the lady that he felt what she felt. Empathy and understanding.

Bush had a facial expression of confusion; his face told the lady that he had no modicum of a clue what she felt. Utter detachment in the place where only empathy and understanding should exist.

And let's take Clinton's least empathetic statement and compare it to Bush's most empathetic statement. Clinton's least empathetic statement: "Well, I've been governor of a small state for 12 years. I'll tell you how it's affected me personally. Every year, congress – and the president sign laws that makes us – make us do more things and gives us less money to do it with."

Bush's most empathetic statement: "...and I read in the bulletin, about teenage pregnancies, about the difficulty that families are having to meet ends – make ends meet, I've talked to parents."

Clinton's least empathetic statement was more empathetic than Bush's most empathetic statement. So, we've established the existence of empathy, and thus the existence of the communication of leadership. But what about the tangible results?

Let's talk about the tangible results if you're skeptical: six million votes. Is that tangible enough for you? Now, let me tell you a little secret. I've snipped the transcripts at the ends of each answer, leaving out a crucial part of the equation. Let's jump to our next section, so I can explain the second piece of the equation: authority.

## PORTRAY AUTHORITY

Empathy and authority are the first dynamic duo of the communication of leadership. It's like a puzzle with only two pieces. Fit empathy and authority together, and you can control the attention of any audience.

Problems and solutions are the second dynamic duo of the communication of leadership. It's a second puzzle with only two pieces. Fit problems to solutions, and you can control the attention of any audience.

And then put together the two puzzles, if you want to master the communication of leadership. How? It's simple: describe problems with empathy and then provide solutions with authority. This is the most basic and yet most powerful formula for the communication of leadership. Given the ease, I wonder why so few people do it.

We just decisively established that Clinton portrayed massive empathy, and Bush did not. This was the problem piece that called for empathy. I snipped the part at the end: the solution piece, that called for authority. You are going to see, once again, the drastic difference that the communication of leadership made. You'll see exactly how one speaker was able to satisfy the problem plus empathy and solution plus authority formula and thus control undivided attention.

Here's what Bush said: "...that's why I'm trying to do something about it by stimulating the export, investing more, better education system. Thank you, I'm glad to clarify."

Here's what Clinton said: "...what I want you to understand is, the national debt is not the only cause of that. It is because America has not invested in its people; it is because we have not grown; it is because we've had twelve years of trickle-down economics. We've gone from first to twelfth in the world in wages, we've had four years when we produced no private sector jobs, most people are working harder for less money than they were making ten years ago. It is because we are in the grip of a failed economic theory. And this decision you're about to make better be about what kind of economic theory you want; not just people saying I wanna go fix it, but what are we going to do! What I think we have to do is invest in American jobs, American education, control American healthcare costs, and bring the American people together again."

Again, a drastic difference, in favor of Clinton. Bush showed authority. Absolutely. But that's not what matters. The question we have to ask is this: who showed more authority? The answer is clear to you, I'm sure.

But I want to talk about why Clinton portrayed more authority. The superficial, surface-level smoke-screen seems to be that Clinton showed more authority because he listed substantive facts, and Bush abstained from doing so. But let's dig deeper. And let's keep digging until we find the truth.

Here's the real reason: Clinton showed exponentially more authority than Bush because he changed the diagnosis of the problem. So that's a strategy I want to convey to you. Want authority on a subject, on an issue, or on a problem?

Change the diagnosis of the problem.

Clinton broadened the frame, took a big picture view, and described what other people were not seeing in their myopic mania. He said, "no, it's not what we all think the problem is, it's actually an entirely different problem altogether."

## HOW RE-DIAGNOSING THE PROBLEM LENDS YOU AUTHORITY

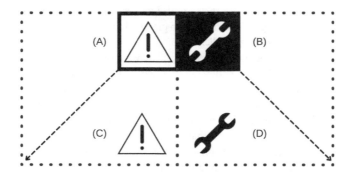

FIGURE 6: Stand out and gain authority by expanding on the common, status quo interpretation of the problem (A) at play and its best solution (B). Expand the diagnosis of the problem (C) ("the national debt is not the only cause of that"), which necessarily expands the scope of the solution (D) ("What I think we have to do is invest in American jobs, American education, control American healthcare costs, and bring the American people together again.")

More specifically: he turned "the national debt is causing the problem" to "it is because America has not invested in its people; it is because we have not grown; it is because we've had twelve years of trickle-down economics."

And what is the drastic importance of re-diagnosing the problem? Just this: that it gives the speaker significantly more authority. Think about it: who would you trust more to solve a problem, the person who accepts the common frame of the problem, or the person who dives deep into it and unveils the true nature of the problem, hidden causes and all? The latter. And that's exactly what Clinton made himself.

This is my favorite study I have conducted in the communication of leadership. Side by side, we see the communication of leadership contrasted with average communication. We see it in video, so we can jump beyond words and see the vocal delivery and body language at play too. And we see the tangible results that speak for themselves and make the power of the communication of leadership self-evident.

Let us turn to another legendary leader: Martin Luther King Jr. Let us discover the secrets of communication that he can teach us. We'll move on from the problem plus empathy and authority plus solution formula, and discover a proven strategy for captivating attention.

---

**KEY INSIGHT:**

There Are Two Types of Problems: Root Causes, and Their Symptoms. If the "Problem Behind the Problem" Remains, New Symptoms Will Emerge.

A Wise, Long-Term-Thinking Leader Shifts the Focus from the Symptoms to the Root Cause.

---

## SET HIGH EXPECTATIONS

Martin Luther King Jr. changed the world. All legendary leaders have. How did he do it? With the communication of leadership. And, as you know, the first element is controlling attention.

Martin Luther King Jr. was a master at controlling attention. Maybe it was partly due to his background as a preacher. Maybe it was due to his natural charisma. Maybe it was simply the gravity of the cause he symbolized. Maybe it was all these things, and one hundred more.

But one thing we know for sure: Martin Luther King Jr. was able to captivate attention because he set high expectations. Think about it: if your audience expects something great, they will give you (and the agenda you are advancing) more attention, right? Of course.

### WHY HIGH EXPECTATIONS GRAB IMMEDIATE ATTENTION

DOPAMINE IS THE CHEMICAL MOTIVATING ATTENTION AND ACTION

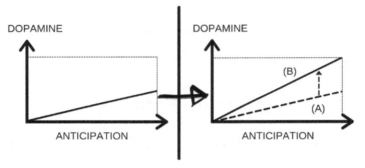

FIGURE 7: Dopamine is the anticipation chemical. When our dopamine is high, our anticipation of pleasure or satisfaction is high; when our anticipation is high, so is our dopamine. As our anticipation rises, so does our dopamine, which motivates action. This strategy of raising expectations (B) raises the anticipation from a lower level (A), which creates action. In this case, it grabs attention.

But how exactly do you establish high expectations? Let me show you how Martin Luther King Jr. did it. The same strategy can work for you.

August 28, 1963, the March on Washington for Jobs and Freedom was in full swing. 250,000 people (with hearts and minds touched by Martin Luther King's communication of leadership) were marching for racial equality, military desegregation, and fair working opportunities. It was monumental. It was ground-breaking. It was the largest demonstration ever seen in Washington, D.C.

And its crown jewel, at least according to the history books? Martin Luther King's speech. His "I have a dream" speech. A speech that would be read by tens of millions of Americans in the years since, as the beacon of morality, strength, and vision that it was.

Those who were there listened, captivated by the oratory. Those who watched it on their televisions were glued to the screen. Those who listen to the recordings today are always awed. What was the secret behind its incredible, unparalleled power as an agent for positive change? The communication of leadership. Do you not see, clear as day, how Martin Luther King controlled the attention of his followers, directed it toward a worthy purpose, backed it by intentional action on a mass scale, supported action with correct thinking, and provided a strong motive for the whole process? Do you not see the tangible results of this?

You must. It is so clearly laid out before us. All we have to do is look. And if we look just a little further, we'll be able to identify exactly how Martin Luther King Jr. was able to control attention, thus laying the groundwork for the next four steps.

So, how did he do it? By setting high expectations. For example, look at the immortal opening line of his famous *I Have a Dream* speech: "I am happy to join with you today in what will go down in history as the greatest demonstration for freedom in the history of our nation."

## HOW TO CAPTIVATE INSTANT ATTENTION WITH EASE

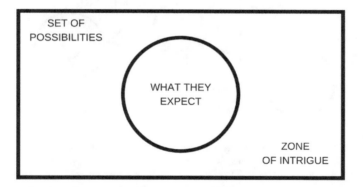

FIGURE 8: You can use expectations with another powerful method as well. This method is to break expectations. The zone of intrigue exists where people's expectations do not. Telling them something they don't expect, doing something they don't expect, or otherwise manifesting a reality outside of what they expect captures attention, generates intrigue, and draws people in.

What kind of person doesn't give undivided attention to the greatest demonstration for freedom in the history of their nation? Now, let's say you are the CEO of a cybersecurity firm, conducting a cybersecurity conference. Let's say you want to be an effective leader; indeed, a legendary one. Let's say you want to control the attention of those you are leading (as the head of the conference) from the very moment you begin your welcoming speech.

What can you do? Set high expectations. How? Like this: "I am honored to welcome you to what will be remembered as the greatest meeting of cybersecurity experts this industry has ever seen." This can be used by leaders in all fields, under all circumstances, speaking to all audiences about all possible occasions.

The model – which calls on you to apply the language pattern of high expectations – is simple and has been used by countless legendary leaders of history, although Martin Luther King is the principal example.

Here it is: "I am [insert positive adjective, like *thrilled*] to [insert verb of welcoming, like *invite*] you to the [insert superlative adjective, like *greatest*] [insert description of event, like *meeting of environmental scientists*] [insert elaboration of superlative, like *this field has ever seen*].

### INFORMATION FORAGING IS THE SECRET OF ATTENTION

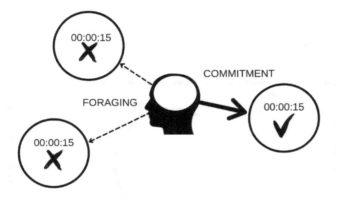

FIGURE 9: This is the simplest visualization of the science of attention. People allocate their attention after a process of "information foraging." They examine – or forage – at one patch of information for a short period of time (roughly 15 seconds). If the "information scent" is not high enough, they move on. They keep foraging until a patch of information hooks them by promising valuable information that will help them survive and thrive. Then, they commit. The language of high expectations accomplishes this.

The limits of this strategy are straightforward: don't falsely hype up the occasion (it really was the greatest demonstration for freedom in the history of the nation), and be specific about the superlative.

"Be specific about the superlative... what does that mean?" you might be wondering. Well, I'll explain. You must never forget to follow the "insert elaboration of superlative" step. Why? Just compare, "I am thrilled to invite you to the greatest meeting of environmental scientists," to "I am thrilled to invite you to the greatest meeting of environmental scientists *this field has ever seen.*"

The latter has dramatically more gravitas; the former falls flat. The latter has a clear sense of conclusion; the former sounds chopped. The latter sounds elevated; the former sounds juvenile.

Indeed, you can even reach the same results if you compare "I am happy to join with you today in what will go down in history as the greatest demonstration for freedom," with "I am happy to join with you today in what will go down in history as the greatest demonstration for freedom *in the history of our nation.*"

And I'll let you in on a little secret of communication theory. The test by comparison is a bullet-proof way to iterate up to the best possible form of articulating an idea. Take two options, pick the better one. Try to beat the winner. Then try to beat that winner. Every cycle produces a more elevated and captivating set of words than the one before it.

## THE TEST BY COMPARISON VISUALIZED

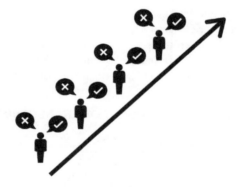

FIGURE 10: Which of the two ways of wording a message is stronger? Keep the winner. Think of another way, and stack it up against the winner. Keep the winner of that contest. Iterate your communication to perfection in this step-by-step, deliberate, algorithmic manner.

You just learned a proven speaking pattern that will control attention from the very beginning of your communication. And now, depending on your political alignments, we greet our best friend or our worst enemy for another key element of the communication of leadership. Ronald Reagan.

## EXPOSE A HIDDEN MIRACLE

Ronald Reagan was a legendary leader. Hate him or love him, he succeeded at fulfilling the five steps of the communication of leadership. Maybe you don't agree with the definite purpose he achieved, or maybe you do. Regardless, he achieved it, and it is not inherently immoral. So, let's talk about his story, his communication, and what we can learn from it to empower our own leadership.

Now, before we begin, there's one thing you must understand about Ronald Reagan. His communication was excellent. So excellent, that he is still known as "the great communicator." As little as people can agree on his policies, most people can agree that he was excellent at communicating them. And that is what we're here to study.

And let me tell you about one secret strategy used in the subtext of nearly every single major piece of communication produced by Ronald Reagan, from his speeches to his press releases to his campaign ads.

This secret strategy is one of the most effective methods for controlling attention. It is also proven to elevate the mental state of an audience.

So, what is this legendary strategy? Exposing a hidden miracle. Let me give you an example of Ronald Reagan pulling this strategy off: "Senator Hatfield, Mr. Chief Justice, Mr. President, Vice President Bush, Vice President Mondale, Senator Baker, Speaker O'Neill, Reverend Moomaw, and my fellow citizens: To a few of us here today this is a solemn and most momentous occasion, and yet in the history of our nation it is a commonplace occurrence. The orderly transfer of authority as called for in the Constitution routinely takes place, as it has for almost two centuries, and few of us stop to think how unique we really are. In the eyes of many in the world, this every-four-year ceremony we accept as normal is nothing less than a miracle."

### REVEAL THE EMERGENT OR TRANSCENDENT

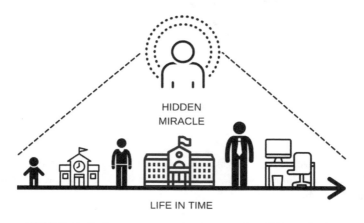

FIGURE 11: Portray an emergent or transcendent hidden miracle toward which your audience can orient themselves. Offer them meaning and significance. Or, more appropriately, reveal the

meaning and significance that has always been there that they
have just forgotten.

So how do you do it? It's incredibly simple, really. It's a two-step language pattern to make the ordinary seem extraordinary: first, identify an underrated commonplace occurrence related to your subject of communication, and second, present it as the miracle it really is.

Think about how Reagan did it. For step one, he chose the underrated commonplace occurrence of peaceful transition of power. For step two, he presented it as the miracle it really is. Maybe this seems easy to you. Maybe it doesn't. And if it doesn't, I have a feeling I know why. Because you're probably wondering... "how do I make something appear like a miracle?" And I will tell you exactly how.

Present something as a miracle by expressing how it looks to other people, to people on the outside. Why? Because everything is subject to habituation over time. In other words: given enough time, human beings can get used to just about anything.

Loss becomes less painful, love becomes less passionate, and yes, miracles become less miraculous. The magic of this strategy is that it brings people back to a place where they experience the feeling with the same intensity as when it was new. And a bullet-proof way of doing so is by explaining what something looks like to people who haven't habituated to it yet.

This is the strategy for making the habituated miraculous again that Reagan chose. That's why he said, "*in the eyes of many in the world*, this every-four-year ceremony we accept as normal is nothing less than a miracle." But there are two more strategies I want to teach you.

Use the "it's unprecedented" strategy. The first is always the best; it is always the most miraculous, and the most memorable. So, to present a hidden miracle (and thus control attention), show your audience that the underrated occurrence you chose in step one is unprecedented. It's simple: "nowhere else in the world, and at no other time, has any group of people accomplished [insert underrated commonplace occurrence]."

Use the "open the hood" strategy. Don't mistake me presenting three strategies for me telling you that you have to pick one. Go ahead and use them all. As for this one, you can make something appear miraculous by opening the hood.

Confused? Let me explain. Do you remember the first time you saw a car's engine? I do. When I first saw what was beneath that hood, I realized that the hidden mechanisms making the car move in the first place are more miraculous than anything on the outside, including the movement itself. The intricacies of the engine, how all the pieces moved in perfect unison, each part playing its role, was somehow more awe-inspiring than the end result. And thinking about how the engine came to be in the first place makes it yet more miraculous. Hundreds of parts, each made up of yet more parts, manufactured by people spread far and wide across the world, according to the designs of a group of brilliant people, using the best materials (again gathered by hundreds of people across the world), are shipped to one location, put together, and attached to the rest of the vehicle, with perfect precision.

What does this have to do with making an underrated commonplace occurrence seem miraculous? I'm sure you've figured it out by now. In step two, explain the hidden, little-known, often-forgotten mechanisms manifesting the result (the underrated commonplace occurrence) you chose in step one.

For example, let's say your position of leadership is the head of an industrial manufacturing company, producing heavy shipping equipment that fuels a local economy. Let's say you want to make the finished result seem miraculous, to control attention, and achieve the communication of leadership. Here's what you could say: "See that crane that just came off the assembly line *(common, underrated occurrence)*? Let's not forget what it represents *(transition to opening the hood)*. Let's not forget where it came from. Let's not forget that its birth started over two years ago in East Asia, 5,203 feet below the surface of the Earth, where miners gathered the raw iron used to produce it. They plucked enough of it from the mine, stuck it in a cart, which traveled back up to the surface of the Earth. A truck driver took the cart, drove it to a refinery in a different country, where refinery workers separated the silt from the raw iron. Then, a team of material chemists analyzed the grade of the iron and reported to us that it is of the highest quality. It was driven from the refinery to an airport, and from there, the pilot flew it to a local airport in Ohio. Airport managers removed it from the plane and shipped it here to us. So far, the miners, the truck driver, the refinery workers, the material chemists, and the pilot, have earned the wages that will feed their families. Our operations in those countries furthered their journey to full development. Then, the pure iron came here. We melted it. We molded it to suit the needs of our clients. We brought together electricians, machine operators, scientists, financiers, managers, and hundreds of workers from the neighboring towns. The production of that crane will feed hundreds of families right here in Ohio. We produced that crane, which will go on to produce, our client tells me, affordable housing in the inner cities of the state, allowing yet more people to attain the American dream. It might look like just a crane to you. But you must always remember that it is nothing short of a miracle." It shows clairvoyance and perspective. It shows the ability to take the big picture and zoom out. It shows perspective. And all leaders need perspective.

**KEY INSIGHT:**

# Connect People to the Miraculous Meaning of the Things They Forget to Be Grateful For.

**TURNING AN EVERYDAY OCCURRENCE INTO A MIRACLE**

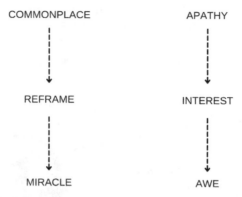

FIGURE 12: Present what is commonplace, and reframe it into a miracle. This creates an emotional trajectory from apathy to interest to awe.

The beauty of this is that the same strategy that worked for Reagan will work for the CEO of an industrial operation, for the founder of the latest tech startup, for a branch manager of a sales firm, for the captain of a football team... indeed, for anyone who finds life calling on them to lead, and who finds within them the courage to answer that call.

But let's not forget the last step. Enumerate the miracle. After you've presented the underrated commonplace occurrence, after you've used one of the three strategies for presenting it as a miracle, enumerate the miracle.

How? By saying something like, "It might look like just a crane to you. But you must always remember that it is nothing short of a miracle." Or, in Reagan's case, "this every-four-year ceremony we accept as normal is nothing less than a miracle."

And now, let's turn to a strategy used probably 100 times from the same stage at the same event. Let's jump out of the past and into the present. Let's see how the Democratic politicians competing for the 2020 nomination in the primary have all used the same strategy countless times to control attention.

## SPEAK TO THE PEOPLE'S PAIN

Here's something that bears repetition 1,000 times. I like to call it the empathy hyper-response tendency: people have problems that cause pain, and they will give attention to people who talk about the problems and the pain they cause.

And this draws a distinction between problems and pain. Seems obvious, right? Indeed, it is obvious. Unfortunately, that is exactly why people always forget this. It's too obvious, so people stop paying attention.

What's so obvious? This: problems are outside, pain is inside. "Not enough money" is a problem, and the pains it causes are "stress, desperation, insecurity." Understand? Problems are external; pain is internal. To speak to people's pain (and control attention), you must speak about both the problems that cause the pain and the pain itself.

## WHAT MAKES A PROBLEM A PROBLEM AND WHY IT MATTERS

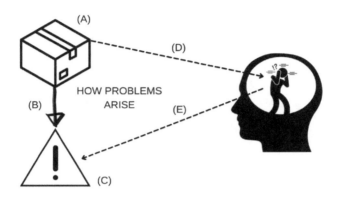

FIGURE 13: An event in the external world (A) becomes unpackaged by our interpretative machinery (B) as a problem (C) when it causes a human-being pain (D): this is what causes us to perceive things as problems (E). It can be said that the only real problem is suffering, and every "problem" is really just a cause of suffering we seek to remove from the human experience.

Just like solutions only make sense in the context of problems, pain only makes sense in the context of problems. And just like enumerating problems without suggesting solutions sounds useless, enumerating external problems without speaking to the internal pain they cause falls flat.

Think about it: the key to influencing people to do anything is always to create action from within them. You cannot coerce them from without; you must help them convince themselves from within. And that is why speaking to people's pain (and not just the external problems) is so effective: it controls attention because it brings to bear the emotional forces from within them. Get it?

We'll discuss different kinds of problems later. But for now, I want to tell you about what's happening in 2020, and how that relates to problems and pain. The Democratic party was so energized in opposition to the Trump presidency that they produced roughly 26 primary candidates. Yes, 26. That's a lot.

And when they were on the debate stage, I witnessed one of the most compelling examples of this technique I've ever seen. Why? Because right then and there, side by side, almost in sequence, so many of the candidates, with different and diverse policy positions, with different political and cultural backgrounds, and with varied communication styles, used the same exact communication technique. When that happens, I notice. In fact, it's my job to notice.

So, are you just going to believe me? You shouldn't. Not until you read these snippets from the transcripts. I picked eight responses to questions from the moderator at random, and six of them include this technique. Quite simply, it is a problem plus the pain it causes. Let me show you.

Cory Booker: "I think we have a serious problem in our country with corporate consolidation (problem). And you see the evidence of that in how dignity is being stripped from labor (pain)..."

Jay Inslee: "And I'm proud of standing up for unions. I've got a plan to reinvigorate collective bargaining so we can increase wages finally. I marched with the SEIU folks (problem). It is not right that the CEO of McDonald's makes 2,100 times more than the people slinging cash at McDonald's (pain)."

Amy Klobuchar: "The president literally went on TV, on Fox, and said that people's heads would spin when they see how much he would bring down pharmaceutical prices. Instead, 2,500 drugs have gone up in double-digits since he came into office. Instead, he gave $100 billion in giveaways to the pharma companies (problem). For the rest of us, for the rest of America, that's what we call at home all foam and no beer. We got nothing out of it (pain)."

Elizabeth Warren: "Look at the business model of an insurance company. It's to bring in as many dollars as they can in premiums and to pay out as few dollars as possible for your health care (problem). That leaves families with rising premiums, rising copays, and fighting with insurance companies to try to get the health care that their doctors say that they and their children need (pain)."

Cory Booker, again: "First of all, we're talking about this as a health care issue, but in communities like mine, low-income communities, it's an education issue (problem), because kids who don't have health care are not going to succeed in school (pain). It is an issue for jobs and employment (problem), because people who do not have good health care do not succeed at work (pain). It's even a retirement issue (problem), because in my community, African-Americans have a lower life expectancy because of poorer health care (pain)."

Bill De Blasio: "We have to change the discussion about in this country because look at the bottom line here. Those tragic - that tragic photo of those - that parent, that child - and I'm saying this as a father (problem). Every American should feel that in their heart, every American should say that is not America, those are not our values (pain)."

And we see a common trend emerge. We see that so much of the pain invoked has to do with suffering injustice. We see that the problems are just causes of injustice.

More on that later. Don't forget about this. This is an absolutely critical technique for step two: directing attention to a definite purpose.

Speaking of 2020 Democratic candidates, we now turn to Bernie Sanders, and a technique he uses in almost every single speech he delivers, to control undivided attention.

## BUILD A COALITION

Bernie Sanders is a man who stands for revolutionary ideas. Revolutionary ideas especially demand the communication of leadership as a mechanism of manifestation. Mr. Sanders understands this.

At this point, and as a brief aside, I must state the obvious: as a student of the communication of leadership, I separate who is using a technique from the technique itself. I ask you to do the same.

If you have strong political views, chances are you hate Mr. Sanders and love Mr. Reagan, or love Mr. Sanders and hate Mr. Reagan. And yet, they both use the communication of leadership. Recognize that a figure you dislike, who is advocating ideas you dislike, can still effectively use the communication of leadership. If you don't have strong political views, you might be wondering why I included this little message. But sadly, I've had readers viciously lash out at me for including excerpts from particularly divisive politicians.

That said, back to Bernie. He understands the critical element of the communication of leadership better than many of his colleagues. He understands the single secret of mass movements that achieve audacious goals against all the odds. He understands the persuasive power of a deeply ingrained, subconsciously hyperactive psychological state.

He understands the power of psychological coalitions. We over me and you. Together over apart. For each other over for ourselves.

The psychology of teams is one of the most persuasive, influential forces known to humanity. It truly is none other than the mastermind principle mentioned in the foreword. The human psychology is thrilled by team-member status. It's scientific... it's evolutionary. Humans who were pleased by being a part of a team, were more likely to form a team, and about 100,000 years ago, being in a team was the difference between life and death, so the gene controlling whether or not someone is pleased by team status was naturally selected to be passed on through the generations, until today, when leaders can play upon that gene; when leaders can use the very fabric of our DNA in their favor, and hopefully in our favor as well.

**KEY INSIGHT:**

# The Most Persuasive English Word? "Together." Phrase? "We the People." Why? Unity.

## THE SEVENTH PRINCIPLE OF PERSUASION: UNITY

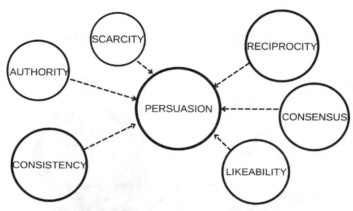

FIGURE 14: In Robert Cialdini's groundbreaking book *Influence*, he revealed six scientifically proven principles of persuasion. Scarcity: we want what is rare or soon to be unavailable. Authority: we listen to authority figures. Reciprocity: we return favors. Likeability: we listen to those we like. Consistency: we want to act consistently with our past actions. Consensus: we follow the crowd. There are actually seven, and the seventh principle closely ties to the powerful and persuasive psychology of teams: unity.

So, the science is clear: the mechanism of evolution makes human beings want, at times above all else, to belong to a larger coalition of human beings. We know, and perhaps have experienced first-hand, how pleasing team status can be.

And that which pleases controls attention. Let's call it the pleasure hyper-response tendency. But why build a coalition in the first place? When people enter a coalition, they abandon reservations and throw themselves with renewed vigor to the pursuit of a goal. The tribal psychology of teams gives people self-identity, a belief system that organizes the world in neat little ways, and a self-reinforcing cycle of intellectual confirmation. It creates a comfortable nook of common belief, common vision, common goal, common enemy, common identity, and common struggle.

Team psychology has massive appeal to our 1,000,000-year-old brains, and thus, holds massive influence over us. Furthermore, coalitions built around common transformative aspirations are yet more influential. And that which influences, controls attention.

So, how does Bernie sanders build a coalition to control attention and achieve the communication of leadership? Specifically, how does he build a coalition around transformative aspirations? I'm going to show you one phrase he used at the start of one of his speeches. Know this: every single piece of communication produced by Mr. Sanders and his campaign includes a drastic amount of nearly identical phrases. Coincidence? No. Deliberate intention. Because they know what to say.

And here's the special phrase: "Thank you all very much for being here today and thank you for being part of a political revolution which will transform America."

## PRESENT INFORMATION HOW THE MIND RECEIVES IT

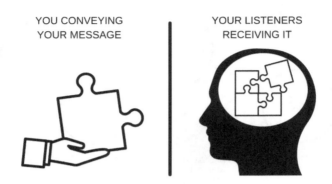

FIGURE 15: All effective influence relies on conveying a message that conforms to (and / or minimizes the clash with) the contents, processes, biases, heuristics, and functions of the mind receiving it. Or, put simply, all effective influence relies on conveying information how the human mind is wired to receive it.

## SYSTEM ONE, SYSTEM TWO, AND WHICH ONE TO USE

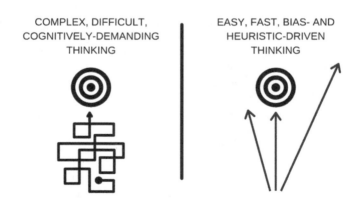

FIGURE 16: While humans are capable of complex, difficult, slow, cognitively-demanding thinking processes (which behavioral economists define as "system two" thinking), we typically operate in the fast-paced, cognitively inexpensive "system one," which is the home of biases and heuristics.

## VISUALIZING ATTRIBUTE SUBSTITUTION AND SOCIAL PROOF

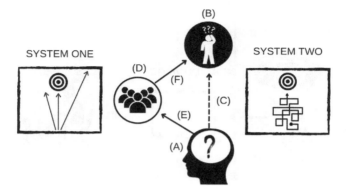

FIGURE 17: Attribute or heuristic substitution is a fundamental algorithm that influences human judgment. When we evaluate a question (A) like "is this a truthful claim?" (B), trying to answer the question directly is cognitively demanding work that lies in the realm of system two (C). So, instead of evaluating the question directly, we substitute an easy heuristic attribute (D), evaluate the heuristic attribute (E), and transfer the answer to the difficult "target" variable (F). Social proof and many of the principles of psychology we discuss in this book run on attribution substitution. We substitute "what do most people think about X?" for "what do I think about X?"

Coalition? Check. Transformation? Check. Team psychology activated? Check. Attention controlled? Check. Think about it: everyone wants to be a smaller part of something bigger than themselves. A good coalition is greater than the sum of its parts, and everyone wants to be elevated by the power of a team.

It is one of the dualities of human desires. We want to balance individualism with our role as a valued part of a group. And we also want to transform; to improve; to grow; or, as Dr. Abraham Maslow put it, to self-actualize.

So, take a lesson from Bernie. Control attention by thanking your audience for joining a coalition built around a transformative aspiration.

**KEY INSIGHT:**

# An Intelligent Unity Beats Radical Individualism & Radical Collectivism.

## THE SOCIAL-PROOF STRUCTURE THAT MOTIVATES ACTION

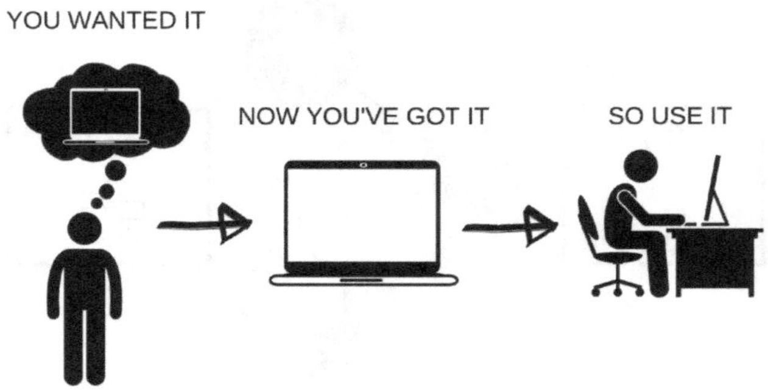

YOU WANTED IT

NOW YOU'VE GOT IT        SO USE IT

FIGURE 18: This persuasive three-step structure "upsells" people to another action and uses both the principles of social proof and consistency. "You wanted it; you clamored for this change; you moved mountains to get this thing. Now you have it. You got what you wanted. But the job isn't finished. Now you have to use it. So, take this next action."

Moving on to a technique you have seen – but probably didn't notice – hundreds of times, from leaders all over the world, and from all time periods.

We're going to turn back to our good friend Franklin Delano Roosevelt, and see how he used the communication of leadership to handle yet another crisis.

## MAKE BOLD PROMISES

Promises matter. Why? Because they are like a check. When someone makes a promise, it is like they are writing you a check for whatever it is they promised, which can only be cashed in at a later date.

Would that "later date" part bother you if you got a check for a massive amount of money? Maybe, but you'd probably be more thrilled about the money than the time you have to wait to collect it.

And Franklin Delano Roosevelt just wrote a massive check to the entire nation. After, mind you, they had cashed in his check with the promise to restore the economy (which he did). But let's back up. What happened on December 7th, 1941? I'll let Mr. Roosevelt tell you.

"The United States of America was suddenly and deliberately attacked by naval and air forces of the Empire of Japan. [...] Last night, Japanese forces attacked Hong Kong. Last night, Japanese forces attacked Guam. Last night, Japanese forces attacked the Philippine Islands. Last night, the Japanese attacked Wake Island. And this morning, the Japanese attacked Midway Island."

The United States was finally pulled into the war by a surprise attack on Pearl Harbor. And upon hearing this, the people were feeling impoverished. Not financially impoverished – FDR already solved that – but spiritually impoverished.

"Another war?" "We just did one of those..." "Will my son have to fight?" Spiritually impoverished. They needed to cash in a check.

And FDR gave them one when he said, "no matter how long it may take us to overcome this premeditated invasion, the American people in their righteous might will win through to absolute victory."

That promise, in that dire moment, was like a million-dollar check to each individual American, cashed not into their bank accounts, but into their spiritual accounts.

## HOW TO RAISE THE BALANCE OF SPIRITUAL ACCOUNTS

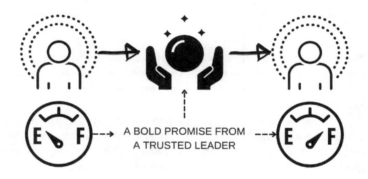

A BOLD PROMISE FROM
A TRUSTED LEADER

FIGURE 19: A bold promise from a trusted leader takes the spiritual accounts of his followers from empty to full.

What is the single most valuable commodity? What is worth more than any stock? What can be exchanged by even those with empty bank accounts? A promise from a trusted person. A promise from a leader.

Something fascinating happens when a trusted and confident person makes a promise to another. If the receiver trusts the giver, then the power of the confidence with which the promise was made does something incredible.

What, exactly? It transfers belief. We'll talk about this later. Just know this: the people trusted FDR, and they saw his absolute faith in his ability to realize his promise, and so they picked up that faith themselves. Now, we know his vocal delivery portrayed faith, but so did the language itself: "the American people in their *righteous might will* win through to *absolute* victory."

## HOW THE MECHANISM OF BELIEF-TRANSFER EARNS TRUST

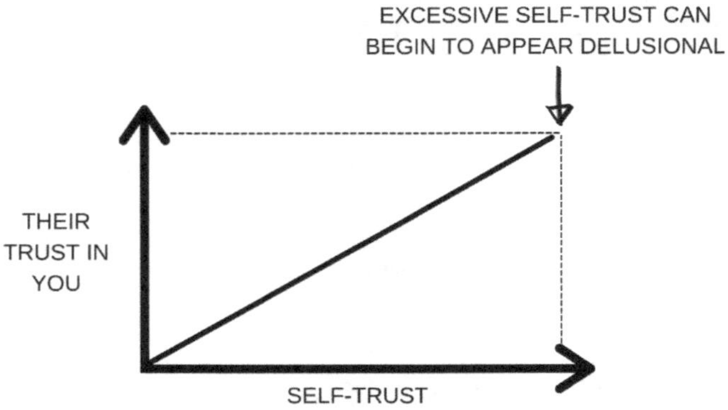

EXCESSIVE SELF-TRUST CAN
BEGIN TO APPEAR DELUSIONAL

THEIR
TRUST IN
YOU

SELF-TRUST

FIGURE 20: As you gain trust in yourself, all else equal, people begin to gain trust in you. This continues up to a point of perceived delusion.

Not to mention the obstacle-discounter-phrase, which tossed aside obstacles (in this case, time – one of the most major): "no matter how long it may take us to overcome this premeditated invasion." And because the critical ingredient of trust was there, FDR's faith was transmuted into the hearts and minds of his audience members.

So, not only was the power drawn from confident delivery, but from the language of absolute conviction. Faith is a form of controlled attention. In fact, one of the most powerful forms. You must have faith in something. That something is where the controlled attention is directed. In this case, on the bold promise made by FDR.

So, how can you use this? It's simple if you're trusted: make bold promises, make them with confidence, and follow through on them. And remember: the best bold promises are the achievement of a goal, the attainment of a benefit, or the defeat of an enemy.

That's all it takes to achieve one of the most powerful principles of the communication of leadership. And almost every single legendary leader has used this one. It is essential to the communication of leadership. But luckily for you, it is simple, accessible, and easy.

In fact, most of these strategies are deceptively simple, and yet, I have only found them hidden in the words of a small segment of people, the tiny group known by history as legendary leaders. Sadly, I have found them nearly nowhere else.

Now, we turn to an element of the communication of leadership that will not only control undivided attention but command complete respect. And we ask Woodrow Wilson to help us with that.

**KEY INSIGHT:**

Conviction is Contagious, a Fact Both Opportune and Dangerous; a Sharp Double-Edged Sword.

Wise Conviction is One of the Greatest Forces for Good; Foolish Conviction, For Evil.

## DIVULGE THE BRUTAL TRUTH

Whenever you see a legendary leader, the communication of leadership is likely at play in one way or another. Woodrow Wilson, former president of the United States, was an exceptionally legendary leader.

He portrayed unparalleled vision, thinking beyond the matters of his nation, and extending his sight to global affairs. He approached every situation with conservative care, compassion, clarity, and calm. He is regarded as one of the nation's best presidents.

He began the world-move toward the perpetuation of stable international law, with the respect of human rights as its moral mantle-piece.

He laid the groundwork for the international organization that, to this day, maintains peace and builds prosperity throughout the world: The United Nations.

And do not forget: where there is a legendary leader, you can almost always find the communication of leadership as a mechanism of manifesting the critical five steps of achieving big, bold, audacious goals.

Woodrow Wilson, for example, teaches us how to divulge the brutal truth. But before we get into specifics, we must talk about why divulging the brutal truth matters in the first place. Because people are fed up with hearing banal bullshit. It's true.

People are sick and tired of language designed to obscure, minimize, or distract. People have had it with politicians and those in positions of power reneging on their moral mandate and then lying about it. People are finished with hearing anything but the truth, the full truth, and nothing but the truth, no matter how brutal a particular truth might seem to the one who has to say it.

So, what does this mean? If you give people the brutal truth, in a spirit of total transparency and complete honesty, you will control their attention. This is truer today than it was when Woodrow Wilson showed us how to divulge the brutal truth to control attention.

And here's how he did it: "The precautions taken were meager and haphazard enough, as was proved in distressing instance after instance in the progress of the cruel and unmanly business, but a certain degree of restraint was observed. The new policy has swept every restriction aside. Vessels of every kind, whatever their flag, their character, their cargo, their destination, their errand, have been ruthlessly sent to the bottom without warning and without thought of help or mercy for those on board, the vessels of friendly neutrals along with those of belligerents. Even hospital ships and ships carrying relief to the sorely bereaved and stricken people of Belgium, though the latter were provided with safe conduct through the proscribed areas by the German Government itself and were distinguished by unmistakable marks of identity, have been sunk with the same reckless lack of compassion or of principle."

If you're wondering what the hell he's talking about, let me put it to you briefly: before the United States got involved in World War One, Germany had the brilliant idea of a doctrine called unrestricted submarine warfare.

And if you're familiar with warfare, or submarines, or submarine warfare, you know that it is, beyond the shadow of a single doubt or skepticism, better left restricted.

But what exactly was unrestricted submarine warfare? "If you see a ship blow it to bits!" except in German, not English. And this meant that all ships, even ships belonging to neutral countries, even ships with civilians on them, even ships delivering medical and humanitarian aid, were targets. Stupid, right?

It was the sinking of the Lusitania on May 7, 1915, that is said to have drawn the United States into the war against Germany and its allies. 1,198 of the 1,959 people aboard were killed, leaving just 761 survivors.

Now, what exactly does this have to do with controlling attention by divulging the brutal truth? To put it bluntly, "a swarm of angry German submarines, which we can't see and can barely detect, are firing missiles at our ships, even though you or your family members are on them, and even though we have nothing to do with the war," was a pretty brutal truth.

And weaker leaders might try to keep the people happy and minimize, mitigate, or draw attention away from the brutal truth. Ignorance is bliss, right? Wrong approach.

Ignorance isn't bliss.

Or, it only is until the world starts falling apart around you, at which point your blissful ignorance is replaced by the most painful, surprising sense of fear and betrayal.

Legendary leaders tell people the things that are hard to tell people, but that they need to hear. Legendary leaders divulge the brutal truth, and therefore control undivided attention, just like Woodrow Wilson did.

Hearing a leader today divulging the brutal truth is a breath of fresh air, isn't it? So, be that leader.

Call out the elephant in the room. Talk about the uncomfortable but necessary reality. Challenge the familiar beliefs. Expose the impending threat.

**DON'T IGNORE THE UNCOMFORTABLE BUT OBVIOUS**

FIGURE 21: Don't ignore the brutally obvious brutal truth. Call it out boldly. Don't try to hide anything, and definitely don't try to hide what is already obvious but unspoken.

And let me present the rule of minimization-reciprocation. Do not obscure the brutal truth, or you will be obscured. Do not mitigate the brutal truth, or you will be mitigated. Do not minimize the brutal truth, or you will be minimized. Divulge the brutal truth, no matter how hard it is to say and how hard it is to hear, no matter how comfortable ignorance might be, and no matter how tempting it might be to beat around the bush. Adopt a spirit of honesty and transparency at all times, and as a leader, you shall be rewarded with honor and total respect.

**KEY INSIGHT:**

# Humans Are Amazingly Adept At Identifying When Speakers Are Deflecting, Obscuring, Minimizing, or Misleading.

## MINIMIZE THE BRUTAL TRUTH AND SEE WHAT HAPPENS

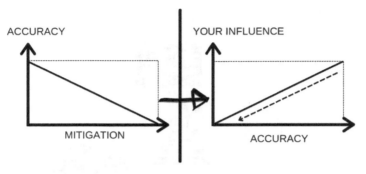

HOW MINIMIZING TOUGH FACTS MINIMIZES YOU

FIGURE 22: As your mitigation rises, your accuracy falls. As your accuracy falls, your influence falls, and as your accuracy rises, your influence rises.

Not to mention that you will control complete attention. And let's bring back making bold promises. That only works if you are trusted. In fact, all communication only works if you are trusted. So, what is one of the most reliable ways to gain trust? Telling your audience things they know would have been easier for you to conceal.

It is for this reason that so many of these legendary speeches follow structures that first divulge the brutal truth, and then make bold promises.

## DON'T MISS YOUR CHANCE TO CAPTIVATE THE AUDIENCE

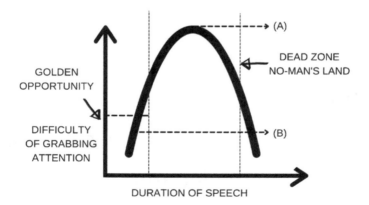

FIGURE 23: It is easiest to grab attention at the start of the speech. It is much harder to do so throughout the middle. It becomes easier once again at the end. The beginning of a speech is a golden

opportunity to grab attention. If you grab attention in the middle, not only will doing so have been less likely, but you only keep attention – assuming you don't lose it again – for about half of the speech (A). Not only is it easier to grab attention at the beginning, but if you keep it, you get attention for the entire speech (B).

In fact, let us add on to our previous equation of the communication of leadership. Remember? It goes like this: describe problems with empathy, and solutions to the problems with authority.

Let's update it to the equation of the communication of leadership V2.0: problems plus the brutal truth about the problems plus empathy about the internal pain the external problems cause, then solutions to the problems plus authority plus bold promises that it will work.

## THE FIRST STRUCTURE THE FIVE-STEPS CAN SUBSUME

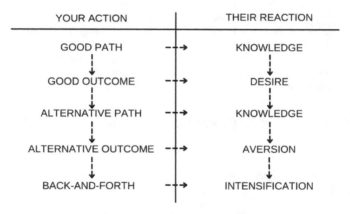

FIGURE 24: The five-step process and equation of the communication of leadership can subsume this structure, which relies on contrast to paint a persuasive narrative that makes your proposal seem self-evidently superior to alternatives that benefit less but cost more.

### KEY INSIGHT:

# The Set of Future Paths People Deem Possible is the Persuasive Battleground.

## THE SECOND STRUCTURE THE FIVE-STEPS CAN SUBSUME

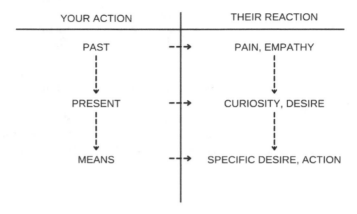

FIGURE 25: This structure creates tremendous curiosity and maintains audience attention throughout. It also conveys the immense value of your idea while generating productive persuasive tension. Tell them how bad it was "then," how good it is "now," and then "how" the change occurred. Before the third step, the audience is deeply curious about what caused the transition.

## VISUALIZING THE SECOND PROVEN PERSUASIVE STRUCTURE

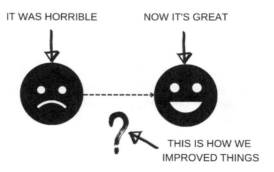

FIGURE 26: This is a visual representation of the past, present, means or then, now, how structure.

## THE THIRD STRUCTURE THE FIVE-STEPS CAN SUBSUME

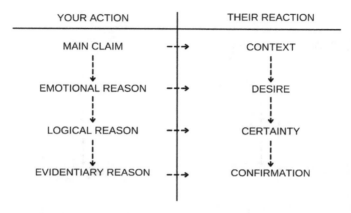

FIGURE 27: This structure uses Aristotle's 2,000-year-old persuasive framework of pathos (emotion), logic (logos), and ethos (evidence), while orienting itself in a list of three.

## THE FOURTH STRUCTURE THE FIVE-STEPS CAN SUBSUME

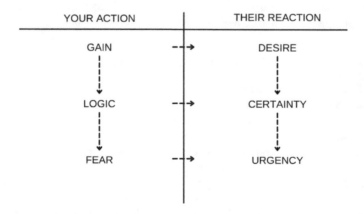

FIGURE 28: This structure uses loss aversion to generate an urgent motivation to adopt your proposal and reap the promised gain, which people feel logical certainty about. First, present the promised gain. Second, prove the credibility of the gain with logic. Third, reveal that the opportunity to reap the gain will expire.

## THE FIFTH STRUCTURE THE FIVE-STEPS CAN SUBSUME

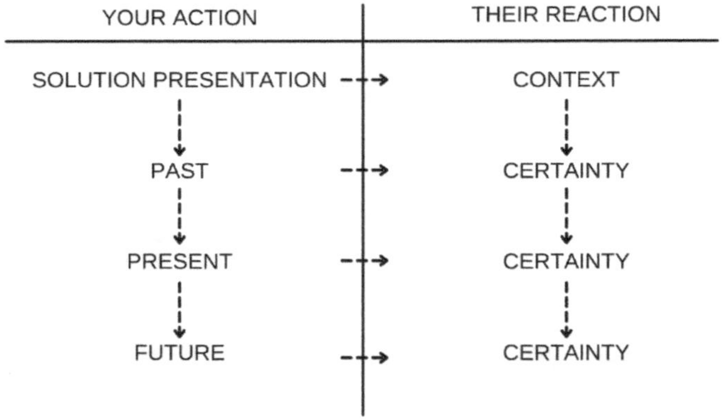

| YOUR ACTION | THEIR REACTION |
|---|---|
| SOLUTION PRESENTATION --→ | CONTEXT |
| ↓ | ↓ |
| PAST --→ | CERTAINTY |
| ↓ | ↓ |
| PRESENT --→ | CERTAINTY |
| ↓ | ↓ |
| FUTURE --→ | CERTAINTY |

FIGURE 29: This structure asserts the value of your solution across three dimensions of time, telling people how "it worked (or would have worked) then, it works now, and it will work in the future," providing three examples.

It's time to move on. John Fitzgerald Kennedy's words are immortal. They embody the communication of leadership. And now, we will unveil one of the most compelling secrets of he used that controlled the undivided attention of the world.

## SHIFT THE PERSPECTIVE

John Fitzgerald Kennedy ranks as one of the world's most legendary leaders, and one of the world's most effective communicators. His work is some of my favorite to analyze. When you read any speech he delivered, look closely and you'll see how much there is to unpack, simply in the realm of aesthetic beauty.

JFK is one of the world's most effective communicators, and what follows is some of the most effective words one of the most effective communicators has ever spoken.

And why are these words so effective? Because he shifts the perspective. Or, more accurately, because he elevates the perspective. You'll see what this means.

But first, let me give you the historical context that will set the stage for the finest example of the communication of leadership by perspective elevation I've ever seen.

The Cold War wasn't pretty. The two biggest nations, with completely contrary belief systems, were amassing nuclear arsenals. And not just any nuclear arsenals (although all are less than ideal), but arsenals so big that they could destroy the entire world hundreds of times over. Like I said, not pretty.

To make matters worse, the mechanisms of guaranteeing accidental launches or bomb drops didn't happen, by today's standards, were iffy at best. For example, did you know that a plane accidentally dropped a live nuclear bomb over the continental United States? And I can't decide if this makes matters better or worse, but to which nation did the plane belong? The United States. Thankfully the bomb didn't blow. So not only was the technical side of it so bad that a nation accidentally dropped a bomb on itself, but it was so bad that the bomb didn't blow even though it was supposed to.

Worry not! There was some consolation. And what was it? Mutually assured destruction, they called it. In other words: the best case for relaxation was the assurance that if either the Soviet Union or the United States shot first, the ensuing cross-fire would guarantee destruction for both sides. In yet other words: "It wouldn't happen because if it did, we would all die almost instantly, and nobody wants that." Not very comforting.

Why am I telling you this? What does it have to do with the communication of leadership, JFK, and elevating the perspective? I'll tell you right now. Despite being on the brink of total annihilation, JFK was able to elevate the perspective. But why does that matter? Because it controls attention. And when matters are more pressing and force a myopic perspective, it becomes extremely difficult to elevate the perspective away from the seemingly urgent demands of the present. And difficult things done well also control attention. That's the difficulty-ease hyper-response tendency.

So, the perspective at the time was, if you couldn't guess from my little historical anecdote, pessimism, and a sense of regression. But JFK changed that, if only for a few moments, and for a few people. He changed pessimism and regression to optimism and progress. And he did it by elevating the perspective, when he said the following, in a speech at Rice University, September 12, 1962: "No man can fully grasp how far and how fast we have come, but condense, if you will, the 50,000 years of man's recorded history in a time span of but a half-century. Stated in these terms, we know very little about the first 40 years, except at the end of them advanced man had learned to use the skins of animals to cover them. Then about ten years ago, under this standard, man emerged from his caves to construct other kinds of shelter. Only five years ago man learned to write and use a cart with wheels. Christianity began less than two years ago. The printing press came this year, and then less than two months ago, during this whole 50-year span of human history, the steam engine provided a new source of power. Newton explored the meaning of gravity. Last month electric lights and telephones and automobiles and airplanes became available. Only last week did we develop penicillin and television and nuclear power, and now if America's new spacecraft succeeds in reaching Venus, we will have literally reached the stars before midnight tonight. This is a breathtaking pace, and such a pace cannot help but create new ills as it dispels old, new ignorance, new problems, new dangers. Surely the opening vistas of space promise high costs and hardships, as well as high reward."

Talk about elevating the perspective. There's a lot to learn here. Don't worry. We'll unpack it all. He elevated the perspective away from "there's a pretty decent chance all of humanity will blow itself up, and so we should be pessimistic about how far we've regressed" to "humanity is progressing at a breathtaking speed."

But that's not all. He elevated the perspective from "humanity is progressing at a breathtaking speed," to "no man can fully grasp how far and how fast we have come, but condense, if you will, the 50,000 years of man's recorded history in a time span of but a half-century."

From a focus on pessimism and regression to a focus on human progress. And not just a focus on human progress, but such a focus from the elevated perspective of condensing all of history from 50,000 years to 50.

He zoomed out.

And the big picture view is almost always more promising than the short-term peaks and valleys.

We fall, we fail, we suffer, and we struggle. Sometimes we wage war, and sometimes we bring all of humanity to the brink of total annihilation. But if you zoom out far enough, even these desperate straits, even these drastically destructive valleys, start looking small. And that's exactly what JFK realized.

If you zoom out far enough, you realize two things. First, that what seems like a disaster is really just a short-term dip – of which there are many along the way – and second, that the big picture trend shows drastic improvement.

This isn't just true of the history of humanity. This is most likely true of whatever history is relevant to you. The history of your business. The history of your team. The history of your group. And on a more personal note, the history of you.

---

**KEY INSIGHT:**

Human Civilization is a Mere Cosmic Blip, but a Hyper-Interesting Blip at That. And Whatever Problem We Now Face is a Mere Blip on the Blip. Take the Long View, the Big View, and the Holistic View. See the Totality. Don't Let a Leaf Blind You to the Forest.

---

## THE SHORT-TERM VIEW MAY BE GRIM AND UGLY

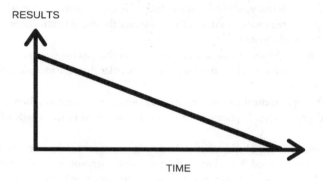

FIGURE 30: The short-term view may show you that in a given period of time your results went from very strong to abysmally bad.

## THE LONG-TERM VIEW IS MORE ACCURATE

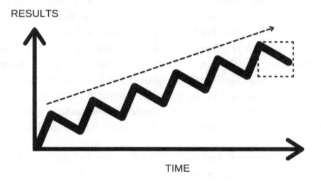

FIGURE 31: The long-term view will show you the long-term trend. It is often significantly more positive than the short-term view. The dotted box represents the previous image, FIGURE 13.

Let me give you a contemporary example of just how practical these hidden pieces of communication wisdom can be. Let's say you're a business leader. Let's say business has been slow, as business often happens to be, and people are pessimistic because of it. Maybe you overhear them talking about how things are falling apart. Maybe there is a pervasive dread that people will lose their jobs when the business goes underwater. Maybe people started looking for new jobs.

Let me tell you exactly what to do to achieve JFK-grade leadership. Go to your office, take a seat, close your eyes for a minute or two. Clear your head. Zoom out. Take the big picture.

Nine times out of ten, you'll find that it is drastically more optimistic than whatever short-term dip you are now experiencing. If not? Divulge the brutal truth, and apply the updated fundamental equation.

But you already know how to do that. So, let's say this just happens to be one of those nine times out of ten, where the big picture is prettier than the myopic mania of short-term thinking.

Call a meeting. Expose the short-term mania as what it is: inaccurate. Then, express your elevated perspective. Replicate your elevated perspective in the minds of your listeners.

"I know this has been a bad quarter (acknowledge the source of the myopic mania). But we have been around a lot longer than a quarter (transition to the elevated perspective). Last year, we signed more new business than any year in company history. This year we were on track to do the same, and we can get back on that track. We hired an unprecedented amount of new talent, people who will continue the success we've had over the past ten years. In a company with a ten-year history, we can't be fooled into seeing it quarter-by-quarter. Don't predict a bad future from a bad quarter. Look how far we've come, just in the last two to three years. Predict a good future from a good ten-year history, in which every subsequent year sowed the seeds for yet further growth, improvement, and prosperity. Sure, this is a bad quarter. But we've been around for 40 quarters. Some of which were bad, and yes, worse than this one. But if you look at the big picture, you will see that even after the worst quarters we've had, we bounced back, better than we were before. You will see that we have drastically improved over the long term. Bonuses have gone up. Salaries have gone up. Sales have gone up. The number of products has gone up. The quality of customer relationships has gone up. Press attention has gone up. Employee satisfaction has gone up. Internal promotion has gone up. Reputation has gone up. The results we've produced over 40 quarters speak stronger than the poor results we've produced in this single quarter (deliver elevated perspective)."

This will control attention. And it will also correct the bad thinking that might actually sow a bad future. People thinking that the future will be bad will probably make the future bad, and this strategy changes their negative expectations into positive beliefs.

Now, one of the most common pieces of advice you'll receive in regards to anything – be it leadership, worldview, or philosophy – is to "have perspective." But what does that really mean? What is a more precise way of saying it? Elevate the perspective.

"Have perspective" should be reworded to "have an elevated perspective that sees the big picture not the short-term," and it should be accompanied by "share that elevated perspective with others if you want to be a strong leader."

And now, we move away from elevating the perspective. We turn back to the themes of problems, pain, and the 2020 Democrats, for a lesson in speaking to injustice. It is a bullet-proof way of controlling attention. I'll tell you why.

## SPEAK TO BROKEN JUSTICE PROBLEMS

Any student of contemporary political science will confirm that, above all, one key difference between Republican messaging and Democratic messaging stands out.

Republican messaging works. Democratic messaging doesn't. Why? Republicans speak to common values. Democrats speak to various, non-value-driven things.

Republicans build intuitive, simple arguments. Democrats build complex, difficult ones.

Republicans appeal to emotion. Democrats appeal to logic.

But I'm noticing a shift. This messaging trend was first essentially accepted as common knowledge about 20 years ago (to the best of my knowledge, as someone with a bachelor's degree in political science). So, do you really think the Democrats would still, after 20 years, not have fixed the errors that were costing them votes, popularity, and elections? Not likely.

I think the Democrats have keyed in on something that makes their messaging work; something that controls attention, and thus achieves the communication of leadership. They have identified a particular subtext that just works. And it is a particular type of problem, causing a particular type of pain that controls attention, and achieves the communication of leadership.

This allows them to speak to common values. This allows them to build intuitive, simple arguments. This allows them to appeal to emotion. But we have some questions. What exactly is the messaging shift? How have they started communicating? And, more importantly, how does it control attention?

Luckily, we also have answers. The shift is a drastic focus on injustice.

They have all started communicating about problems of broken justice. It controls attention because, for all of our moral shortcomings (like nearly destroying all of humanity with nuclear weaponry), we have a keen eye for injustice. In other words: injustice controls our attention, particularly when we are the victims.

The democratic party has, deliberately or by accident, begun, in perfect unison, to brand itself as the party of rectifying injustice. And this is a powerful element of the communication of leadership. And it is also by far the most ubiquitous, uniformly evident strategy I have ever seen. It is present in nearly every single response in the 2020 Democratic primary debate.

But before I show you the examples, let's talk about the foundation of the strategy, and the core structure it produces. This strategy controls attention particularly well when there are three key requirements satisfied.

Injustice controls more attention when there is a clear perpetrator.

Injustice controls more attention when the audience is the victim.

Injustice controls more attention when the speaker is the force for good, who is working to rectify the injustice, defeat the perpetrator, and heal the victim(s).

And we see all of these ingredients in the appeals of the Democrats. The perpetrators are the Republicans and big corporations. The victims are immigrants, minorities, the working-classes, women, and other marginalized groups. The force for good is the Democratic party at large, but particularly the individual speaker, and their plans to create change.

Now, I'm not saying that this is a false representation of the world. I'm also not saying that this is a true representation of the world. I'm saying it doesn't matter whether this is true or false insofar as our goal is to unpack and learn strategies, and that no matter what, this strategy controls attention. As a student of political science for over a decade, I will tell you that we haven't figured it out yet, you're wrong if you think you have an obvious answer, and that it is probably partially true; the truth is likely somewhere in the middle ground, and not just because the middle ground is appealing, but because it's just true.

But let's turn to the examples. When we talked about problems and pain, I pulled at random from the first Democratic debate of this election season.

Now, I'm pulling from the final Democratic debate of this election season. This one was less crowded, and the responses were longer, so I only give six examples here.

Apologies for the lengthy examples, but I cannot resist when something is so drastically, dramatically evident, in such a ubiquitous, uniform way. And I promise this: you will so clearly see, in plain sight, the formula of a victim, plus a perpetrator, plus a speaker who's protecting the victim from the perpetrator, and restoring justice. Let's call it the victim-perpetrator-benevolence triad.

Bernie Sanders: "Well, Judy, what I would say is that we have a president who is a pathological liar (perpetrator). We have a president who is running the most corrupt administration in the modern history of this country (perpetrator). And we have a president who is a fraud, because during his campaign he told working people (victims) one thing, and he ended up doing something else (perpetrator). I believe, and I will personally be doing this in the coming weeks and months (speaker as benevolent force for good), is making the case that we have a president (perpetrator) who has sold out the working families of this country (victims), who wants to cut social security, Medicare, and Medicaid, after he promised he would not do that (perpetrator), and who has documentedly lied thousands of times since he is president (perpetrator)."

Joe Biden: "Well, I don't think they really do like the economy. Go back and talk to the old neighbors in the middle-class neighborhoods you grew up in (victims). The middle class is getting killed (victims). The middle class is getting crushed and the working class has no way up as a consequence of that (victims). You have, for example, farmers in the Midwest, 40 percent of them could pay, couldn't pay their bills last year (victims). You have most Americans, if they've received the bill for 400 dollars or more, they'd have to sell something or borrow the money (victims). The middle class is not, is behind the eight ball (victims). We have to make sure that they have an even shot (benevolent force for good). We have to eliminate (benevolent force for good) significant number of these god-awful tax cuts (perpetrator) that were given to the very wealthy (perpetrator). We have to invest in education (benevolent force for good). We have to invest in healthcare (benevolent force for good). We have to invest in those things that make a difference in the lives of middle-class people (victims) so they can maintain their standard of living (benevolent force for good). That's not being done, and the idea that we're growing, we're not growing. The wealthy, very wealthy are growing (perpetrators).

Ordinary people are not growing (victims). They are not happy with where they are (victims), and that's why we (benevolent force for good) must change this presidency (perpetrator) now.

Tom Steyer: "Let me say that I agree with Senator Warren in much of what she says. I've been for a wealth tax for over a year (benevolent force for good). I'm (benevolent force for good) in favor of undoing all the tax breaks for rich people (perpetrators) and big corporations (perpetrators) [crosstalk] that this administration (perpetrator) has put through. And in addition, I've talked about equilibrating the taxes on passive investment income (benevolent force for good), which would allow us to cut taxes for 95% of Americans (victims) by 10%. But there's something else going on here that I think is really important, and that's this. We know Mr. Trump's (perpetrator) going to run on the economy. I built a business over 30 years from scratch (benevolent force for good). We're (benevolent force for good) going to have to take him (perpetrator) on, on the economy in terms of growth as well as economic justice (benevolent force for good). We're going to have to be able to talk about growth, prosperity across the board for everyone in America (benevolent force for good). My experience building a business, understanding how to make that happen (benevolent force for good) means I can go toe to toe with Mr. Trump (perpetrator) and take him down on the economy and expose him as a fraud and a failure. And I think that's different from the other people on this stage. I think we need a different unconventional way of attacking a different unconventional president (perpetrator) who actually went after the best prepared candidate in American history and beat her."

Elizabeth Warren: "So I see right now is, we've got to get the carbon, we've got to stop putting more carbon into the air (benevolent force for good). We've got to get the carbon out of the air and out of the water and that means that we need to keep some of our nuclear in place (benevolent force for good). I will not build more nuclear. I want to put the energy literally and the money and the resources behind clean energy and by increasing by 10-fold what we put into science, what we put into research and development (benevolent force for good). We need to do what we do best. And that is innovate our way out of this problem and be a world leader (benevolent force for good). But understand the biggest climate problem we face is the politicians in Washington (perpetrators) who keeps saying the right thing, but continue to take money from the oil industry (perpetrators). Continue to bow down to the lobbyist (perpetrators), to the lawyers (perpetrators), to the think tanks (perpetrators) to the bought and paid for experts (perpetrators). America understands that we've got to make change and we're running out of time (benevolent force for good). That climate change threatens every living thing on this planet (victims). But getting Congress to act, they just don't want to hear it (perpetrators). And if we don't attack the corruption first, if we don't attack the corruption head on, then we're not going to be able to make the changes we need to make on climate, on gun safety, on drug pricing, on all of the big problems that face us. We need a Washington that doesn't just work for the rich and the powerful (perpetrators). We need one that works for our families (victims)."

Andrew Yang: "I believe everyone on this stage (benevolent force for good) would do the right thing by DREAMers (victims) in the first hundred days. I would make it a top priority (benevolent force for good). I'm the son of immigrants myself. The fact is almost half of fortune 500 companies were started by an immigrant or children of immigrants (benevolent force for good). Immigrants make our country stronger and more dynamic (benevolent force for good). And immigrants are being scapegoated for issues they have absolutely nothing to do with (victims). If you go to the factory in Michigan, it's not wall to wall immigrants (victims). It's wall to wall robot arms and machines (perpetrators). We have to send the opposite message of this administration (perpetrators) and, as your president, I think I could send a very clear message, where if you're considering immigrating to this country and I'm the president, you would realize my son or daughter can become president of the United States (benevolent force for good). That's the opposite of the current administration (perpetrators) and that's the message I would love to send to the world (benevolent force for good)."

Pete Buttigieg: "Yes, and they should have a fast track to citizenship (benevolent force for good) because what the United States did under this president (perpetrator) to them (victims) was wrong and we have a moral obligation to make right what was broken (benevolent force for good). And on the larger issue of immigration, my understanding of this issue isn't theoretical (benevolent force for good). It's not something I formed in committee rooms in Washington. It begins with the fact that my household, my family came from abroad. My father immigrated to this country and became a U.S. Citizen. It comes from the fact that I'm the mayor of a city where neighborhoods that were left for dying (victims) are now coming back to life (benevolent force for good), largely because of the contributions mainly of Latino immigrants. And I've seen those same neighborhoods shut down (victims). Families huddling in church (victims), panicking just because of the rumor of an ICE raid (perpetrator) that does not make our country safe. Just to look into the eyes of an eight year old boy (victim) whose father was deported (victim) even though he had nothing so much as a traffic ticket against his name and try to think of something to tell that boy because I couldn't tell him what he most wanted to hear, which is just that he was going to have his dad back. How can harming that young man (victim) possibly make America safer (perpetrator)? When I am president? Based on those experiences, I will make sure that this is a country of laws and of values and that means not only ending these unspeakable frugal practices at the border (perpetrator), but finally and truly fixing the immigration system (perpetrator) that has needed, a full overhaul since the 1980s (benevolent force for good)."

That's about as clear as it gets. It's almost so obvious that it becomes hard to see. I know that I almost always have to dive deep into the examples of the communication of leadership to identify their hidden secrets and their little-known sources of persuasive power. And that throws me off. When something is this obviously evident, I make the mistake of looking deep, when in truth, it's all perfectly evident on the surface.

Twenty-five statements, in total, portraying the speaker or the speaker's party as the benevolent force for good. Thirty-two statements, in total, portraying something as a perpetrator, endangering justice. (Usually, Republicans, the wealthy, corporations, or the bills Republicans pass to give tax cuts to the wealthy and corporations.) Twenty-four statements, in total, portraying someone as the victim of the perpetrator, often the audience itself.

## THE FIRST "VPB" VARIANT: "LET ME HELP YOU"

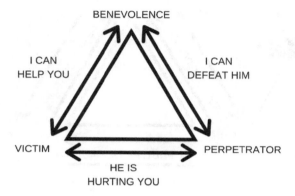

FIGURE 32: This reveals the first victim, perpetrator, benevolence variant. The audience is comprised wholly of people who are being victimized by the perpetrator.

## THE SECOND "VPB" VARIANT: "JOIN ME TO HELP THEM"

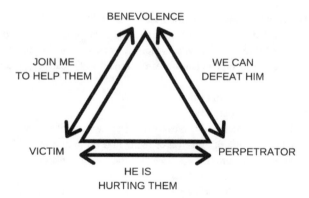

FIGURE 33: This reveals the second victim, perpetrator, benevolence variant. The audience is comprised wholly of people who you are calling to help you help the victims, who are not themselves necessarily victimized.

## THE TWO "VPB" VARIANTS CAN OVERLAP

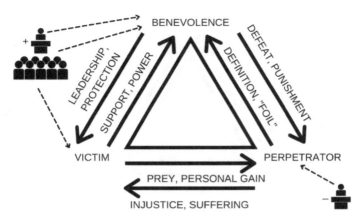

FIGURE 34: This reveals how the model connects its three ingredients; how each part connects to the others, and the relationships between them as well as what they offer one another. The audience can be both the victims, called to offer support to the benevolent force who can heal them, and also candidates for joining the benevolent force, called to help in healing the victims. The speaker's opposition is typically the perpetrator.

And I was conservative in counting up the totals. There could be yet more, that are less clear, which I left out because I wanted to avoid inflating the number. But why? Why does this work? More specifically, why does it work so well that nearly every single politician in the Democratic debates uses the model with near-perfect uniformity? So many reasons.

We have a keen sense of justice.

We want to punish perpetrators.

We feel satisfied when good defeats evil; when justice replaces injustice.

And we like to think of ourselves as living in a world dominated by the forces of justice, not injustice, a world in which we face the consequences of our actions, not of someone else's actions. A fair world.

The message of "[insert perpetrator] has committed injustice against [insert victim], and [insert benevolent force for good] will fix it" speaks to common values, is an intuitive and simple argument, and appeals to emotion.

This message creates cognitive dissonance.

What's that? Cognitive dissonance is the mental discomfort we experience when we perceive a gap between who we want to be or think we already are and reality. And we all want to live in a world governed by justice (or think we already do), so whenever a Democrat exposes injustice, particularly against the common people, what happens? Massive cognitive dissonance. And cognitive dissonance controls attention.

It heightens emotional arousal.

Under the strain of cognitive dissonance, the brain experiences reactions much like those which occur during a physical threat.

And the anger toward the injustice, and the perpetrators that produced it, sets the stage for a feeling of immense good-will toward the benevolent force for good that will rectify the situation. Good-will so immense, that it can sway entire elections.

But what else creates good-will? The victim status (whether legitimate or illegitimate) takes the responsibility off of the shoulders of the victimized. That, too, is immensely appealing. In other words: we want to take responsibility for the good things in our lives, but we want to abdicate responsibility for the bad things.

Now, let's take it a little deeper. What else does this formula accomplish? It speaks in terms of personified archetypes that are immensely accessible to everyone. Let me explain.

Participants in a study had to explain what was happening in a video. The video showed an "interaction" between three triangles. First, there are only two triangles. They move around a little. The people overwhelmingly say one triangle is bullying the other. Then, the third one comes in. It joins forces with the victim triangle and beats back the bully triangle. The people overwhelmingly say that the third triangle saved the victim triangle.

Do you see how deeply ingrained in our minds certain concepts, certain archetypes, and certain personalities are? We have such a high propensity to describe the world in terms of a set of concepts that we even see them played out in the movements of a bunch of triangles on a screen. We might actually be born with an understanding of certain concepts. These are archetypes. Archetypes are easily understood and projected onto the world as we perceive it. God(s), maternal forces, paternal forces, danger, fate, cause and effect, are just some examples of archetypes.

We also tend to understand things through personification. It makes sense: we are social beings, and so we describe the world by assigning human qualities to non-human objects. If you want the deeper answer of why the "perpetrator causing injustice plus victim hurt by the injustice plus benevolent force for good restoring the justice" is so compelling, you now have a complete answer.

And so, here's the complete answer of why it works. Let's review. We have a keen sense of justice. We feel satisfied when perpetrators are punished. We love to see good overcome evil; to see justice beat back injustice. We are more likely to join a team, form a coalition, and support a politician when they portray clear and compelling common values. We are much more likely to accept intuitive, simple arguments, which we find much more persuasive. We are much more likely to accept emotional arguments, which we also find much more persuasive. We direct our attention, subconsciously, toward that which creates cognitive dissonance, mental discomfort, and the physiological response of a physical threat. We feel good-will toward the positive forces that rectify wrong-doing. We love abdicating responsibility for the bad things in our lives because it lightens the burden of "bad thing" plus "responsibility for the bad thing" to just "bad thing." This can be a good practice if responsibility is legitimately not ours. One of the most painful psychological states is being the victim of something and shouldering psychological responsibility, guilt, and blame for it if someone else actually created the perpetration, not you. We cling to worldviews that project particular archetypes onto reality. We cling to worldviews that project particular personalities onto reality.

Don't forget what we discussed. Don't forget the model these highly intelligent political minds seem to be adopting in perfect unison. Don't forget how easily it can be adapted to almost any leadership situation, to control attention, and achieve the communication of leadership.

### THE PERSUASIVE VORTEX OF THIS LITTLE-KNOWN TRIAD

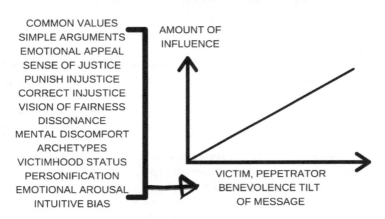

FIGURE 35: This reveals the relationship between the extent to which your persuasive narrative achieves the victim, perpetrator, benevolence model, and your influence, as well as the complex psychology behind this powerful relationship.

Now, we're going to jump back to Ronald Reagan. We're going to discuss a simple, straightforward, and easy strategy to control attention. We're going to discuss how one simple perception can get everyone to lend you their ears. Let's talk about it.

## PRESENT A MOMENT OF DECISION

Decisions demand attention. An impending moment of decision, for which one is yet undecided, creates a tension like none other. Doesn't it? Think about the moments in your own life, where you know you need to decide something, but you can't bring yourself to do it just yet. Doesn't that impending decision, that fork in the road, seem to always creep into your consciousness, no matter how hard you try to suppress it?

## THE THREE THINGS YOU HAVE TO DO WITH THEIR ATTENTION

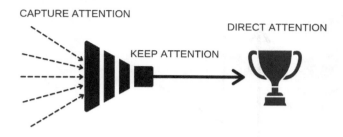

FIGURE 36: This is another way to visualize the function of these attention-captivating techniques. Your goals as a communicator are to capture attention in your persuasive funnel, keep attention, and direct it toward a purpose.

It is precisely this principle that Ronald Reagan used to captivate attention in his November 3, 1980, election-eve address, when he said, "The election will be over soon, autumn will become winter, this year will fade into next... and yet, the decisions we make tomorrow will determine our country's course through what promises to be one of the most perilous decades in our history."

Why does Ronald Reagan say this? Because he understands that moments of decision loom large in people's consciousness and that when they are faced with an impending moment of decision, they direct their attention subconsciously, automatically, toward anything that might help them make the decision.

Let's call it the decision hyper-response tendency. And the key to this strategy is really in that last part. That people subconsciously, automatically, direct their attention to anything related to the decision, is critical. Why? Because your communication is related to the decision, in a major way.

See how this simple strategy can control a tremendous amount of attention, with a tiny amount of effort? Simply apply direct decision enumeration: tell people that they have to make a decision. That's the first step. And it's the only essential step to control attention.

But you can also do some more, to really drive this home. You can also apply advanced decision-framing. Let me tell you about what kinds of decisions are most compelling. That will show you exactly how to up the ante with this strategy, and apply advanced-decision-framing.

## THE IMPACT OF ADVANCED DECISION-FRAMING

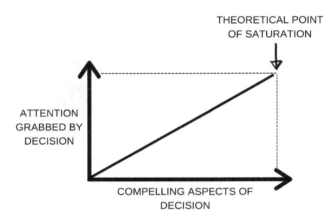

FIGURE 37: As the number of these components of compelling decisions rise in your communication, so does the attention the decision grabs.

Necessary decisions (as in, there is no way around making a decision) control more attention than avoidable decisions.

It is an avoidable decision if you can get by without deciding anything.

Preexisting decisions (as in, they knew about it before you presented it to them), control more attention than new decisions.

It is a new decision if they are hearing about it for the first time.

High-stakes decisions (as in, the impacts of this are major) control more attention than low-stakes decisions.

It is a low-stakes decision if its impacts are minor.

One-chance decisions (as in, this is the only time you get to make this decision) control more attention than many-chance decisions.

It is a many-chance decision if you eventually get another chance to make the same decision. And, many-chance decisions with more delay between the chances control more attention than those with less delay between the chances.

Benefit-gain decisions (as in, decisions that, correctly made, produce a benefit) control more attention than benefit-absent decisions (and the greater the benefit, the greater the attention).

It is a benefit-absent decision if you don't stand to gain anything if you choose correctly.

Loss-prevention decisions (as in, decisions that, correctly made, prevent a loss) control more attention than loss-minimization-absent decisions (and the greater the loss prevented, the greater the attention).

It is a loss-minimization-absent decision if there is no associated harm that you can minimize by choosing correctly.

Dual-benefit decisions (as in, decisions that, correctly made, give both a benefit and protection from a loss) control more attention than unitary decisions.

It is a unitary decision if it only includes a benefit or the prevention of a loss attached to it if you choose correctly, but not both.

Uncertain decisions (as in, the outcomes are unpredictable) control more attention than certain decisions.

It is a certain decision if the outcomes of the available choices are predictable.

High-reach decisions (as in, a lot of people will be impacted by the decision) control more attention than low-reach decisions.

It is a low-reach decision if few people will be impacted by the decision.

Unclear decisions (as in, the outcomes are predictable, but which outcome is preferable is a difficult choice) control more attention than clear decisions.

It is a clear decision if the outcomes are predictable, and one is clearly preferable.

Two-option decisions (as in, you choose this one or that one) control more attention than many-option decisions.

It is a many-option decision if you have to pick one of two or more options or pick anything you can imagine.

Clear-credit decisions (as in, credit for the outcome will be clearly assigned to the decision-maker) control more attention than no-credit decisions.

It is a no-credit decision if nobody can trace down the decision-maker.

Impending decisions (as in, you have five minutes to decide), control more attention than non-impending decisions, that is until such a decision is procrastinated to the point that a non-impending decision becomes impending.

It is a non-impending decision if you have five days to decide, for example.

Hopeful decisions (as in, there is genuinely a good chance you might make the right choice here, and you have some ability to discern the correct choice) control more attention than hopeless decisions.

It is a hopeless decision if "chances are you are screwed either way, so why bother?"

Dynamic decisions (as in, there is one way to win, and one way to lose) control more attention than flat decisions.

It is a flat decision if there are either two ways to win or two ways to lose.

Individual decisions (as in, one person must decide) control more attention than group-based decisions.

It is a group-based decision if someone else can take care of it, or the credit for the decision as well as its resulting harms or benefits are shared amongst a group.

Future-regret decisions (as in, one option will put you through the pain of future regret) control more attention than no-regret decisions.

It is a no-regret decision if there's a very low chance you'll regret making either of the choices.

No-default decisions (as in, a straight road that splits into two, demanding the choice of one or the other) control more attention than default decisions.

It is a default decision if there is a default, and you can make the decision to accept the default. Or, in other words, the two options continue on the road you are on or take that road that branches off of it.

Instant gratification decisions (as in, whether the decision is wrong or right is immediately made evident) control more attention than delayed gratification decisions.

It is a delayed gratification decision if whether the decision is wrong or right will be gradually made clear after a delay, if at all.

Social-pressure decisions (as in, the decision and its outcome are made public for all to see) control more attention than non-social pressure decisions.

It is a non-social-pressure decision if the decision and its outcome will remain private forever.

Concrete decisions (as in, there is a clear, distinct action that corresponds to a decision, like voting for one candidate over another) control more attention than intangible decisions.

It is an intangible decision if there is no clear, distinct action associated with the decision, such as the decision of thinking a certain way over another way.

So, how can a future titan of industry (such as yourself) use this when you inevitably reach that position of leadership? How can anyone at all, in any position of leadership, use what we just discussed to control attention and achieve the communication of leadership? I'll show you right now. In other words, I'll show you how to craft the perfect rhetorical decision that is guaranteed to control maximum attention.

Here's all it comes down to: simply creating the perception that there is a decision and that this decision has the qualities that control more attention instead of the ones that control less attention. Let me give you some step-by-step, fill-in decision-templates for this.

These will seem formulaic. They are. And there's nothing wrong with that. Formulas exist because they work. What makes good communication good is not ambiguous. It can be broken down into a set of simple steps. And in this book, it is broken down.

Anyway, here are the templates that describe exactly how to create each of the qualities of high-attention decisions. Pluck out the qualities you want to portray. Use your knowledge of yourself, your audience, your situation, and the decision to pick the quantities you know fit best.

Necessary decision: "We have to make a choice. We cannot afford to circumvent that. There's no way around it. We simply have to decide on [insert topic], because [insert reasons]."

Preexisting decision: "We have to make a decision on [insert topic]. You've known about this for a long time – we all have – and yet, we still have not moved on it. We've procrastinated. We've delayed. But now it's time to decide, because [insert reasons]."

High-stakes decision: "There's a lot hinging on this decision and only this decision. The stakes are high. We have [insert important value], [insert important value], and [insert important value] to lose, because [insert reasons]."

One-chance decision: "We have to consider this carefully because we do not get a second chance to make the right choice, or to minimize the impacts of us having made the wrong one. This is our only opportunity to decide on [insert topic], because [insert reasons]."

Benefit-gain decision: "If we make the right decision about [insert topic] we have the potential to gain [insert benefit], [insert benefit], and [insert benefit]."

Loss-prevention decision: "If we make the right decision about [insert topic], we can protect ourselves from [insert harm], [insert harm], and [insert harm]."

Dual-benefit decision: "If we make the right decision today, we can gain [insert benefit] and [insert benefit], without suffering [insert loss] and [insert loss], because [insert reasons]."

Uncertain decision: "This is going to be a difficult decision. On the one hand, [insert option] is attractive because [insert reasons]. But at the same time, [insert option two] is equally compelling because [insert reasons]. People are split on this, and there is no expert consensus to guide us either."

High-reach decision: "The eyes of the world are upon us. They are waiting to see how we handle [insert decision], because [insert reasons]. Millions will hold us to account if we do this poorly."

Unclear decision: "We know that if we choose [insert option], we will experience [insert set of outcomes]. But if we choose [insert option two], we will experience [insert set of outcomes two]. And we don't know what is better: [insert set of outcomes], or [insert set of outcomes two], because [insert reasons]."

Two-option decision: "This should be a simple decision. We have two options. We can't do anything else. There's no secret third or fourth option. It's either [insert option], or [insert option two], because [insert reasons]."

Clear-credit decision: "We must tread carefully. This decision we're about to make, and its consequences, will bear our name, and define our reputation, because [insert reasons]."

Impending decision: "We can't put this off any longer. We have until [insert deadline] to decide on [insert topic], because [insert reasons]."

Hopeful decision: "This is by no means hopeless. We have an army of experts and highly-respected consultants with us. We have it in us to discover the correct decision, because [insert reasons]."

Dynamic decision: "We can either win or lose. We can either experience [insert benefits] if we're right, or suffer [insert consequences] if we're wrong, because [insert reasons]."

Individual decision: "There's no disappearing in the crowd for this one. You must each make the decision yourselves, and live with the consequences yourselves, whether good or bad, because [insert reasons]."

Future-regret decision: "Be careful. Do not take this lightly. You don't want to regret the consequences of a wrong choice, because [insert reasons]."

No-default decision: "We can't sit back and do nothing, because [insert reasons]. We either have to [insert option], or [insert option two]. Doing nothing is not an option because [insert reasons]. It's out of the discussion."

Instant-gratification decision: "As soon as we decide, we'll know if we did the right thing, because [insert reasons]."

Social-pressure decision: "People will know if we made the right call because [insert reasons]."

Concrete decision: "We can either do [insert concrete action], or [insert concrete action two]."

Now, it's time for a quick detour. I recently read about the Japanese philosophy of Kaizen, in Robert Maurer's excellent book *One Small Step Can Change Your Life*.

What's that? This: gradually accumulating many small, incremental, positive actions over time, rather than trying to produce good things in big sweeps – what Maurer calls the "innovation approach" – which tend to fail.

And Kaizen presents a fascinating element of human psychology and the underlying neurobiology. We have a prefrontal cortex in our brains governing a set of cognitive functions.

What cognitive functions? The ones responsible for rational, logical, intelligent decision making.

And it is locked in a constant conflict with this thing called the amygdala.

The amygdala responds to danger by shutting down the rest of our brain, including the prefrontal cortex. Let's call it the danger hyper-response tendency. Is this bad or good? It is not just good, but excellent in the face of real danger. You don't want to think; you want to do: run, fight, or hide, for example. Danger demands rapid action, not slow, deliberative thought.

But it can be bad in some cases. Why? Because of the amygdala's Achilles heel. Because intellectual challenges, like decisions, activate the amygdala much like real danger does, and paralyzes our prefrontal cortex. In other words, the intellectual challenge paralyzes the part of the brain which we need to actually solve the intellectual challenge.

## THE PREFRONTAL CORTEX VERSUS THE AMYGDALA

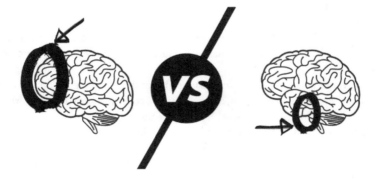

FIGURE 38: The prefrontal cortex evolved later in our evolutionary history. The amygdala is more primordial. Both serve crucial cognitive functions.

The philosophy of Kaizen urges that by thinking and acting on a smaller scale, we avoid activating the amygdala, keep access to our prefrontal cortex, and thus think and act in superior ways with ease.

## WHY INCREMENTALISM BEATS THE INNOVATION APPROACH

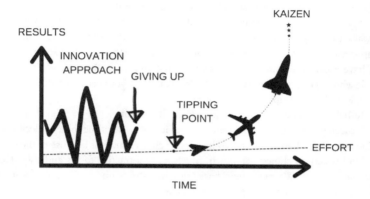

FIGURE 39: A linear, slow, incremental increase in effort over a long period of time eventually hits a "tipping point" producing non-linear gains. The innovation approach achieves sporadic, extreme highs and lows, with varying effort expended throughout. Eventually, the sporadic and effortful nature of the innovation approach, according to Kaizen experts, pushes people to give up on the endeavor.

So, why am I telling you this? Because decisions, specifically of the kind we want to present, grab attention but also trigger the amygdala. And that seems bad. But let's keep talking.

It's true: the decision-difficulty-attention paradox postulates that a decision tends to grab more attention as it becomes more difficult (that's what those qualities are really doing: making it more difficult).

And difficult decisions make people uncertain. Uncertain people are inert, and their rational decision-making apparatus is paralyzed because the uncertainty triggers the amygdala. So, is this whole chapter teaching you a counter-productive communication strategy?

Absolutely not. Time is the most valuable commodity, and I would never waste yours with a counterproductive strategy. Let me explain why this is actually a good thing. People in uncertainty want certainty due to our doubt-avoidance tendency (we hate doubt and want to escape it). And here's the advantage. Who wants certainty more? The person who is uncertain, or the person who isn't uncertain? We talked about problems and solutions. Problems make solutions more attractive. Uncertainty is a problem, and your certainty is the solution.

It's true: you might paralyze them and activate their amygdala with the difficult decision, but they will only remain that way if you don't present certainty.

If you do, they will not remain paralyzed for long, but rather, be compelled to impulsively place their confidence in your certainty as they scramble to escape the discomfort of doubt.

So, I'll briefly summarize this idea. And I'll urge you to note this: the advantage I'm explaining now is in addition to that of grabbing attention. And here's the summary of the process. A big, large-looming, difficult decision creates uncertainty. Uncertainty activates the amygdala. The amygdala inhibits the prefrontal cortex, which is the component that can actually make the decision. If you stop now, you screwed this up. You have a paralyzed audience. That's not what you want. But you won't stop now. People who are uncertain want certainty. If you present your certainty, they will escape their uncertainty by leaping toward your certainty.

Ronald Reagan didn't just present a difficult decision.

He also presented his certain choice. And it is because of the difficult decision that he had attention when he presented his certain choice, and it is because of the difficult decision his certain choice was much, much more attractive to his audience. Get it? Layers and layers. We peel them back, discover the truth, and communicate with piercing knowledge of human psychology. That's all this is.

---

**KEY INSIGHT:**

Your Honest Convictions, Your Honest Certainties, Often Emerge from a Chaos of Honest Uncertainties.

There's No Need to Hide This. Ordering Chaos is More Valuable Than Reordering Order.

---

**BRINGING IT ALL TOGETHER: ANOTHER PERSUASIVE VORTEX**

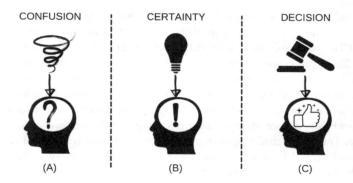

FIGURE 40: Uncertainty causes confusion. Your certainty causes clarity. Clarity causes a decision – the decision to act in a certain way or believe a certain thing, for example.

And now, we're going to turn to a less demanding strategy. In fact, a cliché strategy. I'm willing to admit that. But while the strategy is cliché, we take it to a whole new level. Let's talk about storytelling.

# TELL A STORY

This is the single most overused piece of communication and public speaking advice.

It's in every single book on the subject. Every single "25 tips to captivating communication" article contains it. Go ahead and see for yourself. The vast majority of people default to this when asked to give advice on a presentation, speech, or piece of communication.

So, why is it in my book? Because it's a travesty that you're told to "tell a story," without breaking down how to do it well, or why stories work in the first place. And nobody knows how to tell a story better than Barack Obama.

There's a theme running throughout all of these examples of the communication of leadership. The theme? After nearly every single example, the speaker was explosively propelled forward in their careers.

After JFK's moon speech, his approval ratings shot up massively. After Reagan's "moment of decision" speech, his party was rallied and unified. After Wilson's address regarding unrestricted submarine warfare, he gained a drastic amount of political capital.

And what about this example? What did Barack Obama gain from this example of the communication of leadership, at the 2004 Democratic National Convention? According to some people, people much smarter than me, he gained the White House.

It's true: this is called the speech that made Obama president (just like Clinton's speech in response to the lady in the red dress is called the speech that made Clinton president).

And it was this moment that propelled him to national political fame, setting the groundwork for a successful presidential bid in 2008. Let me show you the example. And then, I'll tell you exactly what's so special about it, and how it's not just a standard story.

"Thank you so much. Thank you. Thank you. Thank you so much. Thank you so much. Thank you, Dick Durbin. You make us all proud. On behalf of the great state of Illinois crossroads of a nation, land of Lincoln, let me express my deep gratitude for the privilege of addressing this convention. Tonight is a particular honor for me because, let's face it, my presence on this stage is pretty unlikely. My father was a foreign student, born and raised in a small village in Kenya. He grew up herding goats, went to school in a tin-roof shack. His father, my grandfather, was a cook, a domestic servant to the British. But my grandfather had larger dreams for his son. Through hard work and perseverance my father got a scholarship to study in a magical place, America, that's shown as a beacon of freedom and opportunity to so many who had come before him. While studying here my father met my mother. She was born in a town on the other side of the world, in Kansas. Her father worked on oil rigs and farms through most of the Depression. The day after Pearl Harbor, my grandfather signed up for duty, joined Patton's army, marched across Europe. Back home my grandmother raised a baby and went to work on a bomber assembly line. After the war, they studied on the GI Bill, bought a house through FHA and later moved west, all the way to Hawaii, in search of opportunity. And they too had big dreams for their daughter, a common dream born of two continents. My parents shared not only an improbable love; they shared an abiding faith in the possibilities of this nation. They would give me an African name, Barack, or "blessed," believing that in a tolerant America, your name is no barrier to success. They imagined me going to the best schools in the land, even though they weren't rich, because in a generous America you don't have to be rich to achieve your potential. They're both passed away now. And yet I know that, on this night, they look down on me with great pride. And I stand here today grateful for the diversity of my heritage, aware that my parents' dreams live on in my two precious daughters. I stand here knowing that my story is part of the larger American story, that I owe a debt to all of those who came before me, and that in no other country on Earth is my story even possible."

Let's first break down the magic of stories, and then how to do them right. This is going to be a lot of complex information. I'm warning you. But I refuse to tell you to use stories without giving you insight into the hidden principles of stories that make them so useful.

And here's the best part: you can apply some of these following principles in other ways, too. So let's get into them.

Stories facilitate mirroring: People have the tendency to themselves feel the emotions of the characters of a story and the storyteller.

Stories create ethos: The perception that the speaker has the interests of the audience at heart and the life experiences behind them that make them worth listening to.

Stories provide context: context contributes just as much meaning to language as the language itself. If language is the picture, context is the frame. And stories set in stone the clear context for the subsequent communication in compelling fashion. And that matters more than we typically realize. In extreme cases, reversing context can reverse the meaning of a set of words.

Stories are emotionally-arousing: According to Jonah Berger, who answers the question "what makes things go viral?" in his book *Contagious*, emotional arousal is a fundamental component of virality. Messages that are emotionally arousing, creating any emotion with intensity, tend to get attention. (Interestingly, another principle of viral messages is that embedding meaning in a story makes the message more viral).

Stories are impactful: Impact is an emotional punch that comes from hearing about people. Impact has to do with what happens to people as a result of something. If it's not ultimately about people, it lacks impact. If your communication does not trace a series of consequences down to how something hurts or helps people, it falls flat. And stories are impactful because they provide people-oriented narratives. Impact comes from mirroring. It is the feeling in someone's heart and mind when they imagine themselves in the shoes of the character of the story. That's the emotional punch of people-driven impact.

Stories provide personal impact: Personal stories provide personal impact. Obama's story was not about some other people in some other place, but his very own family, and the history of his lineage.

Stories activate the intuitive bias: People are more likely to believe a message that is intuitive. And people are also more likely to pay attention to an intuitive message because it reduces the strain on their cognitive resources. A general rule is that high cognitive cost equals low attention paid. If the amount of attention your communication costs is too great, they won't pay the price. Stories minimize attention-cost.

Stories activate the coherence-bias: When people are judging messages, they judge the most coherent message as the most realistic and believable. Stories are inherently coherent, providing a fluent, contiguous, consistent narrative.

Stories activate the simplicity-bias: People are biased to prefer simple messages. We give simple messages more attention. We prefer simplicity because it conserves our limited cognitive resources, and we resent messages that waste those resources without providing anything in return. Stories are inherently simple.

## THE SECRET OF HOW MOST PEOPLE MAKE MOST DECISIONS

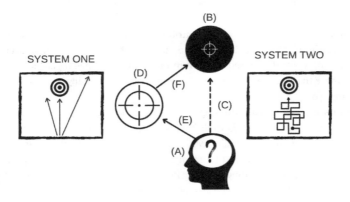

FIGURE 41: Don't forget the process of attribute substitution. When evaluating a question (A) about a target variable (B), instead of doing the difficult thinking and evaluating it directly (C) using system two, most people use a heuristic variable (D) that is much easier to evaluate, evaluate this variable (E), and transfer the answer to the target variable (F). This substitution occurs in system one.

Stories activate the plausibility-bias: When people are judging the truth of something – that which they believe is true gets attention, mind you – they see the most plausible message as the truest message. An idea is plausible if it seems like it could be true. Stories are excellent tools for getting humans to suspend disbelief. Stories are inherently plausible.

Stories activate the availability-bias: When people are trying to answer a question, they overweigh evidence that is readily available; evidence that quickly and fluently comes to their minds. Stories are memorable, and thus available. And you want people to overweigh your evidence. By embedding it in a story, you activate the availability bias in your favor and guarantee that people will overweigh it.

### KEY INSIGHT:

Stories Speak to the Soul. Numbers Hit the Mind. Narratives Touch the Heart. And It Is the Heart That Decides.

## HOW NARRATIVES MAKE YOU MEMORABLE AND ENGAGING

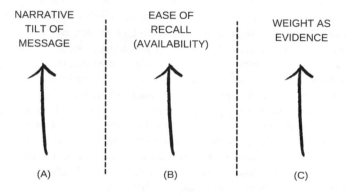

| NARRATIVE TILT OF MESSAGE | EASE OF RECALL (AVAILABILITY) | WEIGHT AS EVIDENCE |
|:---:|:---:|:---:|
| (A) | (B) | (C) |

FIGURE 42: As the narrative tilt of a message rises (A) the availability of the message rises (B), raising its weight (C).

Stories activate the visual bias: We are significantly more adept at mentally handling visual messages; messages that are either visually presented to us, or that verbally paint visual scenes. We produce movies in our minds, and when someone creates one of these movies, they get our attention, and we can easily handle the message without using a high load of cognitive resources. Low cognitive resource expenditure raises attention. That which people find easy to listen to, they listen to. Visual information increases retention. And stories inherently imply, but more often explicitly detail, visual scenes. We see the movie in our minds as we hear the story.

Stories activate the consistency-bias: We drastically overweigh the apparent consistency of a message in judging its value (which means its truth, relevance, and merit). Messages with a fluent coherence of meaning and messages with no self-contradictions between units of meaning grab our attention and hold it – or, more accurately, such messages avoid losing our attention. When we sense a contradiction in one place, we think the whole message is broken, and so we ignore it. Stories, often told in a sequential narrative of events, are inherently consistent.

Stories create attention-command: When you are speaking and you command your audience's attention, you solidify your control of their attention. "But pay attention to this..." is an example. "Look here... Check this out... Listen to this..." are phrases that achieve attention command by directing them to move their attention. And stories themselves are a hidden source of attention command. When you tell a story, you are commanding your audience's attention to picture the events in your story, and in doing so – in beaming mental movies into your audience's minds – you solidify your control of attention. Stories inherently achieve attention command.

Stories appeal to the character-bias: We see the world through a set of filters that manipulate impressions to fit certain predesignated molds. The character-filter is one of them. We have a massive proclivity to see the world through the character-filter, in which events are perceived as the results of characters acting with intent. We reject randomness. We reject meaninglessness. We think that everything that happens is the result of someone, somewhere, doing something; that the world is the product of the deliberate and intentional actions of a cast of characters, not random chance occurrences. And moreover, we don't stop with people; we go so far with this filter that we personify inanimate objects and self-evidently random occurrences, giving them human characteristics. Stories inherently appeal to the character-bias.

Stories appeal to archetypes: We've discussed this previously. Let's have a brief overview. We have evolved with predispositions to easily understand the world through the lens of a set of personalities. The nurturer, the threat, the predator, the prey, the opportunity, the challenge; these are just some archetypes that our minds can effortlessly handle. And know this: stories have been around since language has been around. The cultural evolution of stories and archetypes are closely intertwined. And know this too: most archetypes are characters. Characters and archetypes are often one and the same. Think about the ranks of stock characters that are ever-reoccurring in our stories. Stories inherently lend themselves to archetypes.

Stories appeal to the cause-and-effect worldview: We see the world as a set of cause-and-effect relationships. We believe that we can broadly categorize nearly everything into two buckets: Causes, and results of those causes. And this is accurate. Everything is a result of something and the cause of something else (except for the human free will, which as far as we can see, has the capacity to cause itself). But the cause-and-effect worldview tempts us into hyperactively connecting available causes to available effects and those available effects to available subsequent causes, creating stories where there may be none. Sure: Everything is both a cause and an effect, but any particular effect is not necessarily the byproduct of any particular cause and does not necessarily cause any particular subsequent effect. Human perception forms these connections impulsively. And stories inherently organize themselves as a sequence of causes and effects. Something happens, then the protagonist does something as a result, which causes something else as a result, and then something else, and so on and so forth. There is little *fait accompli* and little randomness in the most compelling stories. Everything is the result of something else. Stories inherently lend themselves to the cause-and-effect worldview.

Stories appeal to the intent-assumption: We alluded to this in our discussion of the character-bias. The intent-assumption is the belief that people act with intent behind all of their actions, clearly seeking a goal, and having in mind a defined mechanism for manifesting that goal. Stories are excellent at assigning intent to the people and characters portrayed in them.

## THE LITTLE-KNOWN PRINCIPLE OF WHAT WE FIND CREDIBLE

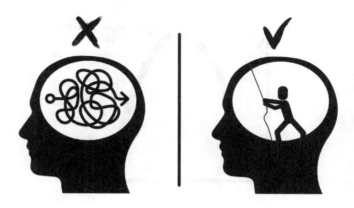

FIGURE 43: People reject complex, convoluted webs of causal relationships. They intuitively accept the notion of an agent acting with intent and pulling the strings.

Stories appeal to the evolutionary practical worldview: In Jordan Peterson's groundbreaking book *12 Rules for Life*, he presents his understanding of how humans see the world. Every possible thing can be viewed in multiple ways, arranged on a spectrum between broad and specific; macro and micro; big-picture oriented and detail-oriented. He argues that our cognitive impression-producing and impression-understanding machinery is designed – through natural selection and genetic evolution – to place us somewhere in the middle of that spectrum. On the macro end, we see things from a perspective so removed from the details that we can't practically engage with things. On the micro end, we see things from a perspective so inundated in the details that we once again can't practically engage with things, though for a different reason. Placed in the middle, between the micro and macro, we see things in a practical way: as a set of tools, objectives, challenges, opportunities, and practical machinations to navigate between, use, avoid, play with, fight against, and otherwise interact with. This is the only practical way to survive, as far as we know. This is how we evolved. We don't see things from a perspective so large or so minute that we can't operate. Instead, we perceive the world with just the level of specificity – somewhere in the middle of the spectrum – to allow us to see the universe around us as a set of action-levers we can play around with to achieve our desired outcomes, without getting overwhelmed by the grandiose big picture or drowning in the irrelevant details. When I read this, I drew one key insight about how we view the world, and why stories appeal to that. We see the world as a set of tools to use, objectives to reach, challenges to overcome, facts to gather, questions to answer, and threats to escape. We see the world in a practical way. And stories directly echo this. The actions of the characters in the stories evoke their practical worldviews, which resonates with our evolutionary practical worldview and grabs our attention.

## HOW PEOPLE SEE THINGS AND HOW TO USE IT

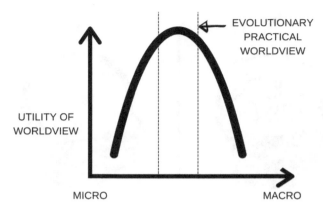

FIGURE 44: As you move toward the middle ground between a micro- and macro-oriented worldview, the utility of your worldview rises. As you move away from the middle ground between a micro- and macro-oriented worldview, the utility of your worldview falls.

Alright. That was a lot. But it was incredibly worthwhile. A few more brief points. Stories are incredibly easy to stack with other techniques we discussed. Think about it. Stories make it easier to turn a common everyday occurrence into a miracle, by explaining the story of what happens when you open the hood.

Stories make it easier to elevate the perspective. In fact, JFK's perspective-elevation that we previously discussed was combined with a story. And it's a case of one plus one equals three. In other words, a story plus another technique intertwined with one another results in more power than their individual forces summed.

So, what's the most compelling story structure?

According to Donald Miller, author of *Building a Storybrand* (a marketing book that I read, and applied the insights from to my book descriptions, which now beat nearly every average market metric), presents the following story structure.

"A character has a problem...

Then meets a guide...

Who gives them a plan...

And calls them to action...

That action either results in a success or failure..."

He also asks us to answer these following questions to build the wire-frame of our story.

## VISUALIZING THE 5,000-YEAR-OLD STORY FRAMEWORK

FIGURE 45: This is one of the most psychologically persuasive and irresistibly influential structures known to man. You can use it for countless rhetorical purposes.

"Who were you, and what did you want? What was the problem you encountered, and how did it make you feel? Who did you meet, or what did you read that helped you? What plan did you come up with after meeting the guide? What did it feel like to take action on that plan? What could have been lost if you'd have failed? What was the happy ending you experienced?"

## A THREE-STEP STRUCTURE THAT USES THE FRAMEWORK

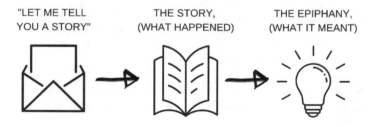

FIGURE 46: A powerful three-step persuasive structure is to invite the audience into a story, tell them the story (which slowly brings them to the realization of the core persuasive epiphany), and then elaborate on the epiphany.

Now, more broadly, we ought to close this section with a general discussion of what makes stories so powerful. We – and by we, I mean our species – have evolved right alongside stories. Stories are tools we have used to package information and pass it down from the year 1 to the year 2020, and they are tools we'll use to pass on these same stories as long as our species exists.

Humans love stories. On so many levels, stories appeal to us. On a psychological, cultural, personal, and even neurological layer, stories are devices that make meaning easy for us. Stories are inherently attention-controlling. And that should make them ubiquitous tools in your arsenal.

## THE ROLE YOU MUST PLAY IN RELATION TO YOUR AUDIENCE

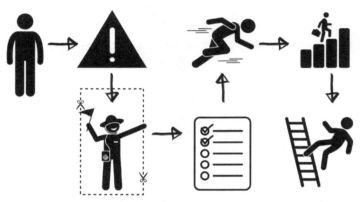

FIGURE 47: You must play the role of your guide in relation to your audience members, who are the heroes in the story. Through this lens, from this perspective, we can reformulate the story framework (which is typically called the hero's journey): "your audience has a problem and meets you, who acts as a guide, gives them a plan, and calls them to action that results in success." What are the two elements of an effective guide? Empathy and authority: "I've been there, I understand how you feel, and I got out, so I know how to get you out."

Now, let's talk about one of Franklin Delano Roosevelt's most attention-grabbing speaking techniques, that made his listeners feel like he was inviting them to play a role in the writing of history.

## FUTURE SIGNIFICANCE TODAY

Future significance today – what does it mean?

To understand future significance today, you need to know some background information about the hidden components of human psychology.

Let's talk about it. Humans want to be a part of something bigger than themselves. Humans want to feel significant. Humans want to feel that their daily activities are contributing something. Humans want to play a role in the writing of history. Humans want to feel like someone, somewhere, will feel some impact from their actions, and hopefully a positive one. Humans want a footprint. Humans want to build a footprint in a group.

So, what is the future significance today strategy? I'll summarize it in one simple, straightforward sentence. Don't let the simplicity fool you into forgetting how insanely powerful this strategy is, based on all of those compelling elements of human psychology invoked. It's telling your audience how significant people in the future will find what they are doing that day. Get it? Elegant. Easy. Effective. Step-by-step. Simple. Straightforward.

## THE "EYE OF HISTORY" STRATEGY GRABS ATTENTION

NOW                                            +100 YEARS

FIGURE 48: Tell them how people a century later will perceive their struggle in the present moment. Put their present endeavor in the context of history. Tell them how the eye of history will see it.

And examples of this abound. We need not belabor this issue.

You know FDR is my favorite example of the communication of leadership. You know FDR was able to achieve incredible results in the real world by accomplishing those five critical steps we discussed. And you now know that when he said the simple phrase "Yesterday, December 7, 1941, a *date which will live in infamy,* the United States of America was suddenly and deliberately attacked by naval and air forces of the Empire of Japan..." he was explaining the future significance of what people today are going through.

And it's fascinating: the actual manuscript used by FDR shows that he crossed out whatever was there before, and wrote in "a date which will live in infamy." The intent is clear.

Life is suffering.

At least some people think so. And there's certainly an element of truth to that. People can sense when an endeavor will beat, batter, and bruise them; when something is going to sap their energy, sap their time, and sap their willpower; when they are going to struggle and suffer in pursuit of a goal. They want to procrastinate such a thing. They want to give their attention to something else – anything else – to avoid that difficult but necessary endeavor.

It takes a leader in a time like this to give them the strength they need to even perform the act of directing their attention toward the struggle. And what does that leader need to do? That leader does not need to tell them it'll be easy.

Be a leader, not a liar.

The leader needs to say, "Sure, it'll be hard… but tomorrow, people are going to look back at this and say 'I'm so happy that this person pushed through because it made my life so much better.'"

The leader needs to give the person the willpower infusion that comes from knowing that the struggle today will be significant to people tomorrow. In doing so, the leader brings to bear the psychological forces we previously touched on.

## DIFFICULTY-CONFIDENCE MATRIX

Certain people, at certain times, doing certain things, need leaders more than others.

Let me give you an example. Bam! World War Two starts. You're a young man in the United States, 18 years of age, and you get drafted. You are pulled out of school. Your life plans are derailed. Who knows if you'll be able to resume them when it's all over? You get a week notice to pack your bags – with strict regulations detailing the Spartan minimum of items you're allowed to bring – and then you say goodbye to your family for who-knows-how-many-years, and perhaps for the last time.

You arrive at a training camp. In three months – just three months – you are turned from a normal young man into, borrowing Obama's language, an apparatus of the "finest fighting force this world has ever seen," to fight an enemy in a "distant, different and difficult land."

Grueling. Absolutely grueling. And not just grueling, but terrifying. And it's not just an everyday terror. It's a bone-jarring, mind-blowing, strength-sapping terror. You've heard the stories of how the German army is the most advanced military in all of recorded human history. You've heard the stories of how they have effortlessly toppled European government after European government, and how the last island of democracy in the sea of Nazi tyranny is barely holding on (and it does so simply because of another leader who used the communication of leadership – Winston Churchill). You've heard the stories of the blitzkrieg – or lighting war strategy – used by the Wehrmacht, and you've heard how their ruthless soldiers are hyped up on ideological fervor and methamphetamine-infused combat supplements, allowing them to fight with ferocity for three days without sleep, food, or rest.

I mentioned that certain people, at certain times, doing certain things, need leaders more than others. If you are in the situation I just described, you're one of these people who needs to hear a leader use the communication of leadership more than most.

Enter Dwight D. Eisenhower. Enter the difficulty-confidence matrix. Let's bring out the transcript. It was short. It was simple. But it meant everything to those brave yet uncertain young men, who saw their world turn upside down in a matter of weeks, who were about to board boats to storm barricaded beaches and planes to parachute into the picturesque plains of Europe, always moving forward – and never backward – despite the bludgeoning barrage of billions of bullets and bombs.

Here's what he said: "Soldiers, Sailors, and Airmen of the Allied Expeditionary Force. You are about to embark upon the Great Crusade, toward which we have striven these many months. The eyes of the world are upon you. The hopes and prayers of liberty-loving people everywhere march with you. In company with our brave Allies and brothers-in-arms on other Fronts you will bring about the destruction of the German war machine, the elimination of Nazi tyranny over oppressed peoples of Europe, and security for ourselves in a free world. Your task will not be an easy one. Your enemy is well trained, well equipped, and battle-hardened. He will fight savagely. But this is the year 1944. Much has happened since the Nazi triumphs of 1940-41. The United Nations have inflicted upon the Germans great defeats, in open battle, man-to-man. Our air offensive has seriously reduced their strength in the air and their capacity to wage war on the ground. Our Home Fronts have given us an overwhelming superiority in weapons and munitions of war, and placed at our disposal great reserves of trained fighting men. The tide has turned. The free men of the world are marching together to victory. I have full confidence in your courage, devotion to duty, and skill in battle. We will accept nothing less than full victory. Good Luck! And let us all beseech the blessing of Almighty God upon this great and noble undertaking."

So, let's dissect this piece of the communication of leadership and discover the strategy embedded in it: the difficulty-confidence matrix. It goes like this. "Hell yes, this will be difficult, dark, and dreary." "Hell yes, I have the most complete confidence and surpassing certainty that despite that difficulty, you're going to vanquish your foe and emerge the victorious champions of the world."

### KEY INSIGHT:

# Bad: "It's Tough." Also Bad: "It's Not Tough." Good: "It's Tough… But We're Tougher."

## THE "HARD BUT EASY" STRATEGY INSPIRES ENTHUSIASM

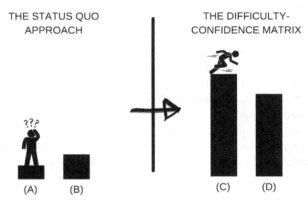

FIGURE 49: The status quo approach is to leave their estimation of their capabilities where you found it (A), and their estimation of their incoming difficulties as somewhat commensurate with their capabilities (B). The difficulty-confidence matrix works best in difficult circumstances. It massively increases their estimation of their capabilities (C), while acknowledging the significant difficulty they face (D).

Simple, right? It's saying that it will, in fact, be difficult, but that you know it is not more challenging than your people are courageous, competent, and capable. It's difficult. It's very difficult. It will test us. It will stretch us. It will threaten to break us. But we will prevail because it is no match for us.

Instant willpower boost.

Willpower used to address the damn thing. Willpower used to place one's attention where it needs to be, instead of trying to shirk the challenge. Awesome.

### KEY INSIGHT:

A Leader's Duty: Help People Bear their Burdens. A Leader's Toolbox: Hope, Wisdom, Love, Vigilance, Commitment, Complete Honesty, and Evidence-Based Conviction.

## TOO MUCH ORDER BORES AND SUFFOCATES US

FIGURE 50: Too much regularity, predictability, comfort, sameness, and safety suffocates our human spirit.

## TOO MUCH DISORDER SCARES AND OVERWHELMS US

FIGURE 51: Too much chaos, change, danger, uncertainty, and unfamiliarity can overwhelm us.

## THIS GOLDEN MEAN CREATES HUMAN FLOURISHING

FIGURE 52: The golden mean is standing right on the line between chaos and order, with one foot in each, and balancing the two. The difficulty-confidence matrix achieves this rhetorically, exposing your audience to the chaos of difficulty but also revealing the certainty and resilience of their capability to confront the chaos.

## UNPACKING WHAT IT MEANS TO PROGRESS IN LIFE

FIGURE 53: Personal growth and career progress is often increasing the scope of the chaos one can manage and the disorder one can turn into a corresponding order.

And I mentioned the last remaining island of democracy in Europe, and how it held on despite the Nazi onslaught, because of Winston Churchill. We turn to him now, and a communication strategy he used to control concentrated attention in Britain's direst, darkest, most testing time.

# DECLARATORY CASCADE

I heard Winston Churchill was hopelessly drunk when he spoke these words. Who knows? If he was, it represents one of the few times in the past 3,000 years of recorded human history that a drunk person was lucky – not unlucky – his words were remembered.

But what were the words? They were, quite honestly, majestic, and these everlasting words embody, I estimate, over fifty rhetorical strategies. But we focus on one today. And one specifically designed to control attention. A declaratory cascade.

And you must understand the context of the era. Nights were no longer dark. The raging fires gave them a reddish glow. Though while the fire stripped the darkness from the night sky, it draped the darkness like a curtain over the spirit of those who thought their standing as the final free people remaining in Europe would not last long.

And these words were a beacon of light in that spiritual darkness, that made the drear seem not impervious, but penetrable with the right mix of courage and unity.

Here's what he said, when Nazi bombs were bursting in the beautiful boulevards of London, fires were ferociously devouring his people's dwellings, and despair seemed no less than undeniable destiny amidst the dramatic destruction that donned London.

Reading these legendary words now, 80 years after they were uttered, still gives me chills. The communication of leadership will do that to you.

"We shall go on to the end, we shall fight in France, we shall fight on the seas and oceans, we shall fight with growing confidence and growing strength in the air, we shall defend our island, whatever the cost may be, we shall fight on the beaches, we shall fight on the landing grounds, we shall fight in the fields and in the streets, we shall fight in the hills; we shall never surrender."

There are, I believe, about fifty rhetorical techniques wrapped up in this short excerpt. But we're going to talking about one in particular: the declaratory cascade.

What you have to know to understand this strategy is this: when you're speaking, each of those comma-delineated phrases sounds like a sentence. The declaratory cascade is simple. It's straightforward. But it's insanely powerful. It creates captivating intensity. It creates captivating rhythm. It creates captivating cadence. And it controls attention. So, what is it? A cascade of short, snappy, assertive, confident, compelling, absolute statements in short sequence.

Anaphora, starting a series of sentences with the same words, is usually attached to the declaratory cascade. For Churchill, his repetitive, sentence-starting phrase was "we shall fight..."

And this does something else: it creates a rhythm, an expectation, which gives incredible importance to the first phrase that breaks away from the pattern. That's called the breakaway phrase. In this case, it was "we shall never surrender." The audience expected "we shall fight..."

But their attention was concentrated on that phrase when it broke from the pattern, especially after following it with the first two words "we shall," essentially implying repetition before breaking it. The declaratory cascade is not just accompanied by anaphora, but often grammatical parallelism.

In addition, strict parallelism.

So, all of the sentences are short, snappy, crisp, and direct declaratory statements filled mostly with absolute, uncompromising, unambiguous language, making confident, aspirational promises.

That's the declaratory cascade. It controls attention because it lowers cognitive load, and makes listening easy. The sentences also start with the same phrase, until that key sentence that breaks away from the pattern. That's anaphora.

### HOW TO AVOID A MAJOR COMMUNICATION OBSTACLE

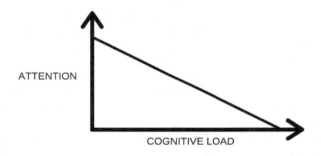

FIGURE 54: As cognitive load rises, the attention your audience pays you drops.

It builds captivating rhythm and then places importance on – and therefore directs attention to – the final phrase which breaks from the pattern. And the sentences also have a nearly-identical grammatical structure. That's grammatical parallelism.

Grammatical parallelism also builds attention-grabbing cadence and lowers cognitive load, which controls attention. Last, the sentences have many of the same words placed in identical positions. That's strict parallelism. Strict parallelism builds attention-grabbing rhythm.

That's all we need to know for the declaratory cascade. The same speech uses the difficulty-confidence matrix. "In the air – often at serious odds, often at odds hitherto thought overwhelming – we have been clawing down three or four to one of our enemies; and the relative balance of the British and German Air Forces is now considerably more favorable to us than at the beginning of the battle. In cutting down the German bombers, we are fighting our own battle as well as that of France. My confidence in our ability to fight it out to the finish with the German Air Force has been strengthened by the fierce encounters which have taken place and are taking place. At the same time, our heavy bombers are striking nightly at the tap-root of German mechanized power, and have already inflicted serious damage upon the oil refineries on which the Nazi effort to dominate the world directly depends."

And now, this next attention-grabbing strategy of the communication of leadership marries JFK's, MLK's, and Churchill's approaches, showing us a strategy that they have all used with extreme efficacy.

---

**KEY INSIGHT:**

# A Cascade of Declarations is a Declaration of Its Own... a Powerful Metadeclaration.

# It Declares One is Comfortable Declaring, which is an Act of Hope and a Leap of Faith.

---

## SUPERABUNDANCE

We already know quite a bit about these three leaders: JFK, MLK, and Churchill. We know how they used the communication of leadership and what they did with it. So, we're going to get right into the strategy.

It's called superabundance. It's one of the four core elements of ancient rhetoric. It is also called addition, repetition, or expansion.

And that's truly all it is. You'll see what I mean by that.

If you're wondering, the Latin word for superabundance is adiectio (I say, despite knowing that you probably weren't wondering). Superabundance came from the ancient "rhetors:" masters of rhetoric. It's no secret why their words have lived on for over 2,000 years.

According to Wikipedia, superabundance, or amplification, "refers to the act and means of extending thoughts or statements: to increase the rhetorical effect, to add importance, to make the most of a thought or circumstance, to add an exaggeration, or to change the arrangement of words or clauses in a sequence to increase force."

What are the other three elements of ancient rhetoric?

First, omission, or in Latin, detractio.

It is also called subtraction, abridgment, or lack.

Omission is less important than superabundance.

Second, transposition, or in Latin, transmutatio.

It is also called transferring. Also, not as important.

And lastly, permutation, or immutatio, in Latin.

It is also called switching, interchange, substitution, or transmutation. Again, not as important.

Here's what you need to know about superabundance: it takes an idea that could be summarized by one single word, but instead, it breaks down that word into a mountain of beautiful, flowing, eloquent and evocative language.

It's one of the only times you want to lower your word economy by saying less with more words. I'll give you the three examples of superabundance empowering the communication of leadership by drawing people in and grabbing attention.

Churchill could have said, "We shall go on to the end, we shall fight this battle *everywhere* it takes us, and we shall never surrender." There's no superabundance in that. Instead, he expanded *everywhere* into this: "we shall fight in France, we shall fight on the seas and oceans, we shall fight with growing confidence and growing strength in the air, we shall defend our island, whatever the cost may be, we shall fight on the beaches, we shall fight on the landing grounds, we shall fight in the fields and in the streets, we shall fight in the hills." That's the power of superabundance.

JFK could have said, "Let every nation know, whether it wishes us well or ill, that we shall do *anything* in order to assure the survival and success of liberty." There's no superabundance in that. Instead, he expanded *anything*, into "Let every nation know, whether it wishes us well or ill, *that we shall pay any price, bear any burden, meet any hardship, support any friend, oppose any foe,* in order to assure the survival and the success of liberty." That's the power of superabundance.

MLK could have said, "So, let freedom ring from every state." There's no superabundance in that. Instead, he expanded *every state* into "So, let freedom ring from *the prodigious hilltops of New Hampshire. Let freedom ring from the mighty mountains of New York. Let freedom ring from the heightening Alleghenies of Pennsylvania! Let freedom ring from the snowcapped Rockies of Colorado! Let freedom ring from the curvaceous slopes of California! But not only that; let freedom ring from Stone Mountain of Georgia! Let freedom ring from Lookout Mountain of Tennessee! Let freedom ring from every hill and molehill of Mississippi. From every mountainside, let freedom ring.*" That's the power of superabundance. MLK also used superabundance two more times in this speech. "And when this happens, when we allow freedom to ring, when we let it ring from (expansion of everywhere) every village *and every hamlet, from every state and every city,* we will be able to speed up that day when all of God's children, (expansion of God's children) black men and *white men, Jews and Gentiles, Protestants and Catholics,* will be able to join hands and sing in the words of the old Negro spiritual, "Free at last! Free at last! thank God Almighty, we are free at last!"

Superabundance – and all these strategies – are enduring. Superabundance was understood and explained around 2,000 years ago by ancient rhetorical masters. And yet, in our time, it is used by legendary leaders everywhere.

What does this prove? That the core elements of the communication of leadership are not arbitrary. They are timeless. What do I mean by that? I didn't create those five steps in the process, just like I didn't create superabundance. I found them. I found them buried in the words that have stood the tests of time. I found them hidden in the language that motivated people to do incredible things (putting a man on the moon, recovering from economic depression, and crushing Nazi Germany, are just among them). I found them layered just under the elements of communication that meets the eye; there for anyone who is willing to do a little digging (or read the words of someone who has done a lot of digging, like you are right now). They were there before me; they will be there after me. And not only does this apply to the five steps, but the strategies to achieve them.

## SPEAK TO THE MOMENT

What's one signal that, without fail, indicates a compelling example of the communication of leadership? A video of a speech going viral. Nearly every single viral video of a speech I've witnessed applied at least one of the strategies in this book, and very often many more than one.

And this particular video of a speech in the British Parliament grabbed one million views in just a week. Why? Well, people say it comes down to just one segment from the speech. Who is the speaker? Julia Gillard, someone who led an incredible career.

She served as the 27th prime minister of Australia, and the leader of the Australian Labor Party from 2010 to 2013. Though I'm sure if you asked her, she would tell you that the moment we are discussing today would rank near the top of her "most fun on the job moments" list.

So, what exactly happened? What did she say? And why did it go viral? "Good sense, common sense, proper process is what should rule this Parliament. That's what I believe is the path forward for this Parliament, not the kind of double standards and political game-playing imposed by the Leader of the Opposition now looking at his watch because apparently a woman's spoken too long." And why did it go viral? There's a surface-level answer.

But there's also the truth, and while the two often overlap slightly, they are rarely identical. The surface-level answer? This speech went viral because she "roasted" her political opponent, Tony Abbott. But there's nothing special in that. This happens in the United States Congress all the time, and it doesn't make waves.

So, what's the truth? What do we find if we dig deeper? It's not that she put her political opponent on blast, it's how. And how did she do it? By speaking to the moment. Let me tell you what probably went on in her head: "Good sense, common sense, proper process is what should rule this Parliament. That's what I believe is the path forward for this Parliament, not the kind of double standards and political game-playing imposed by the Leader of the Opposition... *(WAIT. Do NOT continue this as planned, Gillard, because Mr. Abbott is giving you a fantastic opportunity to speak to the moment)*... now looking at his watch because apparently a woman's spoken too long."

In other words, I believe Gillard had a plan for what she was going to say, but deviated from it when she saw the opportunity to speak to the moment and call out Abbott's immediate behavior.

## THE IRREFUTABLE CURSE (OR BLESSING) OF LEADERSHIP

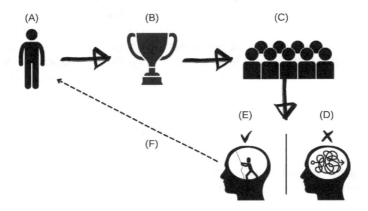

FIGURE 55: People have a psychological tendency to attribute observed phenomenon to agents. This is called agent detection bias. The blessing of leadership is that a leader (A), who is a visible and salient agent, can present accomplishments and positive outcomes (B) and even attribute them to "the company" or "the team" (C), but because people instinctively reject convoluted explanations (D) and intuitively accept single agents acting with intent (E), have those accomplishments attributed to themselves (F), even if they have little or nothing to do with it (like a president being credited for a good economy even though he hasn't implemented any new economic policies). The curse of leadership is that the same psychological process occurs with bad outcomes.

Another example? I am writing this section during the Coronavirus epidemic in the United States. Congress was supposed to pass a bill offering economic relief to Americans. The first iteration did not pass, because Democrats in the House of Representatives voted it down. I recently saw a video of a Republican in the Senate – whose name, despite trying to track it down, I could not find – applying the same exact strategy. He said, and I am paraphrasing, "Look around. The Democrats voted down this bill. But where are they? I'm looking around. I see only my Republican colleagues here ready to negotiate and work through our differences in a bipartisan manner. There's one Democrat, two, three, but that's it. And behind that door, Chuck Schumer [the leader of the Democrats in the Senate] behind closed doors, in secret, is trying to advocate for the very thing his party just supposedly voted down in this bill: corporate bailouts."

He applied this strategy in two ways. He spoke to the moment once, by calling out the absence of Democrats in the chamber, and then a second time, by calling out Chuck Schumer's lack of transparency associated with closed-door negotiations.

Both of these things, just like Tony Abbott checking his watch during Gillard's speech, are right now, in the moment. And that's why it's so powerful to call them out. With that, we conclude this step, and turn to part two.

### REVISITING THE FUNDAMENTAL FIVE-STEP PROCESS

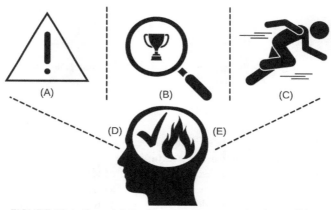

FIGURE 56: Let's revisit the five-step process and put everything we learned in the context of this framework. First, grab attention (A). Then, direct it to a definite purpose (B). Then, back it with intentional action (C). Back this entire process with correct thinking (D) and a powerful motive (E).

**KEY INSIGHT:**

# Only Appeal to Hope, or Fear, or Any Future-Based Sentiment, For One Purpose: Clarifying What Constitutes Duty Now.

## YOU COMPLETED STEP ONE OF FIVE

FIGURE 57: In this chapter, you learned how to complete the first step: capture attention.

...............................Chapter Summary...............................

- Present problems with empathy and solutions with authority. This is the foundational structure.
- People have problems that cause pain and pay attention to people who talk about solving the problems and pain.
- Legendary leaders do not seek to obfuscate difficult realities. Instead, they face the difficult truth head-on.
- Problems of broken justice produce a tremendously powerful persuasive impact, as do their potential solutions.
- Present problems plus the brutal truth about the problems plus empathy about the internal pain the externals cause.
- Present solutions to the problems with authority plus bold promises that they will work.

### KEY INSIGHT:

Human Attention is One of the Most Powerful Creative and Generative Forces Known to Us. No Wonder So Many Mythologies Wrap It in the Clothes of the Divine.

## THE FIVE-STEP FRAMEWORK (PART ONE)

| 1 | Controlling Attention |
|------|------------------------------------|
| 1.1 | Portray Empathy |
| 1.2 | Portray Authority |
| 1.3 | Set High Expectations |
| 1.4 | Expose a Hidden Miracle |
| 1.5 | Speak to the People's Pain |
| 1.6 | Build a Coalition |
| 1.7 | Make Bold Promises |
| 1.8 | Divulge the Brutal Truth |
| 1.9 | Shift the Perspective |
| 1.10 | Speak to Broken Justice Problems |
| 1.11 | Present a Moment of Decision |
| 1.12 | Tell a Story |
| 1.13 | Future Significance Today |
| 1.14 | Difficulty-Confidence Matrix |
| 1.15 | Declaratory Cascade |
| 1.16 | Superabundance |
| 1.17 | Speak to the Moment |
| 2 | Directing Attention to a Definite Purpose |
| 3 | Backing the Attention with Intentional Action |
| 4 | Backing the Intentional Action with Correct Thinking |
| 5 | Backing the Entire Process with a Powerful Motive |

## GIVING THE GIFT OF MEANING

"What feats he did that day: then shall our names.
Familiar in his mouth as household words
Harry the king, Bedford and Exeter,
Warwick and Talbot, Salisbury and Gloucester,
Be in their flowing cups freshly remember'd.
This story shall the good man teach his son;
And Crispin Crispian shall ne'er go by,
From this day to the ending of the world,
But we in it shall be remember'd;
We few, we happy few, we band of brothers;"
- King Henry in Shakespeare's Henry V

a small number of lucky people

united in their devotion to each other

and to a mission worth remembering

MEANING

**Access your 18 free PDF resources, 30 free video lessons, and 2 free workbooks from this link:**
**www.speakforsuccesshub.com/toolkit**

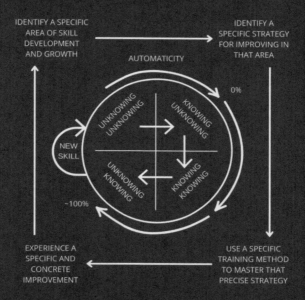

How do anxious speakers turn into articulate masters of the craft? Here's how: With the bulletproof, scientifically-proven, 2,500-year-old (but mostly forgotten) process pictured above.

First, we identify a specific area of improvement. Perhaps your body language weakens your connection with the audience. At this point, you experience "unknowing unknowing." You don't know you don't know the strategy you will soon learn for improving in this area.

Second, we choose a specific strategy for improving in this area. Perhaps we choose "open gestures," a type of gesturing that draws the audience in and holds attention.

At this point, you experience "knowing unknowing." You know you don't know the strategy. Your automaticity, or how automatically you perform the strategy when speaking, is 0%.

Third, we choose a specific drill or training method to help you practice open gestures. Perhaps you give practice speeches and perform the gestures. At this point, you experience "knowing knowing." You know you know the strategy.

And through practice, you formed a weak habit, so your automaticity is somewhere between 0% and 100%.

Fourth, you continue practicing the technique. You shift into "unknowing knowing." You forgot you use this type of gesture, because it became a matter of automatic habit. Your automaticity is 100%.

And just like that, you've experienced a significant and concrete improvement. You've left behind a weakness in communication and gained a strength. Forever. Every time you speak, you use this type of gesture, and you do it without even thinking about it. This alone can make the difference between a successful and unsuccessful speech.

Now repeat. Master a new skill. Create a new habit. Improve in a new area. How else could we improve your body language? What about the structure of your communication? Your persuasive strategy? Your debate skill? Your vocal modulation? With this process, people gain measurable and significant improvements in as little as one hour. Imagine if you stuck with it over time. This is the path to mastery. This is the path to unleashing the power of your words.

**Access your 18 free PDF resources, 30 free video lessons, and 2 free workbooks from this link: www.speakforsuccesshub.com/toolkit**

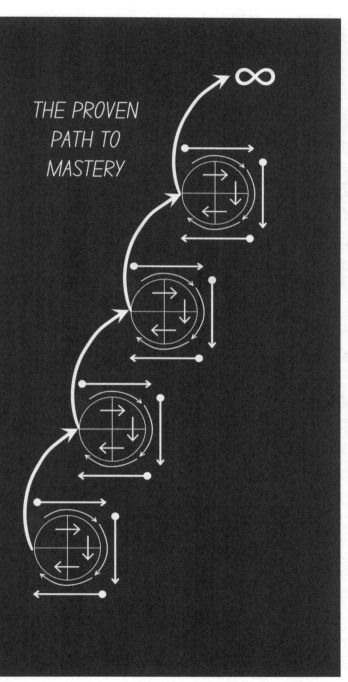

**SPEAK FOR SUCCESS COLLECTION BOOK**

# III

**HOW LEGENDARY LEADERS SPEAK CHAPTER**

# III

# STEP TWO:

## Nine Strategies to Direct Attention to a Definite Purpose

## ACHIEVE SINGULARITY

Y OU'VE GRABBED ATTENTION. THAT'S OFTEN the biggest challenge and biggest accomplishment. And it is necessary. Absolutely necessary.

Because without attention, you can't accomplish the next four steps of the communication of leadership. You can't direct attention to a definite purpose if you don't have attention in the first place. You can't back the attention with intentional action for the same reason. You can't back the intentional action with correct thinking if you don't have any intentional action in the first place. And you certainly can't back the entire process with a powerful motive if people aren't even motivated to listen to you.

Think of the communication of leadership as a chain model. It's a chain, and every link is necessary. And not only that, but this specific order is also necessary.

### THE CHAIN MODEL OF EFFECTIVE COMMUNICATION

FIGURE 58: You must accomplish the five steps in their order. If the process falls apart, it does so at its weakest link: the step you executed least effectively.

But if you apply the strategies in part one, you'll avoid these disasters. You have attention. Now, what do you do with it? Direct it to a definite purpose. So, let's get into the first strategy for doing so: achieving singularity. Why does it work?

People crave simplicity.

People crave oneness.

People crave self-completion.

What do I mean by self-completion? That whatever goal they pursue is self-contained; stand-alone; worthwhile in and of itself, no matter what else is going on out there in the world.

It's not dependent on a complex web of goals to be valuable. It's not useless if one of those goals in the web falls through. It's not dependent on any external circumstances to be valuable. It's not useless if something changes to render it irrelevant. It is inherently, intrinsically, fundamentally valuable, by its very nature, and nothing can change that. That's the first thing people want.

Goals that are self-contained are most attractive. For me, writing books is such a goal. I do it because, to me, it is an inherently worthwhile goal; because, to me, it would still be worthwhile even if I made no sales, got no recognition, and received no positive feedback from readers. It is, simply put, a self-contained goal.

And before we discuss this strategy, we need to talk about what singularity even means. Singularity means that there is one thing. One goal. One objective. One desire.

It means that all the attention you've gathered with the part-one strategies is not dissipated to the point of impotence among a variety of purposes, but is completely, fully, entirely channeled in the direction of one very specific, singular purpose.

**THE ONLY TYPE OF GOAL PEOPLE LIKE TO RALLY AROUND**

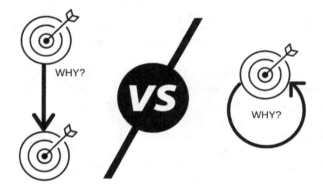

FIGURE 59: A goal that is worthwhile only because it serves as a means to another goal and not as an end in itself is not as persuasive as a goal that is inherently worthwhile, and an end in itself.

**KEY INSIGHT:**

# Connect to Your Axiomatic Moral "First Principles," the Foundations of Your Movement and Cause.

### DON'T MAKE THIS AVOIDABLE GOAL-SETTING MISTAKE

FIGURE 60: A multitude of goals dilutes audience attention. A singular goal is significantly more influential. We will shortly discuss how to mesh this piece of advice with a common need: the need to provide more than one directive or goal.

So, what's the whole point of this? What does it all come down to? Why have I told you all this? Because this strategy is directing your now-obtained attention toward a purpose that has two characteristics people demand from the goals they set: self-containment and singularity.

This prevents trying to direct the attention somewhere it won't go because the goal is neither self-contained nor singular. This prevents you from wasting your earned attention on something that is not inherently worthwhile or dissipating it by spreading it too thin, over more than one purpose.

### KEY INSIGHT:

One Goal, One Vision, One Path, One Unified Coalition. To Split is to Weaken. Connecting Two "Highest Priorities" with the Word "And" Is a Sloppy Sleight of Hand. You Can't Have Two "Most Important Goals," Only One.

## THIS IS HOW YOU LOSE ATTENTION AND MISS THE MARK

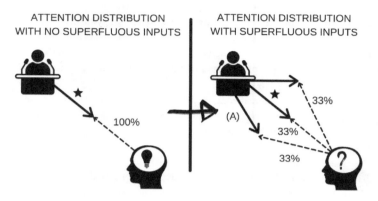

FIGURE 61: When you present one crucial idea, this idea receives 100% of the attention you currently control. If you present one crucial idea and two less important ones, the two irrelevant ideas distract away from the crucial one by diluting attention (A). Less often really is more. This is part of the wisdom of the singularity strategy.

Clinton's example of the communication had a self-contained and singular purpose. So did Woodrow Wilson's. So did Reagan's. So did JFK's. So did MLK's. So did FDR's. So did Obama's.

You get the point: they all do. And I now urge you once more to separate your personal politics from your studies of the communication of leadership. Why? Because the best contemporary example of self-containment and singularity is Donald Trump's 2016 campaign slogan: Make America Great Again. Your hate or love for him is irrelevant. You want to become an effective leader; thus, you want to master the communication of leadership; thus, you are willing to take any lesson in the strategies, no matter where they come from.

I could have chosen a less controversial, but weaker and less contemporary example. I chose not to. Why? Because my goal is to provide the best education in this communication strategy possible.

That said, let's discuss. We can plainly see that it is self-contained. The goal of Making America Great Again has obviously apparent value. But here's the key point. That value is intrinsic. It is inherent. It is fundamental to the goal. It is part of its very nature. In other words, the goal of making a country great – any country – assuming what is meant by "great" truly is great, is not only valuable, but that value is *inalienable from it.*

This guarantees that pursuit of the goal will not be futile if something changes to make the goal unworthy, because there is nothing that can change to make the goal unworthy, because it is inherently worthy.

That's self-containment. What about singularity? It's one goal. It's a simple goal. It's not an array of goals. The multiple aspects of the Trump agenda – the wall, tax cuts, tariffs on China – those are all enveloped by the overarching, singular goal, and contained within it. But that's our next strategy: organizing a pyramid.

And here's the point: you must not only have a goal that is singular and self-contained, but also express those qualities. You must present clarity on the singularity and self-contained goal. Trump repeated it at every single rally and put it on a big red hat.

We can just use a simple self-contained and singularity-indicating language pattern like, "But the big goal for us right now is one thing and one thing only: to [insert goal], because [insert explanation of self-containment]."

Simple, easy, and effective. And a brief, brief review of why directing attention to anything that is not singular or self-contained is a bad idea.

If it is not singular, the attention will be scattered around to the point of impotency. Attention produces action if it is concentrated in one direction. The wider it spreads, the weaker it becomes.

If it is not self-contained, people will have reservations about throwing themselves fully in the pursuit of the goal because is it not inherently valuable.

## THE DESIRE PYRAMID AND SINGULAR SELF-CONTAINMENT

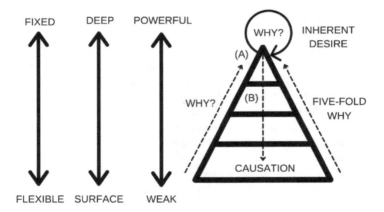

FIGURE 62: Human desires are arranged in a pyramid. Why do most people want the objects of their individual desires? Because desire X – the core, inherent human desire(s) – is satisfied by desire Y, and Y by Z, and Z by… so on and so forth. You reach this deep desire by asking "why?" of more superficial desires (A), and by the five-fold-why process which we will discuss shortly. This deep desire causes all other desires, and it is desired for its own sake.

## DESIRE HIERARCHIES ARE THE KEY TO MOTIVATION

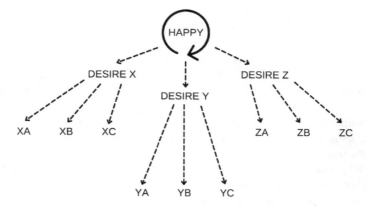

FIGURE 63: This is a more granular example of a desire hierarchy. Desires do not exist as isolated categorical imperatives, but as members of a hierarchy in which they exist in relation to other desires. (On another note, the same holds true for values). For example, this desire hierarchy indicates that "happiness" is the singular, self-justifying, inherent desire. This person wants X, Y, and Z because they satisfy the core desire, and XA, XB, and XC because they satisfy desire X, which satisfies the core desire. And it goes deeper than the third layer.

## THE SIMPLEST VISUALIZATION OF INTRINSIC MOTIVATION

DESIRE X

DESIRE X

FIGURE 64: This is the easiest way to understand what it means for a desire to be self-contained, or desired only for its own sake and not to satisfy some other desire.

## ORGANIZE A PYRAMID

Now, you might be wondering, "If my goal needs singularity, does that mean I have to keep repeating the same thing over and over again, without introducing new initiatives?" No, of course not.

It just means that you must guarantee that those new initiatives all fall under the umbrella of your singular goal. For Trump, the many facets of his agenda are all ways to accomplish the one singular and self-contained banner goal of Making America Great Again.

Border control. Tariffs. Conservative judges. It's all part of the same scheme. And, as I said, whether you hate it or love it is irrelevant: the point you have to understand is that this type of pyramidal goal organization works.

Why does it work? Because people hate uncertainty, and will not act if they are uncertain. Let's call it uncertainty hyper-response tendency.

This pyramidal goal organization allows you to remove uncertainty while retaining nuanced complexity, simply because it arranges the complexity under the banner of a simple, single goal.

### HOW TO GAIN CLARITY ON YOUR HIERARCHY OF OBJECTIVES

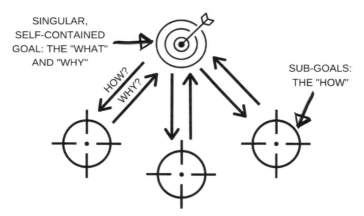

FIGURE 65: Organize your goals in a hierarchy. You should have a primary, singular, self-contained goal: the "what" and the "why." This is the thing you don't budge on. You may litigate between different ways to achieve this, between different sub-goals, but this objective is the uncompromisable goal.

People demand clarity before jumping on board a bandwagon. They need to know what they're getting themselves into. And what better way to give them that clarity than the pyramidal organization? We also have to talk about one of the core elements of message-virality.

What's message virality?

A message has virality if people talk about it, and the people who heard about it talk about it some more, and so on and so forth until it cascades into a snowball-effect of awareness. And the pyramidal structure is important for two reasons.

Reason number one: people don't talk about complicated things that they don't quite have a grasp on (at least, not as much), and deviating from the pyramidal model produces a confusing, tangled, scattered barrage of policy proposals that are not unified by a single overarching goal.

Reason number two: people talk about that which is simple, impactful, and easy to grasp; applying the pyramidal structure allows you to present a complicated array of policies and sub-goals under the umbrella of one overarching goal because that overarching goal is simple, singular, self-contained, and easy to advocate for, while also putting the array of policies in context.

Get it? And why is it called a pyramidal organization? Because your singular and self-contained primary goal, at the peak of your agenda, is supported by a layer of sub-goals beneath it.

So, maybe this seems a little abstract. And at this point, it is. But it won't be once I explain the tangible language pattern, we can use to instantly apply this model.

Step one: choose your one, big, overarching goal that is singular and self-contained.

Step two: select whatever array of policies are included in that big, overarching goal.

Step three: apply the "priming" language pattern: "We want to [insert big, overarching, singular and self-contained goal], and we will do it by [insert policy one], [insert policy two], and [insert policy three]."

And why is this called a priming statement? Because it has an interesting function. It's a clock.

What do I mean by that? Well, let's say you're giving a ten-minute speech to a company about the agenda for the next three years. People are probably a captive audience; in other words, they are there partly because of professional pressures, and not entirely because they want to hear what you have to say. Sorry, but it's true.

What does that lead to? Constant clock-checks; constant pondering, "when will this end so I can go home?"

That produces a very bad thing: reduced attention.

So, how does the priming statement, which also allows you to organize your message in a pyramidal structure, combat the clock-check tendency of captive audiences? By giving them a metric by which to view the progress you've made, and thus how long they have to wait before going home. In other words, it psychologically primes them to see first, how each sub-goal fits into the context of a larger proposal, and second, how much content is left in your speech.

If you say, "We will do X, by enacting policy one, policy two, and policy three, which I'll explain right now," they can judge your progress by seeing which policy you're speaking about right now. Thus, they don't check the clock. Thus, they don't wonder how much time is left. Thus, they keep giving you the attention you earned in part one. In the realm of more traditional public speaking teaching (having both delivered and received traditional public speaking lessons, I can say we are far, far away from "traditional" in this book), we learn the concept of a preview and review.

A preview is what we just discussed: "We want to [insert big, overarching, singular and self-contained goal], and we will do it by [insert policy one], [insert policy two], and [insert policy three]." It previews your content at the start of your speech.

A review is essentially restating the preview at the end of your speech: "And so, as I've demonstrated, by enacting [insert policy one], [insert policy two], and [insert policy three], we can finally achieve [insert big, overarching, singular and self-contained goal]."

Why do this? Because repetition aids memory.

And lists of three, which you are not bound to, but which you should strive to include, also aid memory. But what else aids memory? Parallelism.

What's parallelism?

Well, we discussed it previously. Two sentences create parallelism if they have identical grammatical structure.

I wrote this book

You read this writing.

Those two sentences are grammatically parallel, in the form (pronoun) (verb) (adjective) (noun). Strict parallelism, as we've discussed, takes it a step further than identical grammatical structure, to the realm of placing identical words in identical positions.

I wrote this book.

You read this book.

So, how does this tie into your preview and review statement of your pyramidal goal organization? Like so: each of your policies, or sub-goals in your priming statement, should be presented in grammatically parallel or strictly parallel forms.

For example: "We will regain our competitive edge by introducing new innovations, building new branches, and implementing new incentive-structures." "We will regain our competitive edge by (verb) (adjective) (noun), (verb) (adjective) (noun), and (verb) (adjective) (noun)."

They are also strictly parallel: each of the phrases has the word "new" as the second word in the sequence of three words. Why? Maybe the speaker wants to emphasize the novelty of the approach.

Novelty excites and holds attention. If you're not speaking about something new – at least, new to your current audience – grabbing attention will be an uphill battle.

And, maybe you've noticed, we used alliteration too: "We will regain our competitive edge (big, overarching, singular and self-contained goal) by *i*ntroducing new *i*nnovations, *b*uilding new *b*ranches, and *i*mplementing new *i*ncentive-structures." Awesome. But let's move away from this for now.

I'll give you another phenomenally undeniable example of the pyramidal organization in action. We now turn to Lyndon B. Johnson. Let's henceforth call him LBJ.

He entered the oval office in the wake of one of our most challenging national tragedies: the assassination of JFK; a man whose steady hand guided us through the Cuban missile crisis; a man whose array of major policies, in a sad irony, included curbing gun violence; a man whose immortal words will live on for centuries, redefining our national ethos for decades to come.

But that's not the only reason it was a trying, testing, challenging time. There was a crisis abroad and at home. The Cold War, the Vietnam war, and countless measures of international strife haunted our international policy like a scepter. At home, tranquility was lost with JFK. And LBJ knew something. That people have a fixed attention span. And that if he tried to direct attention in too many directions, something sad would happen: it would become powerless.

If it's any consolation, at least diffused attention is powerless in many different directions at once. So, he knew that the pyramidal organization was a necessity. He knew that he needed a big, bold, brave, simple, straightforward, singular, and self-contained overarching goal, under which to organize the rest of his scattered initiatives.

If Trump's is Make America Great Again, LBJ's was this: "The Great Society." Check out this excerpt from his speech presenting the Great Society concept to the American public. The transcript follows. I've labeled it to indicate the signs of the strategy, though, at this point, they will be abundantly apparent to your trained eyes. And note this, too: the big, overarching, singular, and self-contained goal tends to be broken down into a short phrase.

A bumper-sticker phrase.

And that short phrase is often repeated to aid recall and inspire message virality. You'll see that in this example.

"Your imagination, your initiative, and your indignation will determine whether we build a society where progress is the servant of our needs, or a society where old values and new visions are buried under unbridled growth. For in your time we have the opportunity to move not only toward the rich society and the powerful society, but upward to the Great Society *(first presentation of his big, overarching, singular and self-contained goal)*. The Great Society (first repetition) rests on abundance and liberty for all *(sub-goal one, enveloped by the overarching goal)*. It demands an end to poverty *(sub-goal two)* and racial injustice *(sub-goal three)*, to which we are totally committed in our time. But that is just the beginning. The Great Society is a place where every child can find knowledge to enrich his mind *(sub-goal four)* and to enlarge his talents *(sub-goal five)*. It is a place where leisure is a welcome chance to build and reflect *(sub-goal six)*, not a feared cause of boredom and restlessness *(sub-goal seven)*. It is a place where the city of man serves not only the needs of the body *(sub-goal eight)* and the demands of commerce *(sub-goal nine)* but the desire for beauty and the hunger for community *(sub-goal ten)*. It is a place where man can renew contact with nature *(sub-goal eleven)*. It is a place which honors creation for its own sake and for what it adds to the understanding of the race *(sub-goal twelve)*. It is a place where men are more concerned with the quality of their goals than the quantity of their goods *(sub-goal thirteen)*. But most of all, the Great Society is not a safe harbor, a resting place, a final objective, a finished work. It is a challenge constantly renewed *(sub-goal fourteen)*, beckoning us toward a destiny where the meaning of our lives matches the marvelous products of our labor *(sub-goal fifteen)*. **Preview statement:** So I want to talk to you today *(statement of speaker's intent, common in previews)* about **three** *(the magic, memorable number)* places where we begin to build the Great Society – in our cities, in our countryside, and in our dassrooms *(alliteration and strict parallelism: (adjective) (possessive) (noun), where the adjective is always "in," and the possessive is always "our.")*

I knew about this strategy long before finding this particular example. I just wanted another example for this book. And the first one I looked at had this strategy prominently displayed. I knew of the Great Society concept, and I knew that when a leader presents a short phrase like that, it is usually a big, overarching, singular and self-contained goal enveloping an array of policies.

I was right, confirming this strategy yet again. Now, one final brief point before we move on to the next strategy for directing attention to a definite purpose.

I want to emphasize the value of uniting a large variety of policies or proposals under one simple, singular, and self-contained banner. Imagine that he didn't unify it all under the "Great Society" concept. What would he have produced?

A laudable, honorable, yet forgettable and splintered array of unrelated policies. But he knew that it would be drastically, dramatically, definitively better to instead present the big banner phrase; creating a great society; because this is so memorable, singular, and self-contained that everyone can talk about it and support it, and because it places the array of various policies in a pyramidal organization that has coherence, consistency, and context.

---

**KEY INSIGHT:**

The Strategic Injunction to "Divide and Conquer" Implies a Compelling Corollary.

"Unite and Persist," Or Perhaps Even "Unite and Conquer." And the Greater the Unity, Of Course, the Greater the Prize.

---

## HOW THE BIG BANNER PHRASE INSPIRES FOLLOW-THROUGH

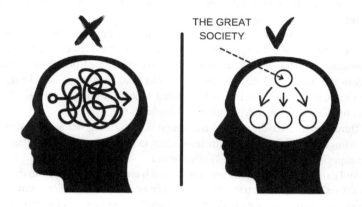

FIGURE 66: Instead of a complex, convoluted array of disconnected policies, Lyndon B. Johnson presented his primary, singular, self-contained goal: building the Great Society. He then expanded on different sub-goals, or different methods to achieve this overarching goal.

## CREATE VISUALIZATION

I want to try something. Read this next sentence.

A bright, red, shimmering sunset.

What happened in your mind? Well, you probably (this isn't bullet-proof) saw a sunset. Your mental-movie machinery produced it, without consulting you. You didn't get prompted, "should I produce the image of a bright, red, shimmering sunset?" It just went ahead and did it without your permission. In fact, it had no choice. It is not autonomous, and it is not in your control, by default, though you can exert mental calories to reign it in. Sometimes, just *sometimes*, you'll be able to, if at all.

But the point is this: I just spelled out the visualization, and your mental movie went ahead and did it. It's kind of scary if you think about it. Anyone can magically create these mental-movies in your mind, and your mental-movie machinery is not only ill-equipped to resist the injection, but well-equipped to immediately shove in the cassette tape, and play the damn movie.

But that's not all. Your mental-movie machinery is also very vivid. If you were concentrating when you read that visualization, you didn't just see a sunset; you saw a bright sunset, a red sunset, and a shimmering sunset. Bright as opposed to obscured by clouds. Red as opposed to orange. Shimmering as opposed to dull due to air humidity (or whatever makes a sunset not shimmer. I won't pretend I have the slightest modicum of a clue as to what that might be).

And this motivates a question, which you probably already asked yourself. "What does this have to do with the communication of leadership?" Well, it's simple: it directs obtained attention toward a definite purpose.

That answer motivates another question, though. "What does this have to do with directing attention toward a definite purpose?" And that's the question to which we turn in this section. It's a fun one. The answer is this: as I demonstrated, people have cognitive functions that make their minds extremely attracted to producing visual imagery; in other words, we all have mental machinery that makes our minds extremely likely to direct our attention to visually-stimulating thoughts.

Think about it: daydreams involve mental visualizations, not abstract thoughts. Daydreams usually involve the daydreamer acting in some situation, with a clear, crisp, and compelling visual scene painted in their mind.

And daydreams command attention. So much attention, that they can distract us from a massively important test sitting right in front of us, as our allotted time drains. So much attention, that they can distract us from the road in front of us, forcing us to slam on the brakes. So much attention, that they can distract us from the person in front of us who is opening up to us, telling us something extremely personal.

Why? That's the whole reason I'm telling you this. Daydreams do this because they are visually stimulating. So, we'll get into how this accomplishes the second step of the communication of leadership now. I'm presenting a strategy that has four points of impact.

Point one: goal statements.

Point two: attached adjectives.

Point three: powerful visual adjectives.

Point four: visual metaphors and imagery.

Let me explain the four points. Goal statements are, quite simply, statements that describe your goal. In other words, the definite purpose to which you are directing audience attention. Attached adjectives are adjectives directly next to a noun or verb, modifying the noun or verb by specifying some quality. And there's a specific process for adding attached adjectives.

Point two, step one: write what you want to say.

Point two, step two: underline all the nouns and verbs.

Point two, step three: place a compelling adjective specifying some quality of the noun or verb before each. Or, if not all of them, however many you want to apply this strategy to.

For example, take the sentence, "We will march onward to victory, waging war for our ideals, our virtues, and our rights." (Step one). Step two: "We will <u>march</u> onward to <u>victory</u>, <u>waging</u> <u>war</u> for our <u>ideals</u>, our <u>virtues</u>, and our <u>rights</u>." Step three: "We will *relentlessly* <u>march</u> onward to *uncompromising* <u>victory</u>, *viciously* <u>waging</u> *righteous* <u>war</u> for our *surpassing* <u>ideals</u>, our *vice-less* <u>virtues</u>, and our *God-given* <u>rights</u>."

So, to summarize the attached adjective strategy, you write what you want to say, you underline all verbs and nouns you want to modify, and you place directly next to them an adjective enumerating a quality of the verb or noun. Great. Now, what about powerful visual adjectives? Powerful visual adjectives are visual (obviously).

But they are also specific: a distinct aspect of the verb or noun to which you are attaching them.

They are detail-oriented, focused on filling in the small details of the noun.

They are concrete, focused on something physically visible. "Striking" is not physically visible, while "orange" is.

They are evocative, focused on evoking a visceral emotional reaction.

And they are open, not so specific that the audience can't fill in the blanks to their individual content.

Here are some PVAs that you can apply to "sunset," that fulfill those requirements: "Orange," "Bright," "Shimmering." Here are some PVAs that are not powerful. They're just "visual adjectives," and don't work the same way: "Colorful," "Beautiful," "Striking." These are not specific, concrete, or detail-oriented.

"Orange, bright, shimmering sunset" paints a distinct mental image. "Colorful, beautiful, striking sunset" does not. Alright. Moving on to the fourth and final point. Visual metaphors and compelling imagery.

I think you know what metaphors and imagery are. So, I'll just give you one of the best examples that comes to my mind. It's from a figure that frequently appears in this book: Ronald Reagan. He wasn't called the "Great Communicator" for no reason.

Here's what he said in his farewell address, after eight years as president. It was the 34th time he spoke to the American public from the oval office. It was also the last. No wonder he wanted to cap it off with such a beautiful sequence of words. Pay attention to the metaphors and imagery. Here's what he said at the end of this address.

"And that's about all I have to say tonight, except for one thing. The past few days when I've been at that window upstairs, I've thought a bit of the *'shining city upon a hill.'* The phrase comes from John Winthrop, who wrote it to describe the America he imagined. What he imagined was important because he was an early Pilgrim, an early freedom man. He journeyed here on what today we'd call a little wooden boat; and like the other Pilgrims, he was looking for a home that would be free. And how stands the city on this winter night? More prosperous, more secure, and happier than it was eight years ago. But more than that: After 200 years, two centuries, she still stands strong and true on the granite ridge, and her glow has held steady no matter what storm. And she's still a beacon, still a magnet for all who must have freedom, for all the pilgrims from all the lost places who are hurtling through the darkness, toward home."

Are the United States really situated on a granite ridge? Nope. Are the United States really glowing? Nope. Are the United States really physically holding steady? I guess. Though continents do physically "shift" by the process of continental drift, so I suppose not. Are the United States really battered by an ongoing storm? Nope. Are the United States really a beacon? Nope. Are the people seeking a free land really hurtling? Nope. Are the people seeking a free land really escaping darkness? Nope.

I say this to emphasize the key point here. The strategy is presenting conceptual meaning through the concrete pathways of the mind's visualization machinery, thus directing attention to something in an incredibly powerful way.

It's metaphorical; it's figurative, not literal. The United States is not really situated on a granite ridge, but we have a strength and stability. The figurative, concrete, clear imagery of a granite ridge evokes a distinct sense of strength and stability, more so than the non-visual words "strength and stability" would.

The United States is not really glowing, but we have a material opulence and quality of life unrivaled throughout the world. The figurative, concrete, clear imagery of a glow evokes a distinct sense of material opulence and quality of life, more so than the non-visual words "material opulence and quality of life."

The United States is not physically holding steady, but we have (mostly) held true to our ideals through testing and trying tempests. The figurative, concrete, clear imagery of holding steady evokes a distinct sense of holding true to our ideals, more so than the non-visual words "holding true to our ideals."

The United States is not really battered by an ongoing storm, but we have been accosted by tempestuous, tumultuous forces overseas and domestically that have challenged our mettle. The figurative, concrete, clear imagery of a storm evokes a distinct sense of the accost of tempestuous, tumultuous, mettle-challenging forces, more so than the words "tempestuous, tumultuous forces overseas and domestically."

The United States is not really a beacon, but we have stood as a bastion of higher ideals for decades. The figurative, concrete, clear imagery of a beacon evokes a distinct sense of our standing as a bastion of higher ideals for decades, more so than the words "we have stood as a bastion of higher ideals for decades."

The people journeying toward a better life in the United States are not really hurtling, but they do feel like their journey is hardly in their control. The figurative, concrete, clear imagery of hurtling evokes a distinct sense of an out-of-control journey, more so than the words "they do feel like their journey is hardly in their control."

The people leaving behind their homes to seek better lives in a distant, different, and difficult land, are not really leaving behind the darkness, but they are escaping something that must be pretty bad if it is to motivate this journey. The figurative, concrete, clear imagery of darkness evokes a distinct sense of escaping something that must be pretty bad, more so than the words "they are escaping something that must be pretty bad if it is to motivate this journey."

**KEY INSIGHT:**

# Visualize the Abstract. Make Concrete the Conceptual. Turn Squishy Theories into Hard, Material, Grounded Realities.

## HOW TO MAKE YOUR MESSAGE COME TO LIFE AND ENGAGE

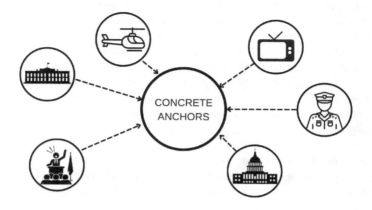

FIGURE 67: Make your message memorable, bring it to life, and engage the audience by presenting your core idea through visual, concrete anchors.

And this final strategy – metaphors and imagery – involves what I call "micro-metaphors," or tiny little bite-sized visual metaphors that you can inject into a sentence much like attached adjectives. For example, "We will march onward to victory, waging war for our ideals, our virtues, and our rights," becomes, "We will march, *like an unstoppable tsunami,* onward to victory..."

Alright. Let's bring it back. I know we seem to have gone on a tangent, but I assure you, we haven't: all four of these techniques are just individual prongs of the strategy that unites them, a strategy I am going to uncover for you now. All of these prongs – goal statements, attached adjectives, powerful visual adjectives, and imagery-based metaphors – all contribute to one overarching strategy.

And that strategy is directing audience attention to a definite purpose by way of their visual cognitive pathways; in other words, by way of their most attention-controlling psychological functions.

So, let me give you the play-by-play, step-by-step strategy, now that you know its four constituent parts like the back of your hand.

First, make a goal statement; a clear statement of what you want to accomplish. For example, let's take the pyramidal-organized preview statement, "I want to resurrect a sense of community in this country, by returning decency to the White House, by bolstering our social safety net, and by empowering state and local governments."

Second, apply the attached-adjective strategy, specifically attaching powerful visual adjectives, to your goal statement's verbs and nouns. For example, "I want to resurrect a sense of community in this country, by returning decency to the White House, by bolstering our social safety net, and by empowering state and local governments," becomes "I want to *swiftly* resurrect a *glowing* sense of *close* community in this country, by returning *beaming* decency to the *darkened* White House, by bolstering our *splintered* social safety net, and by empowering state and local governments." You should not add an attached adjective if it will break up the flow of speech or seem out of place. As you can see, these are all powerful visual adjectives we have injected. Note that, for the sake of illustration, I "overdo" the strategy in this example, taking it beyond the point of subtlety. For the sake of clarity, I'll give you what we're working with now minus the markings: "I want to swiftly resurrect a glowing sense of close community in this country, by returning beaming decency to the darkened White House, by bolstering our splintered social safety net, and by empowering state and local governments."

Third, replace non-visual language with metaphorical, figurative, evocative visual language, include extended visual metaphors and imagery.

And use micro-metaphors where you have not attached a powerful visual adjective. For example, "I want to swiftly resurrect a glowing sense of close community in this country, by returning beaming decency to the darkened White House, by bolstering our splintered social safety net, and by empowering state and local governments," becomes "I want to swiftly resurrect a glowing sense of close community in this *shining beacon of a country (micro-metaphor)*, by returning *the beaming light of decency (micro-metaphor building upon a previously added powerful visual adjective)* to the *darkened corridors of the* White House *(imagery)*, by bolstering our splintered social safety net, and *by mending the widening chasm between federal, state and local governments (extended visual metaphors and imagery)."* Once again, for clarity's sake, here's what we have without parentheticals and markings: "I want to swiftly resurrect a glowing sense of close community in this shining beacon of a country, by returning the beaming light of decency to the darkened corridors of the White House, by bolstering our splintered social safety net, and by mending the widening chasm between federal, state and local governments."

We went from "I want to resurrect a sense of community in this country, by returning decency to the White House, by bolstering our social safety net, and by empowering state and local governments" to "I want to swiftly resurrect a glowing sense of close community in this shining beacon of a country, by returning the beaming light of decency to the darkened corridors of the White House, by bolstering our splintered social safety net, and by mending the widening chasm between federal, state and local governments."

**KEY INSIGHT:**

# Visual Speech is Sound that Creates Sight, and Sight Moves the Mind and Speaks to the Soul.

## AN ALGORITHM FOR GENERATING EXCITEMENT AND IMPACT

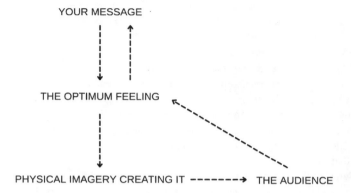

FIGURE 68: This algorithm helps you engineer imagery into your communication. Decide on your message. Figure out the optimum feeling that would motivate your audience to take action more than any other feeling. Brainstorm imagery that creates this optimum feeling. Present this to the audience, and they will experience that optimum feeling which will get them to agree and act on your message.

If you recall superabundance, it's all we're doing right now. Superabundance is the art of rhetorical addition. And all we're doing is rhetorical addition in an extremely algorithmic, deliberate, intentional way designed to expertly play upon hidden psychological characteristics of humans, to direct their attention to a definite purpose with effortless efficacy.

One key note about this.

What is flow?

In other words, what do people mean when they say that a sentence doesn't "flow right?" This: that the rate of information exchange abruptly changes too much in the middle of the sentence.

Now, you want pace changes. You want fast, snappy, concise, and crisp sentences (remember declaratory cascades?), followed by long, complex sentences with twists, turns and accoutrements. But you don't want that rate of information exchange to change first, too much, and second, within a sentence.

It can change abruptly between sentences, but not within sentences. It must be gentle within sentences. In other words, each sentence should have a fairly stable rate of information exchange within it, though that rate should vary between sentences.

And the second element of flow is the balance of phrases within sentences. In other words, don't have a very long phrase, a comma, and then one or two words.

For example, a sentence like "I want to swiftly resurrect a glowing sense of close community in this shining beacon of a country, by returning the beaming light of decency to the darkened corridors of the White House, by bolstering our splintered social safety net, *and by supporting localities*," does not have flow, because (1) the rate of information exchange drastically increases in that last phrase while the detail of the information drastically reduces, and (2) that last phrase does not have a balanced size in relation to the rest of the sentence, making it seem unimportant, and the rest of the sentence seem cumbersome.

So, how does this impact our strategy?

With a simple guideline: make sure to apply the superabundance "rhetorical addition" algorithm of visual impact uniformly within a sentence.

Why? To avoid breaking flow with (1) drastic changes in the rate of information exchange or its detail, and (2) out-of-balance phrase sizes. Alright. Let's say you do apply this strategy, and the sentence either breaks flow or seems far too cumbersome. What do you do? The opposite of rhetorical addition.

Rhetorical reduction.

What do I mean by that? First, liberally and generously apply this algorithm of rhetorical addition, paying no attention to whether the sentence is too long or breaks flow. Your goal at this point is to produce as much as possible, according to the algorithm.

Second, reread the sentence when you finish the algorithm. Is it too long? Does it lack flow because of drastically fluctuating rates of information exchange? Does it lack flow because phrases within it have drastically different, out-of-balance sizes? What do you do? Apply rhetorical reduction, culling the less compelling additions, and keeping only the best, to make the length manageable, and fix the flow problems.

## COMBINING THE TWO PRINCIPAL RHETORICAL ALGORITHMS

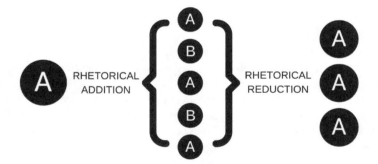

FIGURE 69: You have a strong but short "grade A" sequence of meaning. Rhetorical addition algorithms expand upon this, creating some grade A additions along with some grade B additions. Rhetorical reduction algorithms cut away the grade B additions, leaving only the grade A communication behind.

## AN ALGORITHM FOR QUICKLY PERFECTING YOUR MESSAGE

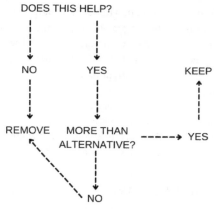

FIGURE 70: This algorithm allows you to evaluate any changes to your message or any parts of your message. Use it to sculpt your message to perfection.

Now, there's a concept called word economy which I love repeating (because it is so deeply important).

And it goes like this: high word economy is imparting a lot of meaning with few words.

On the other hand, low word economy is, you guessed it, imparting little meaning with many words.

In professional settings, high word economy is usually best. But not always. There are some exceptions. Like when you are presenting a goal statement and trying to passionately direct your audience's attention toward a definite purpose.

So, what's the internal mental dialogue of the audience members when they interact with this strategy? Every time you present a visually stimulating piece of information, you are essentially beaming that image into their mental movie screens.

So, what does that lead to? What does it have to do with attention? Every time you beam something into their heads, you grab their attention. And you don't just grab it, but direct it. Seems intuitive, right? So, the mental dialogue and mental imagery goes something like this.

"I want to swiftly *(Image: the speaker moving swiftly and purposely)* resurrect a glowing *(Image: a bright glow)* sense of close *(Image: a group of people close together)* community in this shining beacon *(Image: an elevated, glowing bastion of light shining in the distance)* of a country, by returning the beaming light *(Image: an array of beams of light, much like dappled sunlight through the trees)* of decency to the darkened corridors *(Image: dark, ominous, mysterious-looking empty hallways)* of the White House, by bolstering our splintered *(Image: something cracked into a bunch of little pieces)* social safety net, and by mending the widening chasm *(Image: a growing gap between two things)* between federal, state and local governments."

Every single image-injection controls attention because they can't help seeing the image. It's the power of the mental machinery we talked about at the start of this section. So, how does this direct attention to a definite purpose?

Because by marrying the goal statement with visual information – popping images into their minds, directing their attention, and solidifying attention control – you are not just doing these things randomly, but toward your definite purpose.

Get it? You're directing attention toward a definite purpose in a psychologically irresistible way.

Now, let's move on to another strategy of effortless attention-direction. It's one of the most practical and accessible in the book. I admit that many of these strategies seem overwhelming at first. But I promise you, simply your new-found awareness of them, even without any practice, takes you much further than you realize.

### THE TRUTH OF WHAT A THEME IS AND WHY IT MATTERS

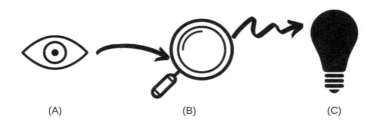

(A)    (B)    (C)

FIGURE 71: People perceive (A), through the lens of a theme (B), your subject (C). Your subject might be America. Your theme might be change. This means your audience will see America through the theme of change.

**KEY INSIGHT:**

## A Theme is Not a Subject. A Theme is the Conceptual Lens You Aim at the Subject.

## HOW TO USE A METAPHOR SO YOUR THEME IS MEMORABLE

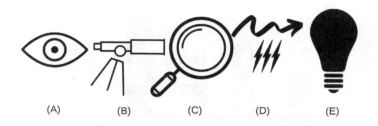

FIGURE 72: People can perceive (A), through a metaphor (B), your theme (C). Through your theme, their perception (D) of your subject (E) is altered. For example, viewing the subject of America through the theme of change, and the theme of change through the visual metaphor of seasons.

## PROMISE BENEFITS

Benefits, benefits, benefits.

To understand the concept of benefits, you have to understand one of the underlying principles of human motivation. And so, I will first answer this question: when people do something, why do they do it?

It's simple. They go through a special mental algorithm. Let me tell you about this algorithm. It acts nearly instantly after your sensory apparatuses present it with a new action-option. After acting nearly instantly, it is looped over and over again, constantly seeking any changes in the landscape it first detected. And the final point: this algorithm is fundamentally economic in nature. In fact, I first learned it in my Microeconomics course Freshman year of college. It was a great moment, because I realized that the scope of the algorithm went way, way, way beyond economics alone.

So, what's the algorithm?

The perceived net gain evaluation.

How does it work? Like this: when people are asking themselves, "should I take this action?" they go through the following mental calculation, often subconsciously, and almost instantly. The mental calculation? It's a conditional, actually. If the perceived marginal gain is greater than the perceived marginal cost (including opportunity cost – the perceived marginal gain of the best forgone alternative), they act.

## THE CRUCIAL ACTION-SELECTING COGNITIVE ALGORITHM

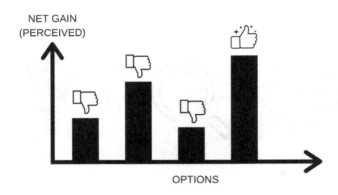

NET GAIN
(PERCEIVED)

OPTIONS

FIGURE 73: If an option has the highest perceived net gain of all the other options available, people select that option. Thus, a major sub-goal of your persuasive effort is to raise the perception of net gain associated with your proposal.

However, if perceived marginal gain is lower than perceived marginal cost, plus opportunity cost, they don't act. It's simple, right? If doing this action does more good than bad, and is the action that does the most good, you do it, right? And this can justify bad behaviors, too. Why can it justify bad behavior? Because it's not purely strict in its nature. Because it deals with perceived net gain. In other words, it is wholly subject to the fickle, misled, and gullible vagaries of human perception. In other words, where we might perceive a massive net gain, there can often, in reality, be a massive net loss. This deals with perception.

And let me remind you of the final piece to the puzzle, which you may have figured out by now. This algorithm deals with actions. And listening to you is an action. More specifically, directing their attention to a definite purpose proposed by you falls under the envelope of this algorithm, as most actions do.

The algorithm works on the action-option of listening to you just as it works on all other action-options. It also works on the action-option of directing attention to your proposed definite purpose just the same. So, what does this all come down to?

Raise perceived net gain.

How? Easier said than done, right? Well, in truth, doing it will be just as easy for you as saying it by the end of this section. There are two ways.

Way one: raise the perceived marginal benefit.

Way two: lower the perceived marginal cost.

## THE TWO FUNDAMENTAL WAYS TO MOTIVATE ACTION

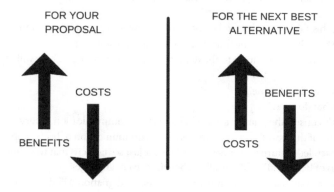

FIGURE 74: Influence perceptions to raise the perceived benefits and lower the perceived costs of doing what you want them to do. Do the same for the most tempting of the alternatives to your idea, except reverse it: raise perceived costs, lower perceived benefits.

And we focus on way one, in this section. So, how do you raise the perceived marginal benefit? Let me re-emphasize the critical point. This deals with perceptions. And you control perceptions; you can change them as you see fit, with your words. Note that the true perceived net gain of your proposal will always remain the same; you are just manipulating the perceptions in your favor.

## AN IRRESISTIBLY INFLUENTIAL PERSUASIVE FRAMEWORK

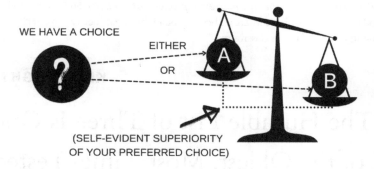

FIGURE 75: If you have sufficiently raised the perceived marginal gain of your proposal and lowered the perceived marginal gain of the primary alternative to your proposal (which may simply be

inaction), or if this balance of gains is implied or commonly known by your audience, then a powerful persuasive structure is simply to tell them they have a choice and present the two options.

So, this fairly complex explanation comes down to an extremely simple strategy. Promise benefits. Answer the following questions for inspiration.

"If I direct my attention to the definite purpose you propose, how will my life get better?"

"What's in it for me?"

"What do I get?"

Let's consult the grandmaster of all aspects of communication theory: the speech transcripts of the world's finest examples of the communication of leadership.

In fact, let's return to our new friend LBJ. It just so happens that this abounds with examples of benefits. I'll italicize all the benefit-driven language.

"Your imagination, your initiative, and your indignation will determine whether we build a society where *progress is the servant of our needs*, or a society where old values and new visions are buried under unbridled growth. For in your time we have the opportunity to *move not only toward the rich society and the powerful society, but upward to the Great Society*. The Great Society rests on *abundance and liberty for all*. It demands *an end to poverty and racial injustice*, to which we are totally committed in our time. But that is just the beginning. The Great Society is a place where *every child can find knowledge to enrich his mind and to enlarge his talents*. It is a place where *leisure is a welcome chance to build and reflect, not a feared cause of boredom and restlessness*. It is a place where *the city of man serves not only the needs of the body and the demands of commerce but the desire for beauty and the hunger for community*. It is a place where *man can renew contact with nature*. It is a place which *honors creation for its own sake and for what it adds to the understanding of the race*. It is a place where *men are more concerned with the quality of their goals than the quantity of their goods*. But most of all, the Great Society is not a safe harbor, a resting place, a final objective, a finished work. It is a challenge constantly renewed, beckoning us toward a destiny where the *meaning of our lives matches the marvelous products of our labor*. So I want to talk to you today about three places where we begin to build the Great Society – in our cities, in our countryside, and in our classrooms."

**KEY INSIGHT:**

# The Humble List of Three Is One of the Oldest, Most Time-Tested Devices In the Speaker's Arsenal.

## LAYER ON THE "REASONS WHY" TO MOTIVATE ACTION

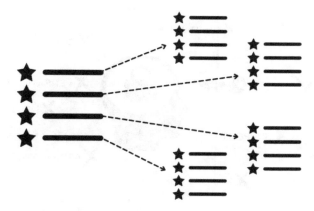

FIGURE 76: Break down the benefits. Explain them at length. Benefits persuade. They raise perceived marginal benefit. They motivate action. They are the things people want to "get" by acting. Do you present four benefits? Try breaking each of the four into four more. See how that sounds. Try to imagine the persuasive impact.

Here's what you have to understand: every single time LBJ produced benefit-driven language, perceived net gain increased, and thus the amount of attention the audience directed toward his definite purpose (building the Great Society) increased.

Know this: it's a spectrum. You earn attention by pushing perceived marginal gains over perceived marginal costs; however, the more you push gains over costs, the more attention you get. So, what does this mean? It means that you should do what LBJ did. Produce a mountain of benefits. What does that do? With every additional benefit, directed attention does not plateau, but continues to increase.

And here's an additional point: you should use more benefits not only to drastically increase attention with every added benefit but because some people have a keystone-benefit that is more compelling to them then all the others combined. Adding more benefits increases your chances of hitting more of these keystone benefits.

**KEY INSIGHT:**

There Are 7,000,000,000 People. That Means Psychologists Could Write 7,000,000,000 Unique Textbooks.

## VISUALIZING KEYSTONE BENEFITS

FIGURE 77: Many decision-makers have one keystone benefit that is the key to getting their approval and action. They may not even be aware of this particular keystone benefit: it may be wholly a subconscious desire.

## WHY SUPERABUNDANCE UNLOCKS MORE MINDS

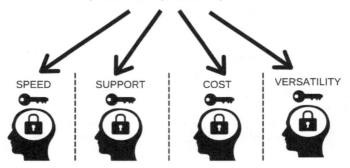

FIGURE 78: Superabundance – listing multiple benefits, costs, opportunities, risks, etc. – increases your influence because it raises your chances of hitting on more keystones. It is very much a "spray and pray" approach, but this does not detract from its effectiveness. Additional benefits, even if they are not keystones, still help.

And, recall declaratory cascades and superabundance? Go ahead and use those strategies, combined with benefits. LBJ did it. Pay attention to the declaratory cascade and the superabundance, and how benefits are embedded in them.

"The Great Society is a place where every child can find knowledge to enrich his mind and to enlarge his talents. It is a place where leisure is a welcome chance to build and reflect, not a feared cause of boredom and restlessness. It is a place where the city of man serves not only the needs of the body and the demands of commerce but the desire for beauty and the hunger for community. It is a place where man can renew contact with nature. It is a place which honors creation for its own sake and for what it adds to the understanding of the race. It is a place where men are more concerned with the quality of their goals than the quantity of their goods."

If a declaratory cascade plus a superabundance is a case of one plus one equals three, adding benefits makes it a case of one plus one plus one equals twenty. So, how do you evaluate if you are promising sufficient benefits or not? It seems simple and straightforward: just count up the times you speak with benefit-driven language. But that's wrong. Let me tell you why. If you have ten benefit-driven statements, are you promising sufficient benefits? That question cannot be answered. You need another piece of information: how many statements are in the communication?

If you have 1,000 statements, and ten are benefit-driven, you do not promise sufficient benefits. Attention is diluted. It is not directed. Whatever attention you managed to grab with part-one strategies, is now dissipated because you haven't used part-two strategies to direct it to a definite purpose.

Thus, the necessity of the benefit-equation grows apparent.

What's the benefit equation?

This: (number of benefit-driven statements) / (number of statements) * 100. This tells you something critical: "what percentage of my statements are benefit-driven?"

This is an infinitely more reliable way to check yourself on whether you've satisfied this strategy. But here's the thing: benefits are most important at the start of your communication, and right around the time you present the goal statement.

While people run through the perceived net gain equation constantly to evaluate whether they should continue doing an action, they particularly do it when they are first presented with a new action-option.

So, here's the benefit-equation strategy we arrive at: apply the benefit-equation localized to the start of your communication when your goal is definite-purpose presentation. For example, LBJ needed to direct attention to the definite purpose of the Great Society, particularly when he first expressed this definite purpose.

That explains why, out of 13 substantive statements, 11, or 84% (that's a lot), are benefit-driven. Alright. Moving on to another crucial point. People want some things more than others. And, more importantly, people have desire-chains. In other words, people have desire X, because desire X satisfies the deeper desire Y; and desire Y satisfies the yet deeper desire Z, so on and so forth.

That is why some human desires are labeled as "core," and others are not. The core desires are inherently worthwhile (sound familiar?) driving desires; they are the things people seek to satisfy most and seemingly can't escape. I'm sure you've guessed it: these are particularly compelling. These, more than most, ought to be enshrined in your benefit-statements.

So, how do you find them? In Josh Kauffman's best-selling business book, *The Personal MBA*, he answers our question without realizing it. Kauffman presents a simple but compelling line of logic.

If you want to succeed in business, you must have crystal-clarity on your why; the deep motivating reasons you want to succeed; the hidden desires that, exposed, give you massive drive. It's often called your "why power." But he presented a conundrum. It can be difficult to actually discover our real, deep motivating "why." The reason?

We're typically only aware of surface-level desires that satisfy desires which satisfy desire which, so on and so forth, eventually chain their way to our deep why. To fix this and dig down into ourselves to figure out our why, Josh presented a great strategy.

He calls it the five-fold-why.

What is it? It goes like this. Answer the question, "why do you want to achieve this goal?" Chances are you'll get a fairly superficial answer from yourself. You need to dig. Dig with four more "why do you want that?" questions. I'll give you a personal example.

Why one: "Peter, why do you want to grow your business?"

Answer one: "I like money."

Why two: "Peter, why do you want money?"

Answer two: "I like to feel carefree."

Why three: "Peter, why do you like to feel carefree?"

Answer three: "I like to feel carefree because I want to enjoy the great things in life – like a sunny day, or a great meal – without feeling urgent concerns over money."

Why four: "Peter, why do you want that?"

Answer four: "Because it's a lifestyle I want."

Why five: "Peter, why is it a lifestyle you want?"

Answer five: "Because I want it." At this point, we've reached the goal that is, to me, inherently worthwhile, and according to Josh, will be the source of massive motivation and dominating drive in the pursuit of my goal.

Note one: it doesn't have to be five why questions; go until you reach an inherently worthwhile desire; a desire that is not desired because it satisfies another desire but that is singular and self-contained.

Note two: this can branch into two or more answers to a question, at which point you just trace each branch to its conclusion.

When I read this, I realized something. While he was telling me to use this on myself, I realized that it has massive applications in communication. So, we now turn to the final point in this chapter: the benefit-extrapolating five-fold-why.

This does something incredible. It is so unprecedented in my studies of communication theory. It is yet another algorithm based on a bedrock principle of human psychology that we can easily, effortlessly, and quickly apply to a benefit-driven statement to drive yet deeper.

Let me give you an example. Let's say you are debating your contender for the presidency leading up to election day. Let's say a major goal of your agenda is to raise gross domestic product (GDP). The truth is this: that's not a very compelling goal; it is, in fact, a superficial benefit, that is not inherently worthwhile. It is singular, though not self-contained. So, apply the benefit-extrapolating five-fold-why.

Why one: "Why do we want higher GDP?" Answer one: "We want higher GDP because it's not just a vanity-number; it correlates with valuable things." Why two: "Why do we want those valuable things?" Answer two: "We want those valuable things because they include higher life expectancy, lower infant mortality rate, and greater access to education Why three: "Why do we want those things?" Answer three: "Because people will live longer; they will spend more time with their families on this Earth, and there will be less human sorrow; because fewer mothers will experience the greatest, most heart-wrenching tragedy that can ever befall them; because, as we expand educational access, people will reach ever-higher toward fulfilling their newfound potential." Why four: "Why do we want those things?" Answer four: "Because they are inherently valuable."

This does something wonderful: it gives your benefits drastically more power by digging down to the benefit of the benefit of the benefit of the benefit, so on and so forth, until you reach the inherently valuable benefits. And that's what it's all about.

It's about diving deeper and deeper, until you find the inherently valuable benefits, and then using them as the starting point of your benefit-driven language.

In other words, instead of leaving your audience members confused, wondering "why is this person obsessed with GDP?" you break down the benefits of that benefit, in extremely impactful, compelling, human terms.

Get it? Simple but effective. Drill down. Dig deep. Find the truth. Use the truth. Win by wielding the truth as your infallible weapon.

## HOW TO FIND INHERENTLY WORTHWHILE MOTIVATORS

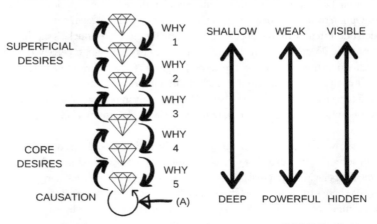

FIGURE 79: With every "why" you go from more superficial desires to more core desires. At the very bottom of the chain is the self-contained motivator: the thing for which the answer to the question "why" is "for its own sake" (A).

### REVISITING THE TWO REQUIREMENTS OF A GOOD GOAL

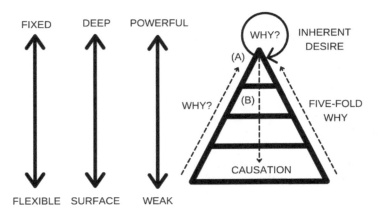

FIGURE 80: Reexamine this image to understand how the five-fold-why process interacts with the desire pyramid. Consider the persuasive impact of appealing to inherent desires, which we may also call axiomatic desires. Asking "why do you want that?" of any lower-tier desire gets you closer to the core desire, which causes all the others (B).

Before we move on, I want to make one point very clear. I want to discuss psychological opportunity cost, and its role in the perceived net gain algorithmic evaluation. Let's say someone in your audience has three options. Option one: listen to you. Option two: check their phone. Option three: give in to a daydream. Let's say that option one, listening to you, does have more benefits than costs. But let's say that option two or three do too. Let's say that listening to you has the highest perceived net gain, and checking their phone has the second highest. They subtract the perceived net benefit of the best alternative they had to forgo in favor of listening to you from the perceived net gain of listening to you. That's opportunity cost, which is included in perceived marginal cost. This is why it's so hard to get attention in the presence of distractions.

Now, we talked about something previously, and I teased the next section. Earlier in this section, I said that there were two ways to raise perceived net gain. Way one: raising the perceived marginal gain. Way two: lowering the perceived marginal cost.

And here's the truth: while this section focused on way one, way two might just be more compelling. And it is way two to which we turn now. Benefits by way of not gains, but loss-minimization.

A brief preview of how we secretly used both in our last example: "Because people will live longer (gain-benefit); they will spend more time with their families on this Earth (gain-benefit), and there will be less human sorrow (loss-minimization-benefit); because fewer mothers will experience the greatest, most heart-wrenching tragedy that can ever befall them (loss-minimization-benefit); because, as we expand educational access, people will reach ever-higher toward their newfound potential (gain benefit)."

## REVISITING DESIRE HIERARCHIES AND INTRINSIC WORTH

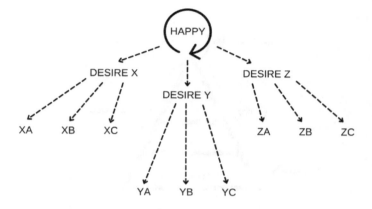

FIGURE 81: Reexamine this example of a desire hierarchy in light of what you know about the five-fold-why. The big bang theory suggests that the universe began expanding from a single indivisible point known as a "singularity." In similar fashion, the entire universe of human desire comes from a pseudo-singular set of core, causal desires.

## THIS IS A WEAK DESIRE-HIERARCHY AND GOAL MAP

FIGURE 82: Strong desire-hierarchies are broad-based, uncompromising on the core desire but open to fulfilling the core desire in multiple ways. Weak hierarchies only have one path to meeting the inherent desire. One point of failure throws off the entire hierarchy.

## DISTINGUISHING BETWEEN DESIRES AND MOTIVES

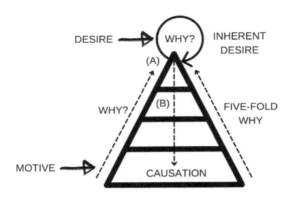

FIGURE 83: We can use the words "motives" and "desires" to distinguish between derived wants (things wanted to satisfy an even deeper want) and underived wants (things wanted for their own sake), respectively.

---

**KEY INSIGHT:**

You Can Motivate People Toward Goals, Goods, and Gains, and That's All Fine.

You Can Also Motivate People Toward the Greatest Goals, The Greatest Goods, and the Greatest Gains. The Choice Is Yours.

# PROMISE LOSS-MINIMIZATION

What is the essence of this strategy? In truth, it just promises benefits. Simply a different kind of benefit. Not "you'll gain X," but "you'll protect yourself from the loss of Y."

Why is this compelling? Because of human loss aversion. What's that? We fear loss more than we take pleasure in gain.

It's why we are so risk-averse. (Most of us, at least. The end of human risk aversion is typically signaled by the words, "Hey man, hold my beer… watch this backflip…") Let me explain. We feel more pain from losing something than we feel pleasure from gaining an equivalent thing.

-$1,000 for some people can be twice as emotionally painful as +$1,000 is emotionally pleasurable. And emotional arousal is the essence of directing attention toward a definite purpose. So is lowering perceived costs, which you inherently accomplish with this type of benefit.

## HOW TO HIJACK LOSS-AVERSION TO MOTIVATE PEOPLE

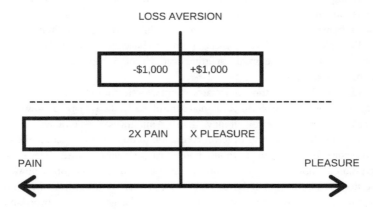

FIGURE 84: People have been shown to regularly fear loss more than they hope for an equivalent gain. While the extent of loss aversion differs between people, it can often be a factor of two.

Get it? What does it all come down to? Promise loss-minimization benefits. But which kind of benefit is better? Here's the secret. It's a false choice. You can use both. In fact, you should. A common speaking pattern among effective salesmen and saleswomen is this: "With this product, you can get [insert benefit] without [insert loss]."

For example, "With this WordPress integration, you can make your Website significantly more profitable, without wasting your time coding." Get it? You shouldn't be surprised about what I'm about to tell you. JFK used this type of benefit extensively. And why shouldn't you be surprised by that? Because where there is an effective communication strategy, chances are you'll see an example of JFK using it. This was in his inaugural address.

Russia, the "red giant," a communist regime, was gobbling up Eastern Europe, drastically expanding its military, and most dangerously, dramatically growing its stock of nuclear weapons, a tiny fraction of which would have been more than sufficient for instantly leveling all of America.

Freedom was under attack. Communism, according to the prevailing American ethos, the antithesis of freedom, was ravaging previously free nations. War seemed inevitable. And not just any war, but a war that would devastate, destroy, and degrade more than any other in human history. It would be a third world war before the dust of the first and second settled, and one more deadly than the first two combined. It was a difficult time to lead.

And when that's the case, it's a good time to use the communication of leadership.

And JFK, in this speech, directed the attention of his audience toward a definite purpose by promising loss-minimization benefits; protection-based benefits; not gains, but protections from losses. Here are the examples. Note that all these excerpts are not ensuring some gain, but ensuring the protection from some loss. And note the instant gravitas this lends him.

Example one: "Unwilling to witness or permit the slow undoing of those human rights to which this nation has always been committed, and to which we are committed today at home and around the world." Loss(es) minimized: the loss of human rights.

Example two: "We dare not meet a powerful challenge at odds and split asunder." Loss(es) minimized: the vague splitting asunder of a begrudging but necessary international coalition.

Example three: "To those new states whom we welcome to the ranks of the free, we pledge our word that one form of colonial control shall not have passed away merely to be replaced by a far more iron tyranny." Loss(es) minimized: iron tyranny.

Example four: "But this peaceful revolution of hope cannot become the prey of hostile powers. Let all our neighbors know that we shall join with them to oppose aggression or subversion anywhere in the Americas. And let every other power know that this Hemisphere intends to remain the master of its own house." Loss(es) minimized: becoming the prey of hostile powers, and aggression or subversion in the Americas.

Example five: "To that world assembly of sovereign states, the United Nations, our last best hope in an age where the instruments of war have far outpaced the instruments of peace, we renew our pledge of support – to prevent it from becoming merely a forum for invective – to strengthen its shield of the new and the weak – and to enlarge the area in which its writ may run." Loss(es) minimized: United Nations turning into a forum for invective.

Example six: "Finally, to those nations who would make themselves our adversary, we offer not a pledge but a request: that both sides begin anew the quest for peace, before the dark powers of destruction unleashed by science engulf all humanity in planned or accidental self-destruction." Loss(es) minimized: dark powers of destruction engulfing all of humanity.

Example seven: "We dare not tempt them with weakness. For only when our arms are sufficient beyond doubt can we be certain beyond doubt that they will never be employed." Loss(es) minimized: use of weapons (a loss).

Example eight: "Let both sides, for the first time, formulate serious and precise proposals for the inspection and control of arms – and bring the absolute power to destroy other nations under the absolute control of all nations." Loss(es) minimized: destruction of other nations.

Example nine: "Now the trumpet summons us again – not as a call to bear arms, though arms we need – not as a call to battle, though embattled we are – but a call to bear the burden of a long twilight struggle, year in and year out, 'rejoicing in hope, patient in tribulation' – a struggle against the common enemies of man: tyranny, poverty, disease and war itself." Loss(es) minimized: tyranny, poverty, disease, and war.

Example ten: "In the long history of the world, only a few generations have been granted the role of defending freedom in its hour of maximum danger." Loss(es) minimized: implicitly (in fact, as many of these are), the loss of freedom.

## ANOTHER WAY TO VISUALIZE LOSS AVERSION

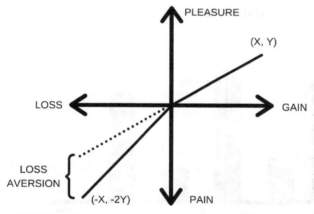

FIGURE 85: This is another way to visualize loss aversion, grafting the psychology of gains versus losses directly onto a mathematical cartesian plane.

(If you think the only lesson in this speech is the loss-minimization benefits, you're wrong. This is one of the most technique-packed speeches I've ever come across, which is why I've devoted an entire chapter in one of my books to uncovering its hidden secrets of rhetorical power). And we need to make one final point. These are the examples from JFK's inaugural address only of loss-minimization benefits. I snipped everything else.

What happened between them, then? As you'll see if you perform close analysis on this phenomenon of an address, between the loss-minimization benefits were gain-benefits. It was a pattern, though a loose one, of alternation between gain-benefits ("we'll get this") and loss-minimization benefits ("we'll avoid losing this").

So, why the pattern? Because it contributes to directing attention to a definite purpose. How? By upping-the-ante on the emotional arousal through the rapid back-and-forth between positive sentiment (gain-benefits) and negative sentiments (loss-minimization benefits, which have negative sentiment because of the description of the minimized loss).

There is a complex and difficult art of narrative-based sentiment mapping, and how to navigate positive sentiment and negative sentiment for maximum efficacy, but the details are not important for our purposes.

In other words, the alternation between these two types of benefits, each of which has a distinct and opposite semantic sentiment map, creates a compelling and attention-directing emotional pull. Sad, happy; sad, happy; sad, happy... Great.

You've mastered the critical algorithm governing human action, and you've mastered the two principal ways of balancing it in your favor. And now, we turn to a section that breaks up the rhythm. What are we going to address in that section? Yet more content tied to benefits. Specifically, we're going to answer two questions.

What do people need?

What do people want?

## HOW TO DISQUALIFY ALTERNATIVES TO YOUR PROPOSAL

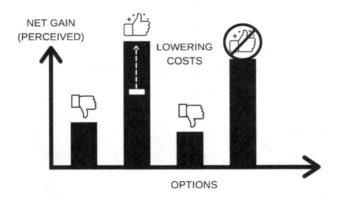

FIGURE 86: Disqualify an alternative to your proposal by increasing the perceived net gain of your proposal over the perceived net gain of the alternative. You can do this by lowering the costs of your proposal, for example. You might object: "Peter, people don't make decisions with this cool, calculating net gain logic! They are emotional!" And you would be correct on the second count, but slightly off on the first. Why? Because this isn't necessarily cool and calculating: perceived net gain subsumes emotional benefits and costs as well as concrete benefits and costs.

# APPEAL TO NEEDS

What are basic human desires?

Human desires are basic wants. They are engineered into every single person, in part, by evolution. Through psychological research, the human desires emerge to us. They are then organized into theories, but still exist on their own. They still act on their own, as independent drivers of human action.

## REVISITING THE THREE GOALS OF ATTENTION CONTROL

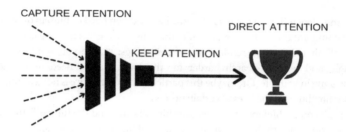

FIGURE 87: Reconsider the need to capture, keep, and most importantly direct attention through the lens of the hot air balloon model of persuasion and influence.

## PERSUASION EQUALS X PLUS Y: COMPLETE THE EQUATION

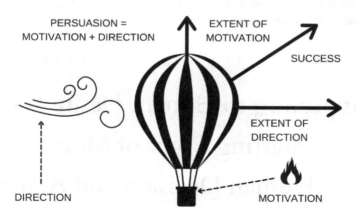

FIGURE 88: Hot air balloons use a flame to heat the fire in a balloon. Hot air rises. When the balloon starts to float, the wind

directs it. Persuasion is like a hot air balloon. It takes motivation and direction; you must motivate people and direct that energy toward a goal. If you don't motivate sufficiently, the balloon will fly low too the ground. It can't clear trees, hills, or buildings (which represent objections or obstacles to action). If it lacks direction, it flies straight up but doesn't actually go anywhere. You must combine both. And think of the canvas – the actual balloon – as your logical case. You need an airtight logical case. Logical, evidentiary, or factual errors poke holes in the logical case, meaning that both the motivating hot air and the directing wind lose their impact and leak through the holes. If you have too many holes, your balloon might not even take off at all, no matter how strong the fire or wind are.

And, depending on the person, some basic human need or human desire might be more dominant than others. So, if you're thinking "this seems nothing like me, and I'm human!" then I want to remind you of two things: maybe you aren't looking deep enough, and need to search harder for the basic human need or human desire manifesting in your life. Or, maybe this particular need or desire is not a dominant force in your life (but is in the lives of certain others).

So, if you're thinking "this seems nothing like me, and I'm human!" then I want to remind you of two things: maybe you aren't looking deep enough, and need to search harder for the basic human need or human desire manifesting in your life. Or, maybe this particular need or desire is not a dominant force in your life (but is in the lives of certain others).

Human motives are manifestations of human desires. A human desire is clean surroundings. A human motive might then be a clean, pearly white kitchen remodel. Human motives are what people seek to satisfy desires. In other words: human motives are different actions and goals people seek. Human motives differ between people. On the other hand, human desires are what human motives satisfy. Human desires are largely the same between people. But this begs the question: why do the basic human needs and human desires matter?

**KEY INSIGHT:**

# Appealing to Human Desire Is the Starting Point of Motivating Human Decision and Action.

## WHAT DOES IT REALLY MEAN TO "LOWER COSTS?"

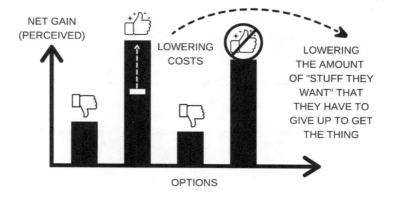

FIGURE 89: What does it really mean to lower costs? It means lowering the amount of "stuff they want" that they have to give up to get the benefits offered by the item. Another way to tip the net gain evaluation in your favor is to increase the amount of "stuff they want" that they have to give up in order to get the benefits offered by an alternative item. Or, more simply, raise the costs of any alternatives to your proposal, and they will pick yours.

You probably want to succeed in life, be it as a leader, in business, or at anything involving other people. To do that, you need to motivate people. You need to drive people. You need to inspire people to take action.

But how? Here's how: with the basic human needs and desires. Think of it this way: if you understand the basic human needs and human desires, you have a simple manual to the human brain. By using the basic human needs and human desires (like I'll show you how), you can become infinitely more persuasive, influential, and successful.

In other words: you are handed a simple input-output system to the human brain. Let me explain in our next section. So, how can you use the basic human needs and human desire in communication?

I'll cut right to the big answer: you can use the basic human needs and human desires in leadership, to motivate your team, in writing, to write with power, in public speaking, to speak with power and persuasion, in everyday conversations, to inspire other people, and in meetings, to get what you want. In other words: you can use the basic human needs and human desires any time you are communicating to a human with the desire to receive a specific action (even if you just want some undivided attention). And here's a hint: that's a lot of the time.

At its core, using the basic human needs and human desires in communication is presenting the action you want people to take as the way to fulfill one of the desires. But this raises the question: is it ethical? Yes. And here's why: you're not lying to anyone. You're not manipulating anyone. You're not harming, swindling, or using anyone.

Instead, here's what you are doing: engineering your communication to focus on the fundamental, genetically-wired things people care about.

### HOW DO HUMAN DEISRES COME ABOUT?

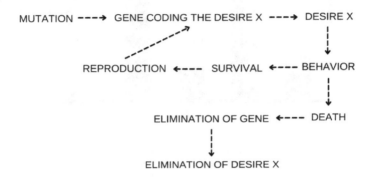

FIGURE 90: Genetic evolution provides a potential explanation for where desires come from. A genetic mutation causes a gene to code us to have a desire. This desire results in behavior that either causes survival which allows for reproduction and the propagation of the mutation (and therefore the desire) or death which eliminates the gene (and therefore the desire).

In fact, one might argue (and I do) that it is unethical to not speak in terms of the basic human needs and human desires. Why? Because you are trying to force your communication on someone without paying proper respect to the evolutionary, drilled-in-their-head desires they seek to fulfill. Let us reveal the frameworks.

**KEY INSIGHT:**

# It's Selfish to Speak in Terms of Only Your Interests and Expect Undivided Attention.

**KEY INSIGHT:**

# The Raw Material of Disparate, Divided, and Default Desires Must Be Shaped.

# It Must Be Organized, Integrated, Nested, and Negotiated Into a Single-Pointed Hierarchy.

## PROMISE MEANS

"The ends justify the means," according to Niccolo Machiavelli, author of *The Prince*. What does he mean by that? He means that the ends – the moral, worthwhile end achievements – justify the immoral means: how the end achievements were created. Joseph Stalin once said, along similar lines, that "You've gotta break a few eggs to make an omelet." But that has nothing to do with the communication of leadership, and I do not endorse the quotes.

What does, then? This: "the means validate the ends." Get it? I'll explain. So far, we've been discussing directing attention toward a definite purpose by describing the ends; the benefits; what you'll achieve, and how people will be positively impacted.

But the ends – by themselves – sound like silliness. In the 2020 Democratic Primary, which is happening right now as I'm writing this, Bernie Sanders seems to be struggling against Joe Biden. Why? Well, potentially, many reasons. Biden is more moderate, pushing less revolutionary, more "realistic" proposals.

Bernie is more liberal, pushing a more ambitious agenda. On paper, to many people, Bernie's proposals sound much, much better. Free healthcare. Free college. Many free things.

So, what's the problem? The reason why Biden is performing significantly better than Bernie is this: while Bernie has wonderful ends (what we'll do), he has few means (how we'll do it) to validate those ends.

In other words, he violates this: "the means validate the ends," because he has ill-explained, vague, and unconvincing means to validate the ends.

Every time Biden asks him a question like "how are you going to pay for that?" it becomes evident.

When he asks Bernie "how are you going to pass that through Congress?" Bernie's unconvincing response exposes his lack of means.

It all comes down to this: a decent proposal fully believed is better than a wonderful proposal half-believed.

And let's call this phrase, that "the means validate the ends," the iron law of a definite purpose.

To rephrase the iron law of a definite purpose, you need to have a convincing, credible, and compelling plan; you need to have means for producing your proposed ends, because without the means, your ends are invalidated.

## WHY YOU ABSOLUTELY NEED TO PRESENT THE "HOW"

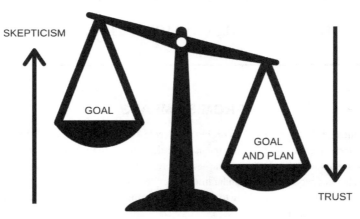

FIGURE 91: Presenting an audacious goal on its own is more likely to draw skepticism and lose trust than presenting a goal and a plan to achieve it. For the purposes of this illustration, the "X axis" is a spectrum from skepticism to trust.

Get it? And that's my theory explaining part of why Biden is outperforming Bernie. Not because his proposals are more attractive, but because while they are less attractive, they are more believable. To put it in yet other words, the ends – benefit-driven language, in all its forms – answer the question "what are you going to do, and why do we want that?" while the means answer the question "how are you going to do it, and why should we place our faith in that plan?"

## REVISITING THE TIMELESSLY PERSUASIVE STORY FORMULA

FIGURE 92: A hero has a problem and meets a guide who offers him a plan and calls him to action that results in success or failure.

## THIS IS WHAT PEOPLE ASSUME IF YOU SKIP THE "HOW"

FIGURE 93: A hero has a problem and meets a guide who doesn't offer him a plan, probably doesn't have one, and calls him to action that results in painful and abject failure.

## CLARIFYING THE PERSUASIVE FUNCTION OF THE "HOW"

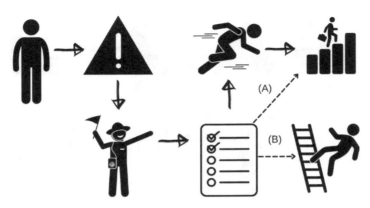

FIGURE 94: The function of a plan in the hero's journey – and remember, you are playing the empathetic and authoritative guide who gives them a plan – is that it makes success seem much more likely (A) and failure unlikely (B).

Get it? I'm going to bring back that excerpt from LBJ's Great Society speech. Remember it? I'm going to ask you to think about this: what was the bulk of his speech devoted to? Ends, or means? Benefits, or plans that produce the benefits? It was devoted to benefits. Which is great. Unless they are not validated by a compelling plan. So, remember that final phrase in his speech? "So I want to talk to you today about three places where we begin to build the Great Society – in our cities, in our countryside, and in our classrooms." That phrase signaled a shift from ends-driven language (benefit-driven language) to means-driven language.

We can call it plan-driven language. Let's see what came after. I'll give you a hint: lots and lots of means; lots and lots of plan-driven language. Why? Because LBJ (or his speechwriters) knew that the benefits so far described would lose impact unless a plan validated them. Like a trident, his preview goal-statement had three prongs.

Prong one: cities.

Prong two: countryside.

Prong three: classrooms.

If you recall problem-solution constructions, the solution portion is the means; it is the plan. LBJ went through the problems with each prong, saying things like, "The catalog of ills is long: there is the decay of the centers and the despoiling of the suburbs. There is not enough housing for our people or transportation for our traffic. Open land is vanishing and old landmarks are violated *(prong one problems – cities)*," "A second place where we begin to build the Great Society is in our countryside. We have always prided ourselves on being not only America the strong and America the free, but America the beautiful. Today that beauty is in danger. The water we drink, the food we eat, the very air that we breathe, are threatened with pollution. Our parks are overcrowded, our seashores overburdened. Green fields and dense forests are disappearing *(prong two problems – countryside)*," and "In many places, classrooms are overcrowded and curricula are outdated. Most of our qualified teachers are underpaid, and many of our paid teachers are unqualified. So we must give every child a place to sit and a teacher to learn from. Poverty must not be a bar to learning, and learning must offer an escape from poverty *(prong three problems – classrooms)*."

And after delineating the problems, here are the means he presented; the means validating the positive ends he started with, turning them from wishful thinking into believable proposals. "These are three of the central issues of the Great Society. While our Government has many programs directed at those issues, I do not pretend that we have the full answer to those problems. But I do promise this: We are going to assemble the best thought and the broadest knowledge from all over the world to find those answers for America. I intend to establish working groups to prepare a series of White House conferences and meetings – on the cities, on natural beauty, on the quality of education, and on other emerging challenges. And from these meetings and from this inspiration and from these studies we will begin to set our course toward the Great Society. The solution to these problems does not rest on a massive program in Washington, nor can it rely solely on the strained resources of local authority. They require us to create new concepts of cooperation, a creative federalism, between the National Capital and the leaders of local communities. Woodrow Wilson once wrote: 'Every man sent out from his university should be a man of his Nation as well as a man of his time.' Within your lifetime powerful forces, already loosed, will take us toward a way of life beyond the realm of our experience, almost beyond the bounds of our imagination. For better or for worse, your generation has been appointed by history to deal with those problems and to lead America toward a new age. You have the chance never before afforded to any people in any age. You can help build a society where the demands of morality, and the needs of the spirit, can be realized in the life of the Nation."

So, to summarize, LBJ's speech traced the following structure, a structure that will prove useful to you if you seek to use it.

Benefits: directing attention by telling people that you can give them what they want. For LBJ, it was things like an end to poverty, an end to racial inequality, and better educational opportunities (and much more, as you saw in the excerpt of his speech).

Three-pronged goal statement: expressing a clear and definitive goal, including the singular and self-contained banner concept, and three sub-goals that fall under it. For LBJ, it was creating a great society by focusing on cities, the countryside, and classrooms.

Problems in each prong: listing out the problems in each prong, that need to be fixed. This validates the solutions. I quoted LBJ's above.

Solutions: listing out the means to validate the ends; to validate the benefits at the beginning. I also quoted LBJ's above. His solutions included the following: assembling the best knowledge in a conference, establishing working groups of experts on these problems; establishing not a massive Washington-driven top-down program, not a strained bottom-up locality-driven program, but new models of cooperation, a new approach to federalism, and inspiring national sentiment in educated people.

Remember this: without a plan, ends-driven, or benefit-driven language sounds like wishful thinking. It's a cycle: benefits create a desire that directs attention; problems validate the need for solutions; solutions (means / plans) validate the benefits (ends). And I have a useful strategy – another equation – for conceptualizing the relationship between beliefs and benefits.

It's simply this: perceived benefit = (trust coefficient) * (benefit scale). Let me explain. Your benefit scale is a percentage. (I express it as a scale from 0 to 1 for ease and clarity: 50% = 0.5) At 1, your benefit scale represents you delivering the highest possible amount of benefits, and of the most attractive kind. It's the most benefit-driven any language can be, at 1. At 0? Nothing. No benefits. Zero. It's the least benefit-driven any language can be, at 0. What about trust? 1 represents full trust. 0 represents no trust.

So, how do the two numbers interact? It evokes the idea that a decent proposal fully believed is better than a wonderful proposal half-believed. As benefits go up, the trust coefficient goes down, making overall perceived benefit lower. This is realistic because it adjusts for the lower trust people place on benefits that sound too good to be true. Promising weak benefits, on a low benefit scale, is not good either. People will trust it. Sure. But they'll trust something they can't really bring themselves to care about. Get it?

Some examples. Let's say you go up and say, in a business meeting planning the next two fiscal years, "We are going to quadruple profits, we are going to multiply the number of branches by a factor of five, we are going to get 75 industry awards, and we are going to 10X our market capitalization." The benefit scale is somewhere near 1. But trust coefficient is somewhere near 0. It all sounds like wishful thinking, doesn't it? The net result? Zero perceived benefit (0 * 1).

Let's say you say, instead, "We are going to maintain fairly consistent growth, perhaps deflating by 10% semi-annually in our three most regulated industries, while market capitalization will remain flat." Your trust coefficient is somewhere near a 1. But your benefit scale is somewhere near 0. The perceived benefit? Zero perceived benefit (1 * 0).

So, how do means – or plans – interact with this? When you propose plans, you can raise your benefit scale without lowering your trust coefficient, thus raising net perceived benefit. So, the best combination is a set of strong, bold, and ambitious, but believable benefits, validated by a compelling plan. Let's apply this thinking to our original example of Bernie and Biden.

Bernie's benefit scale puts him somewhere near a 1. Biden's benefit scale puts him, let's say, at 0.7. Compelling benefits, but not as compelling as Bernie's. However, because perceived benefits adjust themselves for trust, or for the likelihood that they'll actually happen, we have to factor that in as well. Because Bernie is very high on the benefit scale, proposing extremely ambitious and bold plans, he is quite low on the trust coefficient. Let's put him at a 0.5 It's truly not a stretch, based on polls of public sentiment, to say that he is literally half-believed.

So, the net perceived benefit of a Bernie presidency is 50%. (Note that, in isolation, that number means nothing: it's all about how it stacks up against alternatives). What about Biden? Since his benefits are not too unbelievably ambitious, but still compelling, he's at a 0.7 on the benefit scale, and a 0.7 on the trust coefficient scale. That puts him at 49%; pretty much neck-and-neck with Bernie.

But we need to factor in the means; we need to pay attention to the plans. Bernie provides few compelling answers to plan-based questions.

"How are you going to pay for it?"

"How will you get Republicans in Congress to vote for it?"

This is a fact that Biden and other moderates are thrilled to draw attention to.

His trust coefficient drops from a 0.5 – a function of his ambitious benefits – to a 0.3, a function of his ambitious benefits and lack of plans to validate them. Biden provides an abundance of plan-driven language, raising his trust coefficient from 0.7 – a function of his believable benefits – to a 0.9 – a function of his believable benefits matched by compelling plans to validate them.

Bernie: $0.3 * 1 = 30\%$. Biden: $0.9 * 0.7 = 63\%$. Now, this is a conceptual model. It doesn't deal with the thousands of external variables at play. But it is incredibly valuable at teaching us the impact of plan-driven language. Again, what is the function of plan-driven language? Raising the trust coefficient. Validating your benefits. Building the public belief you need for action. Directing attention toward a definite purpose. Turning an improbable hope into an undeniable reality.

---

**KEY INSIGHT:**

# A Tempting Promise Plus a Credible Plan is Persuasive, Powerful, and Unitive.

## Motivation Plus Belief Produces Action. No Promise, No Motivation. No Plan, No Belief.

## HOW CREDIBLE PLANS INTERACT WITH COMPELLING GOALS

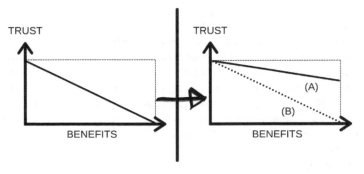

FIGURE 95: As benefits rise, in many cases, trust begins to fall. It sounds too good to be true. However, when you have a credible plan, this relationship weakens (A) as opposed to when you lack a credible plan (B).

Alright, I've made my case for the necessity of a plan. But what defines a good plan? Let's talk about that now.

---

**KEY INSIGHT:**

Of Our Systemic and Uniquely Human Logical Leaps, One Stands Out As We Discuss Plans.

It Is Our Tendency to Assume that All Plans Are Created Equal; that a Plan Is a Plan Is a Plan. *Wrong.*

---

## PRESENT SOLVENCY

Remember the loose structure we're developing? First, benefits. Benefits hook and direct attention. Second, a self-contained and singular goal statement that previews the sub-goals. This channels the attention, directing it toward a definite purpose. Third, problems with each of the sub-goals. These validate the solutions. Fourth, solutions for these problems that will produce the benefits. These validate the benefits. And in this section, we focus on the addition of solvency to the end of this structure. Solvency-statements, which answer a critical question.

"Why is this plan a good plan? Why will it work?"

**DON'T GET THIS CRUCIAL, IRREVOCABLE PATTERN MIXED UP**

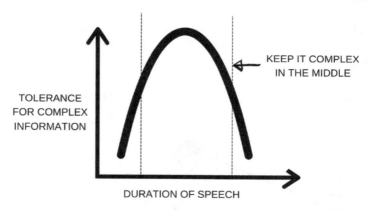

FIGURE 96: At the beginning of a speech, people are still in the "foraging" dynamic. They have not yet committed to a new source of information. They want to see a source of information with high benefit and low cost – a source of information that is interesting and useful and that doesn't demand high cognitive energy. At the end, they are cognitively tired. Their tolerance for complex information peaks in the middle. Plan-driven language – "how-driven" language – tends to be more complex. So, roughly speaking, it tends to belong somewhere in the middle of the speech, when complexity-tolerance is higher.

The definition of solvency is, according to the Merriam-Webster dictionary, "the quality or state of being solvent," and solvent is defined by the same source as "able to pay all legal debts; something that provides a solution; something that eliminates or attenuates something especially unwanted."

(Ironically, the given recent example from the web when I looked up solvency was "Biden was part of the Democratic wing that long sought to work with Republicans on Social Security *solvency* before the party's shift back to an expansion stance.")

Something solvent is something that works; that is internally consistent, not attempting more than its resources can handle, but that can still provide a solution by removing something unwanted (fixing a problem) or providing a benefit.

So, we talked about plans in the last section. And in this section, we address how to present good plans; solvent plans.

There's one salient guideline: present evidence. Loads of it. Heaps of it. More than you need. Make it irrefutable, and inarguable. Marshall your arguments. Know your arguments, and the counters to your arguments, and the counters to the counters, so on and so forth. Map out the battlefield. You don't just need to know you're right, you need to know why you know you're right. And then present all of this to the audience.

It's just like providing a superabundance of benefits; some people have one particular benefit that will compel them the most, while the other benefits fall flat, and providing more benefits increases your chances of hitting more people's keystone benefits.

Likewise, providing more pieces of evidence increases your chances of hitting more people's keystone solvency-indicator, that does more than the rest combined to persuade them.

## HOW TO DEFEND YOUR PROPOSAL FROM OBJECTIONS

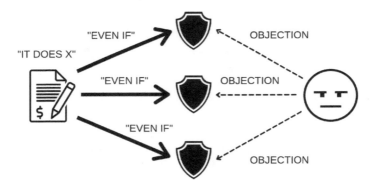

FIGURE 97: Do you recall the hot-air-balloon persuasive model? Objections are like daggers that slash holes in the canvas of the balloon, preventing it from rising high and floating far. Defend your proposal from objections with the proven "even if" strategy. Say that "it does X" (your main claim) ""even if (insert objection), even if (insert objection), even if (insert objection), etc."

**KEY INSIGHT:**

# Rhetoric Is a Vehicle. A Plan Is the Passenger. Rhetoric Is a Vessel. A Plan Is the Contents.

# Good Rhetoric Plus a Bad Plan Is a Recipe for Disaster. And That's Exactly Where Arrogance Leads.

## PROMISE RECTIFICATION

This is the final section in this chapter. And in this section, you learn how to invoke one of the most powerful, motivating, attention-dominating forces in your favor.

You learn how to invoke a yearning; a pain; a stark schism in someone's soul.

It is one of the most powerful forces ever used in communication. Think back to the victim-perpetrator-benevolence model the 2020 Democrats love oh-so-much. It invoked this. So, what is it? Restoring the loss of 10,000 dollars is significantly more attractive than gaining 10,000 new dollars in the absence of a loss.

That will give you a hint. This force is inextricably tied to loss aversion: the pain of a loss is often much higher, and sometimes double, the pleasure of an equivalent gain.

It is also closely related to the endowment effect: that which is ours gains additional value in our eyes; it is endowed with a strange, irrational, objectively non-existent value.

We've talked about gain-benefits. We've talked about loss-minimization benefits. Now, we have to talk about rectification-benefits. What are these? Benefits rectifying some loss people experienced are incredibly compelling and invoke an incredibly powerful emotional response that directs attention toward a definite purpose. Make America Great is significantly, drastically, dramatically less compelling than Make America Great Again.

Why? Because Make America Great Again – due to that "again" – promises rectification. It's a slight, subtle difference, but an incredibly impactful one. The "again" promises a restoration of a greatness we had, but lost, whereas the slogan without that crucial word promises a greatness we never had.

It invokes loss-aversion. It invokes the endowment effect. We want that which we had but lost more than we would want an identical thing we never had to begin with. And this deep desire, this ever-growing want, is accompanied by emotional pain, and deep psychological suffering.

## THE LITTLE-KNOWN PSYCHOLOGY OF RECTIFICATION

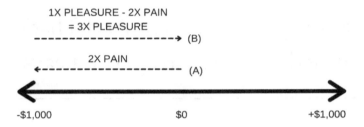

FIGURE 98: A loss rectification benefit promises the reversal of a -$1,000 loss that caused 2X pain (A). This reversal causes the pleasure of the gain it represents – X pleasure for +$1,000 – in addition to the subtraction of 2X pain, which is a 2X gain in pleasure, resulting in a net gain of 3X pleasure (B).

If you know anything about psychology, it's this: people will do anything to escape emotional pain and psychological suffering. This strategy – this advanced, expert approach – doesn't just invoke a shallow, superficial want, but a yearning; a painful grasp for the lost majesty of what was; an escape from the pain of losing that which this strategy (in Trump's case, the "again" word) makes people realize they were ignorant of losing in the first place.

The restoration of something lost is more compelling than the gain of something never possessed; that restoration is a benefit with unparalleled attraction and undeniable magnetism because it promises not only the pleasure of a gain, but an escape from the pain of the loss, which is more painful than an equivalent gain would ever be pleasurable.

Alright. You get it. Let's talk about how to do this, not just what it is. In essence, it's what I just said: presenting your benefits not only as novel gains but as restoration of lost attainments from the past.

Now, it's not one of the three; you don't have to choose one from the triad of gain-benefits, loss-minimization benefits, and rectification benefits. You can use all three, and you should use all three, to direct your audience's attention toward a definite purpose with effortless efficacy. It's called the benefit-triad.

## THE THREE KINDS OF BENEFITS

GAINS

LOSS
PREVENTIONS

LOSS
RECTIFICATIONS

FIGURE 99: This is the benefit-triad. The most effective speakers use all three kinds of benefits.

Some examples of promised rectification?

You'll see an abundance of it in the excerpts from the victim-perpetrator-benevolence model in our first section, but I want to give you some new examples. First, one from Bernie Sanders. This speech kicked off his 2020 presidential run. His persuasive power is extremely polished, precise, and refined, and he understands the power of promising loss-rectification. In fact, examples abound in this speech. I'm tempted to say that this speech was intentionally built around this technique. I wanted to bold all of the rectification-driven language until I realized that basically the entire excerpt would be bolded. Instead, I opted for counting the loss-rectification benefits. This is a phenomenally expressive example.

"No. We will no longer stand idly by and allow three people in this country to own more wealth than the bottom half of America while *(loss-rectification #1)*, at the same time, over 20 percent of our children live in poverty *(loss-rectification #2)*, veterans sleep out on the streets and seniors cannot afford their prescription drugs *(loss-rectification #3)*. We will no longer accept 46 percent of all new income going to the top 1 percent *(loss-rectification #4)*, while millions of Americans are forced to work 2 or 3 jobs just to survive *(loss-rectification #5)* and over half of our people live paycheck to paycheck *(loss-rectification #6)*, frightened to death about what happens to them financially if their car breaks down or their child becomes sick *(loss-rectification #7)*.

Today, we fight for a political revolution. We say to the private health insurance companies, whether you like it or not, the United States will join every other major country on earth and guarantee healthcare to all people as a right. All Americans are entitled to go to the doctor when they're sick *(loss-rectification #8)* and not go bankrupt after staying in the hospital *(loss-rectification #9)*.

Yes. We will pass a Medicare for all single-payer program. Today, we say to the pharmaceutical industry, that you will no longer charge the American people the highest prices in the world for prescription drugs *(loss-rectification #10)*, the result being that one out of five Americans cannot afford the prescriptions their doctors prescribe *(loss-rectification #11)*. The outrageous greed of the pharmaceutical industry is going to end. We are going to lower prescription drug prices in this country *(loss-rectification #12)*.

Today, we say to WalMart, the fast food industry and other low wage employers: Stop paying your employees starvation wages *(loss-rectification #13)*. Yes. We are going to raise the federal minimum wage to a living wage – $15 an hour. Nobody who works 40 hours a week in this country should live in poverty *(loss-rectification #14)*. And yes. We're going to make it easier for people to join unions, not harder.

And by the way. Today we say to corporate America that artificial intelligence and robotics are not going to be used just to throw workers out on the street *(loss-rectification #15)*. This exploding technology must serve human needs, not just corporate profits.

Today we say to the American people that we will rebuild our crumbling infrastructure *(loss-rectification #16)*: our roads, our bridges, our rail system and subways, our water systems and wastewater plants and our airports – and when we do that we create up to 13 million good paying jobs. Today we say to the parents in this country that you and your kids deserve quality, affordable childcare. The children are our future, and they deserve the best possible head start in life with a high quality, universal pre-K program.

Today, we say to our young people that we want you to get the best education that you can, regardless of the income of your family. Good jobs require a good education. That is why we are going to make public colleges and universities tuition free, and substantially lower the outrageous level of student debt that currently exists *(loss-rectification #17)*. America once had the best educated workforce in the world, and we are going to make that happen again.

Today, we say to our senior citizens, that we understand that you cannot live in dignity when you are trying to survive on $13,000 or $14,000 a year in Social Security benefits *(loss-rectification #18)*. My Republican colleagues want to cut Social Security but we have some bad news for them. We're not going to cut Social Security benefits. We're going to expand them *(loss-rectification #19)*.

Today, we say to Donald Trump and the fossil fuel industry that climate change is not a hoax but is an existential threat to our country and the entire planet *(loss-rectification #20)* – and we intend to transform our energy system away from fossil fuel and into energy efficiency and sustainable energy and, in the process, create millions of good paying jobs. All of us have a moral responsibility to make certain that the planet we leave to our children and grandchildren is healthy and habitable *(loss-rectification #21)*.

Today, we say to the prison-industrial-complex that we are going to bring about real criminal justice reform. We are going to end the international embarrassment of having more people in jail than any other country on earth *(loss-rectification #22).* Instead of spending $80 billion a year on jails and incarceration *(loss-rectification #23),* we are going to invest in jobs and education for our young people. No more private prisons and detention centers *(loss-rectification #24).* No more profiteering from locking people up *(loss-rectification #25).* No more "war on drugs *(loss-rectification #26)."* No more keeping people in jail because they're too poor to afford cash bail *(loss-rectification #27).*

And by the way, when we talk about criminal justice reform, we're going to change a system in which tens of thousands of Americans every year get criminal records for possessing marijuana *(loss-rectification #28),* but not one major Wall Street executive went to jail for destroying our economy in 2008 as a result of their greed, recklessness and illegal behavior *(loss-rectification #29).* No. They didn't go to jail *(loss-rectification #30).* They got a trillion-dollar bailout *(loss-rectification #31).*

Today, we say to the American people that instead of demonizing the undocumented immigrants in this country *(loss-rectification #32),* we're going to pass comprehensive immigration reform and provide a path toward citizenship. We're going to provide legal status to the 1.8 million young people eligible for the DACA program, and develop a humane border policy for those who seek asylum. No more snatching babies from the arms of their mothers *(loss-rectification #33).*

Today, we say to the top 1 percent and the large profitable corporations in this country – people who have never had it so good — that under a Bernie Sanders administration we're going to end the massive tax breaks and loopholes that you currently enjoy *(loss-rectification #34).*

We will no longer accept the absurd situation where large corporations like Amazon, Netflix and General Motors pay nothing in federal income taxes after raking in billions in profits *(loss-rectification #35).* We will no longer tolerate the situation in which the wealthy and large corporations stash billions in tax havens throughout the world *(loss-rectification #36).*

Yes, the wealthy and multi-national corporations in this country will start paying their fair share of taxes *(loss-rectification #37).* We are going to end austerity for working families *(loss-rectification #38),* and provide some austerity for large, multi-national corporations *(loss-rectification #39).*

Today, we say to the military-industrial-complex that we will not continue to spend $700 billion a year on the military *(loss-rectification #40)* – more than the next ten nations combined. We're going to invest in affordable housing, we're going to invest in public education, we're going to invest in rebuilding our crumbling infrastructure *(loss-rectification #41)* – not more nuclear weapons and never-ending wars *(loss-rectification #42)."*

Here's the truth: there are countless strategies encapsulated in that speech. But we've discussed them in their own sections. I'll just give you one brief example, and urge you to analyze it to see how he uses other strategies of the communication of leadership. He uses an expansive amount of problem-solution-driven language. In fact, you have to when using loss-rectification benefits; each loss is a problem, and each rectification is a solution. I'm going to enumerate the occasionally-implicit losses rectified since they were not always clear. And here's the key point: all losses are problems, but not all problems are losses. A loss is the removal of something once obtained. I'll elaborate on how Bernie's enumerated problems were losses. If you got it all, skip this.

Rectified loss #1: the loss of greater wealth equality, which existed pre-Reagan

Rectified loss #2: the loss of a child's entitlement to a basic material comfort.

Rectified loss #3: much like loss two, the loss of a veteran's entitlement to housing, and the loss of a senior's entitlement to medical care.

Rectified loss #4: the loss of a more equal division of new income.

Rectified loss #5: the loss of an economy in which one job was enough per family.

Rectified loss #6: the loss of the American promise of peace of mind.

Rectified loss #7: the same as loss number six; the loss of a safety net.

Rectified loss #8: the loss of our entitlement to see a doctor when we are sick.

Rectified loss #9: the loss of our entitlement to get affordable medical care.

Rectified loss #10: the loss of affordable prescription drugs.

Rectified loss #11: the same as loss number ten.

Rectified loss #12: the same as loss number ten.

Rectified loss #13: the loss of living wages.

Rectified loss #14: the loss of an accessible middle class.

Rectified loss #15: the loss of jobs due to AI, automation, and robotics.

Rectified loss #16: the loss of functioning infrastructure.

Rectified loss #17: the loss of affordable, debt-free education.

Rectified loss #18: the loss of reaching one's advanced years in dignity.

Rectified loss #19: the loss of Social Security benefits.

Rectified loss #20: the loss of our planet's health.

Rectified loss #21: the same as loss twenty.

Rectified loss #22: the loss of competent criminal justice.

Rectified loss #23: the loss of funds spent on a failing criminal justice system.

Rectified loss #24: the existence of private prison which is a loss in itself.

Rectified loss #25: the loss of the existence of profiteering from locking people up.

Rectified loss #26: the loss of the existence of a war on drugs.

Rectified loss #27: the loss of an innocent person facing an unaffordable bail.

Rectified loss #28: the loss of people getting criminal records for harmless crimes.

Rectified loss #29: the loss of the public being defrauded.

Rectified loss #30: the loss of justice; people who committed crimes escaping.

Rectified loss #31: the loss of public funds going to pay bail.

Rectified loss #32: the loss of the dignity of undocumented people.

Rectified loss #33: the loss of moral immigration enforcement.

Rectified loss #34: the loss of a fair system of taxation.

Rectified loss #35: same as loss 34.

Rectified loss #36: the same as loss 34.

Rectified loss #37: the same as loss 34.

Rectified loss #38: the same as loss 34.

Rectified loss #39: the same as loss 34.

Rectified loss #40: the loss of public funds on bad expenditures.

Rectified loss #41: the loss of effective infrastructure.

Rectified loss #42: the loss of the endless-war-free international policy.

---

**KEY INSIGHT:**

# Humans Are Risk-Averse, Loss-Averse, Protective and Conservative by Nature.

# Rectifying an Injustice Has More Persuasive Pull Than Seizing an Opportunity, All Else Equal.

# Of Course, We Can Do Both.

---

I love examples that are particularly exemplary, like this one. I will say this: Bernie could have done a yet more compelling job by making the losses more explicit; that is, by specifically explaining how the problems are not just things we don't have and should have, but things we once had and lost. Much of it is implicit, and in this case, that is weaker. What do I mean by that? I mean that, for more of these losses, he should have said things along the lines of, "We used to have this, and now we don't." Regardless, all of these qualify as loss-rectifications, because the thing he says he wants to restore was indeed something we once had.

At the risk of belaboring this discussion of problems and losses, problems are extremely compelling, but problems that are losses of something we once had are yet more compelling because they inspire a strong emotional yearning in us for what once was. Let's quickly turn to FDR, in many ways, Bernie's political parallel from the past, and see how he uses loss-rectification, before moving on to part three: backing the attention with intentional action. FDR shows us how this strategy breaks down into two distinct parts: the loss enumeration, and the loss rectification.

"I am certain that my fellow Americans expect that on my induction into the Presidency I will address them with a candor and a decision which the present situation of our people impel. This is preeminently the time to speak the truth, the whole truth, frankly and boldly. Nor need we shrink from honestly facing conditions in our country today. This great Nation will endure as it has endured, will revive and will prosper. So, first of all, let me assert my firm belief that the only thing we have to fear is fear itself— nameless, unreasoning, unjustified terror which paralyzes needed efforts to convert retreat into advance. In every dark hour of our national life a leadership of frankness and vigor has met with that understanding and support of the people themselves which is essential to victory. I am convinced that you will again give that support to leadership in these critical days.

In such a spirit on my part and on yours we face our common difficulties. They concern, thank God, only material things. Values have shrunken to fantastic levels *(loss enumeration – they "shrunk" from what they once had, to low levels)*; taxes have risen *(loss enumeration – they "grew" from what they once had, to high levels)*; our ability to pay has fallen *(loss enumeration – the ability to pay has "shrunk" from what they once had, to low levels; as you can see, all of these are not just problems, but problems representing the loss of something the country once had)*; government of all kinds is faced by serious curtailment of income *(loss enumeration – curtailment of previously sufficient levels of income)*; the means of exchange are frozen in the currents of trade *(loss enumeration – the previously intact means of exchange are frozen)*; the withered leaves of industrial enterprise lie on every side *(loss enumeration – they "withered" ... problems, including a verb that suggests a change of state, like "withered" usually imply that, at one point, it was not withered; thus, it is a loss and not just a standard problem. The same applies to previous loss-enumerations)*; farmers find no markets for their produce *(loss enumeration – farmers who once had an abundance of opportunity have lost it)*; the savings of many years in thousands of families are gone *(loss enumeration – this final example from this excerpt is perhaps most compelling, and most explicit, which I argue, is better than implicit, with regards to loss enumerations. He is saying that what families have saved has been lost, instead of using a verb that describes state transition, like "frozen," or "withered," which only indirectly imply the loss, and which he used for his previous loss-enumerations. When you only imply loss, people can simply not realize the impact. Remember: losing that which we once had is significantly worse than never having it in the first place, and explicit loss-enumerations guarantees that everyone understands that crucial piece of it; that they did, in fact, once have it)*.

More important, a host of unemployed citizens face the grim problem of existence *(loss enumeration – there was an abundance of opportunity for all in the labor market, now that has been lost)*, and an equally great number toil with little return *(loss enumeration – a job used to provide a comfortable income, and now most do not)*. Only a foolish optimist can deny the dark realities of the moment.

Yet our distress comes from no failure of substance *(this is a compelling strategy: injecting a "what we still have" statement, or a sequence of such statements, right after a grim loss-driven section. Remember: emotional contrasts create significantly more vivid, intense emotions; just like not having something is made worse when contrasted with the experience of once having it, a section of hope, like this one, is made more compelling when contrasted with the previous section of loss-enumeration. If he had just started with hope, there would be no emotional contrast. But because he didn't, and in fact started with loss-enumeration, the hope is warranted, justified, and significantly more compelling due to contrast).* We are stricken by no plague of locusts *("what we still have...").* Compared with the perils which our forefathers conquered because they believed and were not afraid, we have still much to be thankful for *("what we still have...").* Nature still offers her bounty and human efforts have multiplied it *("what we still have...").* Plenty is at our doorstep *("what we still have...")*, but a generous use of it languishes in the very sight of the supply *("what we still have..." but "what we still have lost..." more emotional contrast).* Primarily this is because the rulers of the exchange of mankind's goods have failed *(recall the victim-perpetrator-benevolence model? Though it is not the core of FDR's speech, he introduced a perpetrator just now),* through their own stubbornness and their own incompetence, have admitted their failure, and abdicated. Practices of the unscrupulous money changers stand indicted in the court of public opinion, rejected by the hearts and minds of men.

True they have tried, but their efforts have been cast in the pattern of an outworn tradition. *(This is interesting. The victims are the audience, the perpetrators are the propertied business elites, and the benevolent force for good is FDR. In this section, he presents the perpetrators in an interesting light, not as malevolent, but as incompetent. "They have tried, but failed..." This seems like an attempt to preserve unity.)* Faced by failure of credit *(loss-enumeration)* they have proposed only the lending of more money *(failed attempt at loss-rectification by the perpetrator).* Stripped of the lure of profit by which to induce our people to follow their false leadership *(loss enumeration)* they have resorted to exhortations, pleading tearfully for restored confidence *(failed attempt at loss-rectification by the perpetrator).* They know only the rules of a generation of self-seekers. They have no vision, and when there is no vision the people perish.

The money changers have fled from their high seats in the temple of our civilization *(after failing to rectify the loss, the perpetrators have fled)* We may now restore that temple to the ancient truths *(a vague hint at loss-rectification).* The measure of the restoration *("restoration..." sounds familiar, doesn't it?)* lies in the extent to which we apply social values more noble than mere monetary profit *(loss-rectification).*

Happiness lies not in the mere possession of money; it lies in the joy of achievement, in the thrill of creative effort. The joy and moral stimulation of work no longer must be forgotten in the mad chase of evanescent profits *(loss-rectification).* These dark days will be worth all they cost us if they teach us that our true destiny is not to be ministered unto but to minister to ourselves and to our fellow men *(loss-rectification).*

Recognition of the falsity of material wealth as the standard of success goes hand in hand with the abandonment of the false belief that public office and high political position are to be valued only by the standards of pride of place and personal profit *(loss-rectification);* and there must be an end to a conduct in banking and in business which too often has given to a sacred trust the likeness of callous and selfish wrongdoing *(loss-rectification).* Small wonder that confidence languishes, for it thrives only on honesty, on honor, on the sacredness of obligations, on faithful protection, on unselfish performance; without them it cannot live.

Restoration *(or rectification – same thing)* calls, however, not for changes in ethics alone. This Nation asks for action, and action now *(loss-rectification)*.

Our greatest primary task is to put people to work *(loss-rectification)*. This is no unsolvable problem if we face it wisely and courageously. It can be accomplished in part by direct recruiting by the Government itself *(loss-rectification)*, treating the task as we would treat the emergency of a war *(loss-rectification)*, but at the same time, through this employment, accomplishing greatly needed projects to stimulate and reorganize the use of our natural resources *(loss-rectification)*.

Hand in hand with this we must frankly recognize the overbalance of population in our industrial centers and *(loss-rectification)*, by engaging on a national scale in a redistribution *(loss-rectification)*, endeavor to provide a better use of the land for those best fitted for the land *(loss-rectification)*. The task can be helped by definite efforts to raise the values of agricultural products *(loss-rectification)* and with this the power to purchase the output of our cities *(loss-rectification)*. It can be helped by preventing realistically the tragedy of the growing loss through foreclosure of our small homes and our farms *(loss-rectification)*. It can be helped by insistence that the Federal, State, and local governments act forthwith on the demand that their cost be drastically reduced *(loss-rectification)*. It can be helped by the unifying of relief activities which today are often scattered, uneconomical, and unequal *(loss-rectification)*. It can be helped by national planning for and supervision of all forms of transportation and of communications and other utilities which have a definitely public character *(loss-rectification)*. There are many ways in which it can be helped *(loss-rectification)*, but it can never be helped merely by talking about it. We must act and act quickly *(loss-rectification)*.

Finally, in our progress toward a resumption of work we require two safeguards against a return of the evils of the old order; there must be a strict supervision of all banking and credits and investments *(loss-rectification)*; there must be an end to speculation with other people's money *(loss-rectification)*, and there must be provision for an adequate but sound currency *(loss-rectification)*.

There are the lines of attack *(loss-rectification)*. I shall presently urge upon a new Congress in special session detailed measures for their fulfillment *(loss-rectification)*, and I shall seek the immediate assistance of the several States *(loss-rectification)*.

Through this program of action we address ourselves to putting our own national house in order and making income balance outgo *(loss-rectification)*. Our international trade relations, though vastly important, are in point of time and necessity secondary to the establishment of a sound national economy *(loss-rectification)*. I favor as a practical policy the putting of first things first *(loss-rectification)*. I shall spare no effort to restore world trade by international economic readjustment *(loss-rectification)*, but the emergency at home cannot wait on that accomplishment.

The basic thought that guides these specific means of national recovery is not narrowly nationalistic. It is the insistence, as a first consideration, upon the interdependence of the various elements in all parts of the United States – a recognition of the old and permanently important manifestation of the American spirit of the pioneer *(loss-rectification)*. It is the way to recovery *(loss-rectification)*. It is the immediate way *(loss-rectification)*. It is the strongest assurance that the recovery will endure *(loss-rectification)*.

In the field of world policy I would dedicate this Nation to the policy of the good neighbor *(loss-rectification)* – the neighbor who resolutely respects himself and, because he does so, respects the rights of others *(loss-rectification)* – the neighbor who respects his obligations and respects the sanctity of his agreements in and with a world of neighbors *(loss-rectification)*.

If I read the temper of our people correctly, we now realize as we have never realized before our interdependence on each other; that we cannot merely take but we must give as well *(loss-rectification)*; that if we are to go forward, we must move as a trained and loyal army willing to sacrifice for the good of a common discipline *(loss-rectification)*, because without such discipline no progress is made, no leadership becomes effective. We are, I know, ready and willing to submit our lives and property to such discipline *(loss-rectification)* because it makes possible a leadership which aims at a larger good *(loss-rectification)*. This I propose to offer, pledging that the larger purposes will bind upon us all as a sacred obligation with a unity of duty hitherto evoked only in time of armed strife *(loss-rectification)*.

With this pledge taken, I assume unhesitatingly the leadership of this great army of our people dedicated to a disciplined attack upon our common problems *(loss-rectification)*.

Action in this image and to this end is feasible under the form of government which we have inherited from our ancestors *(loss-rectification)*. Our Constitution is so simple and practical that it is possible always to meet extraordinary needs by changes in emphasis and arrangement without loss of essential form *(loss-rectification)*. That is why our constitutional system has proved itself the most superbly enduring political mechanism the modern world has produced *(loss-rectification)*. It has met every stress of vast expansion of territory, of foreign wars, of bitter internal strife, of world relations *(loss-rectification)*.

It is to be hoped that the normal balance of executive and legislative authority may be wholly adequate to meet the unprecedented task before us *(loss-rectification)*. But it may be that an unprecedented demand and need for undelayed action may call for temporary departure from that normal balance of public procedure *(loss-rectification)*.

I am prepared under my constitutional duty to recommend the measures that a stricken nation in the midst of a stricken world may require *(loss-rectification)*. These measures, or such other measures as the Congress may build out of its experience and wisdom, I shall seek, within my constitutional authority, to bring to speedy adoption *(loss-rectification)*.

But in the event that the Congress shall fail to take one of these two courses, and in the event that the national emergency is still critical, I shall not evade the clear course of duty that will then confront me *(loss-rectification)*. I shall ask the Congress for the one remaining instrument to meet the crisis – broad Executive power to wage a war against the emergency *(loss-rectification)*, as great as the power that would be given to me if we were in fact invaded by a foreign foe *(loss-rectification)*.

For the trust reposed in me I will return the courage and the devotion that befit the time *(loss-rectification)*. I can do no less.

We face the arduous days that lie before us in the warm courage of the national unity; with the clear consciousness of seeking old and precious moral values; with the clean satisfaction that comes from the stern performance of duty by old and young alike. We aim at the assurance of a rounded and permanent national life *(loss-rectification)*.

We do not distrust the future of essential democracy. The people of the United States have not failed. In their need they have registered a mandate that they want direct, vigorous action *(loss-rectification)*. They have asked for discipline and direction under leadership *(loss-rectification)*. They have made me the present instrument of their wishes *(loss-rectification)*. In the spirit of the gift I take it.

In this dedication of a Nation we humbly ask the blessing of God. May He protect each and every one of us. May He guide me in the days to come."

## KEY INSIGHT:

# An Archetypal Narrative: Being "Home," Getting Torn Away, Growing Through Adventure and Adversity, Returning Home, And "Knowing It For the First Time."

**YOU COMPLETED STEP TWO OF FIVE**

FIGURE 100: In this chapter, you learned how to complete the second step: direct attention to a definite motive.

..................................Chapter Summary..................................

- Tie everything back to the pursuit of one singular, self-contained goal. Use it to unite your message.
- Organize a pyramid of subgoals; establish a hierarchy of objectives that culminate in the primary goal.
- People act to move toward pleasure, away from pain, or both. Promise benefits and protection from losses.
- Present a compelling and trustworthy plan for achieving the mission presented in your speech.
- Present the solvency of this plan: Show people why they should place their faith in it and operate by it.
- Promise benefits in the form of the rectification of a loss; benefits in the form of a "return home."

## KEY INSIGHT:

# We Are "Aiming Creatures." We Are Structured to Point, Grasp, Reach, Strive, Hunt, Gather…

# We Need Something to Aim At. A Virtuous Vision Worth Striving Toward. A Good Fight Worth Fighting. An Ideal Worth Embodying. A Promised Land Worth Journeying Toward.

## THE FIVE-STEP FRAMEWORK (PART TWO)

| 1 | Controlling Attention |
|---|---|
| 1.1 | Portray Empathy |
| 1.2 | Portray Authority |
| 1.3 | Set High Expectations |
| 1.4 | Expose a Hidden Miracle |
| 1.5 | Speak to the People's Pain |
| 1.6 | Build a Coalition |
| 1.7 | Make Bold Promises |
| 1.8 | Divulge the Brutal Truth |
| 1.9 | Shift the Perspective |
| 1.10 | Speak to Broken Justice Problems |
| 1.11 | Present a Moment of Decision |
| 1.12 | Tell a Story |
| 1.13 | Future Significance Today |
| 1.14 | Difficulty-Confidence Matrix |
| 1.15 | Declaratory Cascade |
| 1.16 | Superabundance |
| 1.17 | Speak to the Moment |
| 2 | Directing Attention to a Definite Purpose |
| 2.1 | Achieve Singularity |
| 2.2 | Organize a Pyramid |
| 2.3 | Create Visualization |

| 2.4 | Promise Benefits |
|-----|------------------|
| 2.5 | Promise Loss-Minimization |
| 2.6 | Appeal to Needs |
| 2.7 | Promise Means |
| 2.8 | Present Solvency |
| 2.9 | Promise Rectification |
| 3 | Backing the Attention with Intentional Action |
| 4 | Backing the Intentional Action with Correct Thinking |
| 5 | Backing the Entire Process with a Powerful Motive |

**KEY INSIGHT:**

Hope is the Enabler of Action. Evidence is the Enabler of Hope.

A Vision of Tomorrow, a Hope-Worthy Vision, an Inspiring Destiny Worth Fighting For, Defines Our Duties Today.

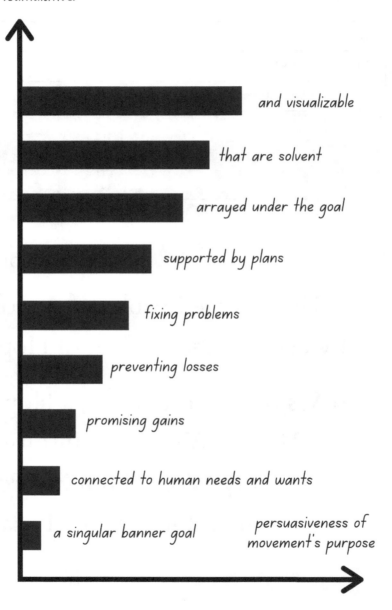

## Claim These Free Resources that Will Help You Unleash the Power of Your Words and Speak with Confidence. Visit www.speakforsuccesshub.com/toolkit for Access.

### 18 Free PDF Resources

*12 Iron Rules for Captivating Story, 21 Speeches that Changed the World, 341-Point Influence Checklist, 143 Persuasive Cognitive Biases, 17 Ways to Think On Your Feet, 18 Lies About Speaking Well, 137 Deadly Logical Fallacies, 12 Iron Rules For Captivating Slides, 371 Words that Persuade, 63 Truths of Speaking Well, 27 Laws of Empathy, 21 Secrets of Legendary Speeches, 19 Scripts that Persuade, 12 Iron Rules For Captivating Speech, 33 Laws of Charisma, 11 Influence Formulas, 219-Point Speech-Writing Checklist, 21 Eloquence Formulas*

**Claim These Free Resources that Will Help You Unleash the Power of Your Words and Speak with Confidence. Visit www.speakforsuccesshub.com/toolkit for Access.**

### 30 Free Video Lessons

We'll send you one free video lesson every day for 30 days, written and recorded by Peter D. Andrei. Days 1-10 cover authenticity, the prerequisite to confidence and persuasive power. Days 11-20 cover building self-belief and defeating communication anxiety. Days 21-30 cover how to speak with impact and influence, ensuring your words change minds instead of falling flat. Authenticity, self-belief, and impact – this course helps you master three components of confidence, turning even the most high-stakes presentations from obstacles into opportunities.

**Claim These Free Resources that Will Help You Unleash the Power of Your Words and Speak with Confidence. Visit www.speakforsuccesshub.com/toolkit for Access.**

**2 Free Workbooks**

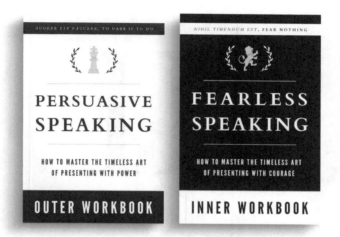

We'll send you two free workbooks, including long-lost excerpts by Dale Carnegie, the mega-bestselling author of *How to Win Friends and Influence People* (5,000,000 copies sold). *Fearless Speaking* guides you in the proven principles of mastering your inner game as a speaker. *Persuasive Speaking* guides you in the time-tested tactics of mastering your outer game by maximizing the power of your words. All of these resources complement the Speak for Success collection.

**SPEAK FOR SUCCESS COLLECTION BOOK**

# III

**HOW LEGENDARY LEADERS SPEAK CHAPTER**

# IV

# STEP THREE:

## 13 Strategies to Back the Attention with Intentional Action

## ASK QUESTIONS

I 'M GOING TO REITERATE ONE OF THE CENTRAL POINTS of nearly all my books on communication.

The central point? It is broken down in two parts.

Part one: that effective communication plays upon the inherent, psychologically irresistible traits of human cognition.

Part two: those traits of human cognition exist as designed by millennia upon millennia of careful evolutionary sculpting.

To the great communicator, these features of psychology are simply tools of the trade, not abstract, arcane theories to be tossed aside. To the great communicator, these features of psychology are not the optional tools of the expert, but the necessary foundation of every speech, every paragraph, every sentence, indeed, every *word*; they are the starting point, to be carefully encapsulated in thought from the beginning of the endeavor to the very end. To the great communicator, these features are ever-present in awareness, seemingly seeking expression, seeking invocation, seeking activation.

And in this section, we are going to deal with a simple but compelling feature of human psychology. What is it? That our cognitive machinery is incredibly adept at dealing with questions.

That our cognitive machinery can take a question, bury it into our subconscious minds, turn it over and over, look at it from every angle, perform every possible thought experiment, without us even knowing, and then return the answer to us hours, days, weeks, months or even years later in a flash of what we call, in our ignorance, inspiration.

### HOW THE SUBCONSIOUS MIND INTERACTS WITH QUESTIONS

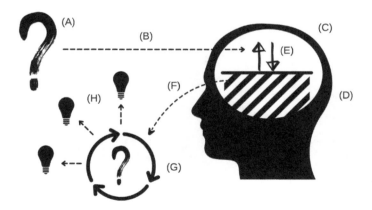

FIGURE 101: When someone hears a question (A), they receive it (B) consciously (C) and subconsciously (D). The conscious and subconscious minds shape each other: your conscious thought habits imprint upon the subconscious mind, and your subconscious mind tosses up conscious thoughts (E) that

correspond to what you have imprinted upon it. Your subconscious mind (F) turns the question over, (G) churning its big cognitive factory and producing not one conscious thought (which the may or may not be acted upon) but multiple over time (H).

It's not inspiration. It's intentional. It's just not an intention we're even aware we have, or that we can act on. It's the nature of the subconscious mind. And in this section, we focus on the third step in the communication of leadership: how to back attention with intentional action. How? By way of incredibly compelling, action-inspiring sequences of sentences, based on our psychological proclivity to cling to questions.

## WHY THE SUBCONSCIOUS IS KEY TO EFFECTIVE INFLUENCE

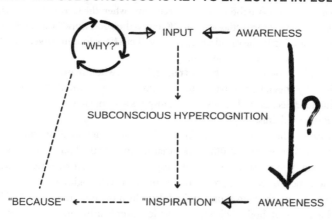

FIGURE 102: When people hear a repeated question, it enters their subconscious mind as an input. The subconscious mind starts running permutations, trying to answer the question. Promising answers leap into the conscious mind as "inspirations." People are only aware of the input and the inspiration. They are generally not aware of what happens in between.

This is a proven strategy. Again, I didn't create this; I just discovered it, though not after a difficult archaeological dig, but in a place plainly visible for all who seek to look. And what's that plainly visible place? The final section of nearly every single example of legendary pieces of the communication of leadership.

Let me show you. We revisited LBJ's Great Society speech a few times, and we'll do it yet again. How did he end his speech? "So, will you join in the battle to give every citizen the full equality which God enjoins and the law requires, whatever his belief, or race, or the color of his skin? Will you join in the battle to give every citizen an escape from the crushing weight of poverty? Will you join in the battle to make it possible for all nations to live in enduring peace – as neighbors and not as mortal enemies? Will you join in the battle to build the Great Society, to prove that our material progress is only the foundation on which we will build a richer life of mind and spirit?"

An example from Winston Churchill? "We have before us an ordeal of the most grievous kind. We have before us many, many long months of struggle and of suffering. You ask, what is our policy? I will say: It is to wage war, by sea, land and air, with all our might and with all the strength that God can give us; to wage war against a monstrous tyranny, never surpassed in the dark and lamentable catalogue of human crime. That is our policy. You ask, what is our aim? I can answer in one word: victory. Victory at all costs, victory in spite of all terror, victory, however long and hard the road may be; for without victory, there is no survival. Let that be realised; no survival for the British Empire, no survival for all that the British Empire has stood for, no survival for the urge and impulse of the ages, that mankind will move forward toward its goal."

And an example from Reagan's 1980 speech at the Republican National Convention? "Can anyone look at the record of this Administration and say, 'Well done?' Can anyone compare the state of our economy when the Carter Administration took office with where we are today and say, 'Keep up the good work?' Can anyone look at our reduced standing in the world today and say, 'Let's have four more years of this?'"

Why apply these rhetorical questions?

The examples abound. But we have to remember the whole reason we're doing this. Why do this? Why does it help us back attention directed toward a definite purpose with intentional action? Because it does just that; it inspires action. How?

What is the mechanism?

Let me explain how this technique inspires intentional action. First, questions put the ball in the audience's court. What does that mean? Think about it: when you are asked a question, you must act; you must respond. And asking rhetorical questions primes the audience to react. Re*act*. It puts them in a psychological state of response. But there's a bigger mechanism at play and a drastically more important one. And here's the truth: chances are nobody took a specific action after hearing any of these speeches I just showed you.

Does that mean they fell flat? No, not at all. Why not? Because they did something significantly more important than inspiring one individual action. What did they do? The questions buried themselves in the audience's subconscious minds, where they turned them over and over, looked at them from every angle, performed every possible thought experiment, without their conscious minds even knowing, and then, in a flash, produced an inspiration to pursue a related intentional action, and then another, and another.

The great speeches of history – the great examples of the communication of leadership – did not become great because they inspired people to take one intentional action and call it a day. Not at all. World-changing movements are not built on one intentional action. Instead, they are built by multiple intentional actions over time, by a massive number of people.

And that's what rhetorical questions of this kind empower, through the subconscious pathway I described; a subconscious pathway which creates conscious thoughts – flashes of inspiration – that create intentional action aligned with your purpose, but not once, which is useless. Over and over and over again. Neat, right?

**KEY INSIGHT:**

# Don't Merely Motivate One Action, One Agreement, One Consensus. Aim Higher.

# Create the Psychological Basis For Multiple Positive Actions and Multiple Agreements Over Time.

**WHY THE SUBCONSCIOUS IS KEY TO MOTIVATING ACTION**

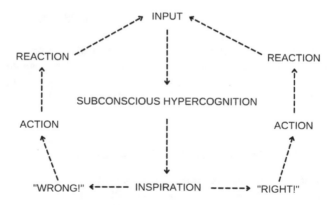

FIGURE 103: People decide upon some actions consciously. Other actions occur subconsciously and semi-automatically. They are habitual, functioning in a sort of "if-then" loop, but this loop can be interrupted (though it generally isn't). In cognitively-demanding, fast-paced situations, our conscious minds can't keep up with the second-by-second inputs. Instead, it sets the direction and the subconscious mind takes over. Inputs enter the subconscious

mind, which "turns them over" and produces inspirations that we can consciously affirm or deny, resulting in actions that produce reactions from the world that feed back into the loop as inputs.

**VISUALIZING THE ULTIMATE PERSUASIVE VICTORY**

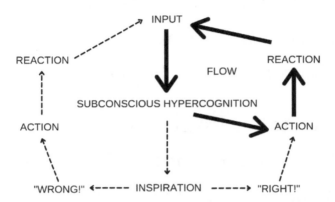

FIGURE 104: A state of "flow" is when the conscious mind steps out of the picture almost entirely and inputs produce subconscious hyper-cognitions which immediately get acted upon without interference or judgment from the conscious mind. These actions produce reactions that cycle back into the subconscious mind as new inputs.

Remember the declaratory cascade? Well, it's time for me to introduce you to the interrogative cascade, which builds upon this strategy we just discussed. In fact, the examples I showed you were examples of the interrogative cascade. A brief note before moving on: the more questions you apply in sequence, the more potent grows their impact when they hit the subconscious mind, and thus the more potent the conscious inspiration the subconscious creates, and thus the more potent the intentional action the conscious inspiration creates. This is the basis of the interrogative cascade.

## INTERROGATIVE CASCADE

For the sake of exploring the interrogative cascade, and the internal dialogue it creates in the audience's mind, I selected the example from LBJ.

Why? Because it is the clearest example of an interrogative cascade available to us. So, what are the three ingredients of an interrogative cascade?

First, it is a sequence of rhetorical questions. This is the only required ingredient to classify as an interrogative cascade.

Second, it typically includes anaphora, in which each question starts with the same words to create rhythm, build captivating cadence, and emphasize those words. This is not required, but typically present.

Third, it typically includes grammatical parallelism. Once more, not required, but empowering.

"So, *will you join in the battle* <u>to give every citizen the full equality</u> which God enjoins and the law requires, whatever his belief, or race, or the color of his skin? *Will you join in the battle* <u>to give every citizen an escape</u> from the crushing weight of poverty? *Will you join in the battle* <u>to make it possible for all nations</u> to live in enduring peace – as neighbors and not as mortal enemies? *Will you join in the battle* <u>to build the Great Society</u>, to prove that our material progress is only the foundation on which we will build a richer life of mind and spirit?"

The first characteristic, a sequence of questions, is self-evident; the second, anaphora, I have italicized; the third, grammatical and strict parallelism, is visible in vague vestiges. I have underlined this. So, you understand what an interrogative cascade is. You also understand what it does. What now?

Let's introduce some more advanced principles of the interrogative cascade.

First, a common and useful anaphora phrase to launch each question: "will you join me in…" Second, the idea of ascending yes questions.

What are ascending yes questions?

It's simple: make each question one which your audience will obviously mentally respond "yes" to, which builds persuasive momentum. Why does it build persuasive momentum? Due to the consistency principle. In other words, the more "yes" answers they have behind them, the more likely they will be to answer "yes" again, due to the principle of consistency, the human desire to act in consistent ways.

### WHY THE CONSISTENCY PRINCIPLE IS IRRESISTIBLE

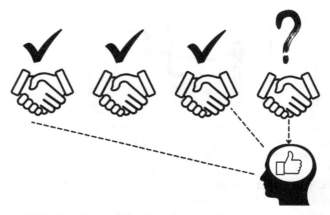

FIGURE 105: When evaluating a new option, people will be much more likely to accept it if it is consistent with their history of related actions.

What about the "ascending" part? Arrange the questions in order of ascending importance, where each additional question is more intense than the one before it, reaching a rhetorical climax at the final, most important question.

"So, will you join in the battle to give every citizen the full equality which God enjoins and the law requires, whatever his belief, or race, or the color of his skin?" Audience mental dialogue: "sure, of course! I can get behind that..."

"Will you join in the battle to give every citizen an escape from the crushing weight of poverty?" Audience mental dialogue: "I suppose so! That might go against my fiscal inclinations, as a fiscal conservative, but I guess I support it!" – if this was first, it would drive away fiscal hawks, but as long as the fiscal hawks responded yes to the first question, that positive "yes" momentum carries over to this question.

"Will you join in the battle to make it possible for all nations to live in enduring peace – as neighbors and not as mortal enemies?" Audience mental dialogue: "Of course!"

"Will you join in the battle to build the Great Society, to prove that our material progress is only the foundation on which we will build a richer life of mind and spirit?" Audience mental dialogue: "Absolutely. I'm all in. Let's do this. Let's fight to end racial inequality, poverty, and international strife, and since I'm all in on those things, let's create the Great Society."

## VISUALIZING THE POWER OF THE YES-LADDER

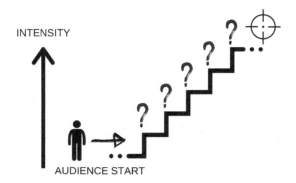

FIGURE 106: The interrogative cascade raises the intensity of the audience's agreement with the sentiment of the cascade while raising the intensity of the sentiment.

Note how he ended with the singular and self-contained big, bold, ambitious banner goal he sought to direct attention to: building The Great Society. Allow me to briefly remind you of the underlying mechanism of the interrogative cascade; allow me to remind you how it creates not one intentional action, but a series of intentional actions over time. Questions go to the subconscious, where the subconscious machinery works on them, eventually inspiring conscious thoughts aligned with what you want, which inspire an abundance of intentional actions over time aligned with what you want.

And it is by way of such questions that some of the world's most incredible speakers have produced some of the world's most incredible results in the real world. LBJ used them for a reason. Churchill used them for a reason. Reagan used them for a reason. Countless other legendary leaders used them for a reason. Why? Because these people understood subconscious psychology.

## "LET'S" STATEMENTS

What if an absurd amount of the world's most moving inspirational speeches, by world-leaders and earth-shakers, time and time again used one simple phrase?

That's actually exactly what happened. And not only one simple phrase, but many simple phrases, and many incredibly complex strategies are shared between them. But for now, we're focusing on one of the most widespread methods: using "let's" statements.

Are you the leader of a team? If so, this is for you. Want to describe to your audience members (your subordinates) what you want them to do, in a way that is authoritative and assertive but not bossy and annoying? If so, this is for you.

Instead of saying, for example, "go to the national sales conference and get as many contacts as possible," say "let's go to the national sales conference and get as many contacts as possible."

Why? Because adding one simple word completely shifts the tone of the message. It's not an individual, despotic order anymore.

Instead, it is a team directive. It's "let us," not "I, your boss, want you to do this, or else." It emphasizes the team and builds unity. And it takes off the pressure without blurring the clarity of your directives.

Get it? It makes it seem like a team effort. And if the responsibility will belong to one specific person, follow the "let's statement" with a question like this: "[insert name], do you think you can take care of that for us?"

This is a sort of micro-reframing because it changes the situation from "*I* want you to do this for *me*," to "let's do this for *us*." In short: this strategy makes it seem like you are a leader who is not begrudgingly but enthusiastically rushing to share responsibility with those in your charge. Examples of this abound.

Winston Churchill used this strategy in another speech during the most tumultuous time in human history. "What General Weygand called the Battle of France is over. I expect that the Battle of Britain is about to begin. Upon this battle depends the survival of Christian civilization. Upon it depends our own British life, and the long continuity of our institutions and our Empire. The whole fury and might of the enemy must very soon be turned on us. Hitler knows that he will have to break us in this Island or lose the war. If we can stand up to him, all Europe may be free and the life of the world may move forward into broad, sunlit uplands. But if we fail, then the whole world, including the United States, including all that we have known and cared for, will sink into the abyss of a new Dark Age made more sinister, and perhaps more protracted, by the lights of perverted science. Let us therefore brace ourselves to our duties, and so bear ourselves that, if the British Empire and its Commonwealth last for a thousand years, men will still say, 'This was their finest hour.'"

President Abraham Lincoln used this strategy in his second inaugural address, a speech of unparalleled importance. "With malice toward none, with charity for all, with firmness in the right as God gives us to see the right, let us strive on to finish the work we are in, to bind up the nation's wounds, to care for him who shall have borne the battle and for his widow and his orphan, to do all which may achieve and cherish a just and lasting peace among ourselves and with all nations."

Ronald Reagan used this strategy in his speech at the Brandenburg gate. "We're bound today by what bound us 40 years ago, the same loyalties, traditions, and beliefs. We're bound by reality. The strength of America's allies is vital to the United States, and the American security guarantee is essential to the continued freedom of Europe's democracies. We were with you then; we're with you now. Your hopes are our hopes, and your destiny is our destiny. Here, in this place where the West held together, let us make a vow to our dead. Let us show them by our actions that we understand what they died for. *Let our* actions say to them the words for which Matthew Ridgway listened: 'I will not fail thee nor forsake thee.' Strengthened by their courage and heartened by their value [valor] and borne by their memory, let us continue to stand for the ideals for which they lived and died. Thank you very much, and God bless you all."

This is the first of a series of sections that center on specific phrases for doing one of the most challenging things for new leaders, in particular: boldly asking for specific, intentional action, which is inherently an act of asserting the mandate to lead.

It can be difficult. Truly. But "let's" statements are very simple phrases that are very effective, and they make this difficult endeavor easy and effortless. Why? For a few reasons.

They emphasize the unity of the team, including the leader: it is let us, not let you.

They emphasize the action; they place all attention on what we are being let to do, in other words.

They, because of their short length, are easy; they minimize the struggle so many new leaders face in asking for direct, specific, intentional action.

Let's move on to another such phrase favored by the world's most legendary speakers.

## "WE WILL" STATEMENTS

"We will" is a bit more assertive and intense than "let us." And sometimes, that's exactly what you want. FDR, in his address to the nation after the pearl harbor surprise attack, used this strategy. "With confidence in our armed forces, with the unbounding determination of our people, we will gain the inevitable triumph – so help us God."

Ronald Reagan, in his address to the nation after the explosion of the Challenger space shuttle, used this strategy too. "The crew of the space shuttle Challenger honored us by the manner in which they lived their lives. We will never forget them, nor the last time we saw them, this morning, as they prepared for the journey and waved goodbye and 'slipped the surly bonds of earth' to 'touch the face of God.'"

I'll say it again: these sections are going to be short and straightforward, teaching you the exact words you should use to seamlessly direct attention to the intentional action you want your audience to take. After these sections, we're going to discuss what to do leading up to the moment when you need to use these phrases. We're going to discuss ending models after we finish the necessary barrage of formulas for action-driven language, like "let us," and "we will."

## "WE MUST" STATEMENTS

"We must" portrays a sense of urgency and builds gravitas while lending indelible importance to the subject of your speech. Theodore Roosevelt used this strategy in one of his speeches on Americanism and American values. "More important than aught else is the development of the broadest sympathy of man for man. The welfare of the wage-worker, the welfare of the tiller of the soil, upon these depend the welfare of the entire country; their good is not to be sought in pulling down others; but their good must be the prime object of all our statesmanship. Materially we must strive to secure a broader economic opportunity for all men, so that each shall have a better chance to show the stuff of which he is made. Spiritually and ethically we must strive to bring about clean living and right thinking. We appreciate also that the things of the soul are immeasurably more important. The foundation-stone of national life is, and ever must be, the high individual character of the average citizen."

Demosthenes, a Greek statesman, and ancient orator, used this strategy as well. "But I do not mean that we should call upon the other states, if we are not willing to take any of the necessary steps ourselves. It is folly to sacrifice what is our own, and then pretend to be anxious for the interests of others, to neglect the present, and alarm others in regard to the future. I do not propose this. I say that we must send money to the forces in the Chersonese, and do all that they ask of us. That we must make preparation ourselves, while we summon, convene, instruct, and warn the rest of the Hellenes."

## "WE SAY" STATEMENTS

You remember Bernie's speech we recently analyzed. The bulk of this speech was, in fact, this "we say" phrase. "We say to the private health insurance companies... Today, we say to the pharmaceutical industry... Today, we say to Walmart, the fast food industry and other low wage employers... Today we say to corporate America... Today we say to the American people that... Today we say to the parents in this country that... Today, we say to our young people that... Today, we say to our senior citizens, that... Today, we say to Donald Trump and the fossil fuel industry that... Today, we say to the prison-industrial-complex that... Today, we say to the American people that... Today, we say to the top 1 percent and the large profitable corporations in this country – people who have never had it so good – that... Today, we say to the military-industrial-complex that..."

And in his speech following the challenger explosion, Reagan used this strategy too. "There's a coincidence today. On this day 390 years ago, the great explorer Sir Francis Drake died aboard ship off the coast of Panama. In his lifetime the great frontiers were the oceans, and a historian later said, 'He lived by the sea, died on it, and was buried in it.' Well, today we can say of the Challenger crew: 'Their dedication was, like Drake's, complete.'"

## "WE SHOULD" STATEMENTS

Theodore Roosevelt, in another speech on the meaning of American citizenship, used "we should" statements in abundance. These make the proposed action seem like a moral imperative.

"In facing the future and in striving, each according to the measure of his individual capacity, to work out the salvation of our land, we should be neither timid pessimists nor foolish optimists. We should recognize the dangers that exist and that threaten us: we should neither overestimate them nor shrink from them, but steadily fronting them should set to work to overcome and beat them down. Grave perils are yet to be encountered in the stormy course of the Republic – perils from political corruption, perils from individual laziness, indolence and timidity, perils springing from the greed of the unscrupulous rich, and from the anarchic violence of the thriftless and turbulent poor. There is every reason why we should recognize them, but there is no reason why we should fear them or doubt our capacity to overcome them, if only each will, according to the measure of his ability, do his full duty, and endeavor so to live as to deserve the high praise of being called a good American citizen."

## "LET" STATEMENTS

These are not "let us," but "let *something else...* "William Wilberforce used this in the conclusion of his speech, calling for the abolition of the slave trade. "As soon as ever I had arrived thus far in my investigation of the slave trade, I confess to you sir, so enormous so dreadful, so irremediable did its wickedness appear that my own mind was completely made up for the abolition. A trade founded in iniquity, and carried on as this was, must be abolished, let the policy be what it might – let the consequences be what they would, I from this time determined that I would never rest till I had affected its abolition."

Martin Luther King, in his legendary "I have a dream" speech, used this strategy too. "And if America is to be a great nation, this must become true. And so let freedom ring from the prodigious hilltops of New Hampshire. Let freedom ring from the mighty mountains of New York. Let freedom ring from the heightening Alleghenies of Pennsylvania. Let freedom ring from the snow-capped Rockies of Colorado. Let freedom ring from the curvaceous slopes of California. But not only that: Let freedom ring from Stone Mountain of Georgia. Let freedom ring from Lookout Mountain of Tennessee. Let freedom ring from every hill and molehill of Mississippi. From every mountainside, let freedom ring. And when this happens, and when we allow freedom ring, when we let it ring from every village and every hamlet, from every state and every city, we will be able to speed up that day when *all* of God's children, black men and white men, Jews and Gentiles, Protestants and Catholics, will be able to join hands and sing in the words of the old Negro spiritual…"

Hillary Clinton, in her *Women's Rights are Human Rights* speech in Bejing: "There are some who question the reason for this conference. Let them listen to the voices of women in their homes, neighborhoods, and workplaces. There are some who wonder whether the lives of women and girls matter to economic and political progress around the globe. Let them look at the women gathered here and at Huairou the homemakers, nurses, teachers, lawyers, policymakers, and women who run their own businesses."

## ACTION WORDS

These are different than the rest. These rely on compelling verbs. These are broader in their application. How did JFK end his inaugural address? "And so, my fellow Americans, ask not what your country can do for you; ask what you can do for your country. My fellow citizens of the world, ask not what America will do for you, but what together we can do for the freedom of man. Finally, whether you are citizens of America or citizens of the world, ask of us here the same high standards of strength and sacrifice which we ask of you. With a good conscience our only sure reward, with history the final judge of our deeds, let us (as you can see, *he combined the two strategies in his ending…*) go forth to lead the land we love, asking His blessing and His help, but knowing that here on earth God's work must truly be our own."

And Obama finished one of his State of the Union addresses with two simple words. "Believe it."

So, what do you actually do to apply this strategy? It's simple. Take an action word (a verb), preferably one with a compelling quality; preferably one that is bold, brave, ambitious; preferably one that drives people to act. For JFK, it was "ask." For you, it can be "seize" or "get" or "make." You get the point. And then, list out the actions you want your audience to pursue, and introduce them with these words. The idea here is that, by using one of these short phrases, like "let us," or "we should," or "we will," or "ask," or "seize," what you are really doing is limiting the number of words you need to deliver the action you want them to take. This improves memory retention. And you are also delivering it with repetition, by repeating the action word. This also improves memory retention.

And if there's anything you want your audience to remember, it is the action you want them to take. So, after this quick, example-saturated flurry of short sections focusing narrowly, with scalpel-like precision, on this one element of calls to action, we ought to review what we discussed.

Introduce your desired action with "let us," which frames your leadership as inclusive, and implies that you lead by example, and are joining in the labor you command of your subordinates.

Introduce your desired action with "we will," which asserts your mandate to lead with more confidence, and which can be attractive if people seek a strong leader.

Introduce your desired action with "we must," which presents the immense urgency and dramatic need for whatever action follows, and thus increases the stakes, which increases both attention and follow-through.

Introduce your desired action with "we say," which portrays you as the spokesperson for a bigger cause, and which allows you to essentially create the action you propose in the moment. If your action is saying something to someone, not only are you introducing that as an audience command, but you're doing it yourself.

Introduce your desired action with "we should," which creates the sense that it is not a command from you, but a moral obligation which is bigger than you.

Introduce your desired action with "let," which obfuscates the actors of the action, which does not clearly lay down responsibility for an action at anyone's feet, which is actually ideal for proposed actions of an abstract nature. Introduce your desired action with any action word, which allows you flexibility, and which removes any ambiguity.

And what do all these have in common? They are all universally recognized as statements that introduce direct commands to a group of people – an audience – and thus, they guarantee that people are primed to hear the command. In other words, these are universally recognized as transitions to action proposals.

---

**KEY INSIGHT:**

Verbs Breathe Life into Language. They Convert Monotony into Music.

Vivid Verbs Paint Pictures. Vivid Verbs Speak Twice. They Speak into Sound and the Sound Speaks into the Mind's Eye, into Sight.

---

## PRESENT POLICIES

This what it all comes down to. Your communication is successful if it results in the carrying out of your proposed policies.

What's a policy?

A policy is a statement of "who should do what, when, and how." Get it? We briefly alluded to this previously.

This is the actual implementation; this is the frontline work that needs to get done for your communication to be called a success. And what follows your action-transitions, whether you're using let's statements or action words? Your policies.

### THE VALUES, BELIEFS, POLICIES TRIAD

VALUES

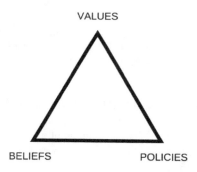

BELIEFS                 POLICIES

FIGURE 107: Values, beliefs, and policies are the three components of worldview.

**KEY INSIGHT:**

# We Value What We Know As "Good," Believe What We Know As "How The World Is," And Create Policies Accordingly.

## HOW THE THREE COMPONENTS OF WORLDVIEW INTERACT

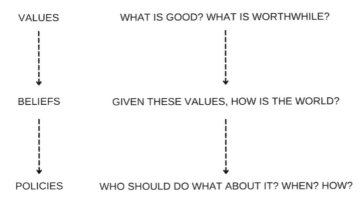

VALUES       WHAT IS GOOD? WHAT IS WORTHWHILE?

BELIEFS       GIVEN THESE VALUES, HOW IS THE WORLD?

POLICIES       WHO SHOULD DO WHAT ABOUT IT? WHEN? HOW?

FIGURE 108: Values are what is good; what is worthwhile. Beliefs are how people see the world in light of these values. Policies are statements of who should do what about how the world is in light of those beliefs.

But let me tell you about a challenge I had in writing this chapter. Looking at some of these examples of legendary leaders producing legendary communication of leadership, I often struggled to find an example of a precise, specific, direct policy statement. Why? Well, to me, I always had a conception of a policy statement as something concrete, something tangible, something physical. And many of these speeches didn't have that at all.

For example, "Let freedom ring." That's not a tangible, implementation-based policy statement. Instead, many of these leaders had much more vague action statements. Just like "Let freedom ring."

"Could we even call them policy statements if they weren't concrete?" I wondered. And the answer is yes.

I resolved my challenge when I realized the true nature of policy statements.

I resolved my challenge when I realized that the nature of a leader's policy statements depends on the scope of his or her leadership.

When you are overseeing a national movement, like Martin Luther King was when his policy statement amounted to the fairly vague "let freedom ring," you are not supposed to be preoccupied with in-the-trenches, front-line implementation stuff. Not at all.

Your goal is vision-setting.

Your goal is inspiration.

Your goal is not setting specific membership goals for specific chapters of specific civil-rights-oriented non-profit organizations, in specific regions, in specific ways, by a specific time, for example. And why not? Because there are leaders below you in the organization – as there were below MLK – who are in charge of that.

If you are a frontline leader, perhaps a manager of a small team tasked with the specific implementation of a goal, you have a narrow scope of leadership, which means you must have a precise, concrete policy statement.

If you are a high-level leader, perhaps a CEO or near-CEO level manager, you are not tasked with specific implementation.

Instead, you are tasked with big-picture vision-setting.

Thus, you have a broad scope of leadership.

This means you must have a visionary policy statement, even though it may be abstract.

Why? Because the frontline leaders are in charge of the specific implementations of your vision, not you. You're tasked with clearly articulating the vision to all, so they know what to follow. This was followed by my realization that this can all be encapsulated by a spectrum model.

The specific-policy end of the spectrum:

You are a frontline leader.

You are tasked with specific implementation of a goal.

You have a narrow scope of leadership.

You must have a precise, concrete policy statement.

The broad-policy end of the spectrum:

You are a high-level leader.

You are tasked with big-picture vision-setting.

You have a broad scope of leadership.

You must have a visionary, though abstract, policy statement. This realization instantly cleared the confusion for me, and I think presenting it in this table will be best for you.

## ORGANIZATIONAL INFORMATION FLOW

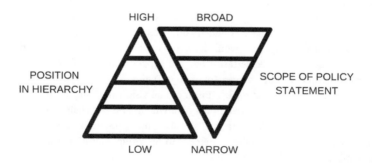

FIGURE 109: At the top of the hierarchy, the scope of your policy statements should be broad. At the bottom of the hierarchy, the scope of your policy statements should be narrow.

## WHAT SHOULD YOU ADVOCATE FOR?

| Type of leader | Frontline leader | High-level leader |
|---|---|---|
| Team size | Small sub-group | Large organization |
| Task-orientation | Implementation | Vision-setting |
| Scope of leadership | Narrow | Broad |
| Policy statement | Specific, detail-oriented | Visionary, abstract |

Obviously, MLK was a high-level leader. Imagine if he had presented a policy suited for a frontline leader. Imagine if, instead of the high-level leader, vision-driven policy statement of "let freedom ring," he had said "let the local chapter of the voter-enfranchisement drive association of Selma, Alabama, seek to center its efforts in lower-income urban centers of the county, and print new voter-registration pamphlets and literature with a red background color instead of blue, by the fifth of the month. Thank you, crowd of 100,000-plus people. That is all."

I don't need to tell you, because you already know that it would have fallen flat. This part might seem obvious. But let's reverse the scheme. What if a low-level leader, perhaps the chair of the Selma chapter of the voter-enfranchisement drive association (which I made up, by the way), said, "And if America is to be a great nation, this must become true. And so let freedom ring from the prodigious hilltops of New Hampshire. Let freedom ring from the mighty mountains of New York. Let freedom ring from the heightening Alleghenies of Pennsylvania. Let freedom ring from the snow-capped Rockies of Colorado. Let freedom ring from the curvaceous slopes of California. But not only that: Let freedom ring from Stone Mountain of Georgia. Let freedom ring from Lookout Mountain of Tennessee. Let freedom ring from every hill and molehill of Mississippi. From every mountainside, let freedom ring. And when this happens, and when we allow freedom ring, when we let it ring from every village and every hamlet, from every state and every city, we will be able to speed up that day when *all* of God's children, black men and white men, Jews and Gentiles, Protestants and Catholics, will be able to join hands and sing in the words of the old Negro spiritual...?"

Not only would it have sounded completely out of place, perhaps a little self-effacing and self-serving, but it would have frustrated the small team because they would be clueless as to the specific tasks they are supposed to complete. That's not how information flows within a movement or organization.

MLK presented a big-picture inspirational vision that aligned the movement's efforts with a broad vision-driven policy statement, and the chair of this local group worked out the implementation details and presented a specific, narrow implementation-oriented policy statement to his group. Get it? Thus, we turn to the fundamental principle of this section: the iron law of policy statements. The scope of your policy statement must line up with the scope of your leadership. To summarize the resolution of my confusion, I once thought that these legendary high-level leaders were simply bad at policy statements. The truth? I had an insufficient understanding of policy statements. I now realize that they produced the exact kind of policy statements they should have.

## ACHIEVE KAIROS

Let's say that you can choose one of two scenarios in which to deliver your speech. Assume that everything about the speech is the same. The same words. The same delivery. The same everything.

The only difference is when you give the speech. The goal is to persuade a company to change its operations.

Here's scenario one: Everything is absolutely wonderful. Profits are high, management is handing out chunky bonuses, and everyone is getting a raise.

Here's scenario two: Everything is absolutely awful. Profits have tanked, management is taking bonuses back, and there are no raises to speak of.

A speech to persuade a company to change its operations is most likely to succeed when it is abundantly clear that the operations aren't working. You do not speak in a bubble. The facts of the outside world always influence your audience. Context is everything.

Will people want to change the way a company works when everything is wonderful? No. How about when everything is awful? Most likely.

Kairos is incredibly powerful. You make the outside world your partner in persuasion. You use an amazing persuasive element: the reality of the lives your audience members are living.

They will never ask "what's the evidence?" if they are living the evidence. Politicians use Kairos all the time.

Every time a politician speaks of economic reform during a stock market crash, that's Kairos. Every time a politician speaks of raising police funding after a surge in crime, that's Kairos. Every time a politician speaks of raising regulations on deep-sea oil rigs after a spill, that's Kairos.

It's not necessarily the case that the politician only sought these policies when the crisis struck. Perhaps they always supported those policies, but knew the truth of Kairos: advocacy demands a crisis.

A Roman nobleman bought a fleet of the ancient equivalent of firetrucks. He ordered the fleet to drive around the city finding fires. When one of the carriages found a fire, the operator would demand payment from the occupant of the house to put it out.

Now, he could have run his business differently. He could have sent out a Roman door-to-door salesforce saying "Hi! Your house is not on fire now, but it may be on fire tomorrow night, or the night after that, or perhaps some night in the next ten years. Want to pay me an annual stipend to drive by your house? If it's on fire, I'll put it out."

People on dry land don't want to hear about a life jacket, no matter how forcefully you tell them they might one day need it. Alternatively, people treading water in the middle of the ocean will want that life jacket no matter what you say about it or what it will cost them.

These are extreme examples, but they point at the essential truth: Timing is everything. Save your persuasion for when it is most likely to succeed. You will add the most powerful persuasive element to your speech without changing a single word.

Kairos is even more complex than this. Ancient Greek rhetorical teachers conceived of Kairos as a metaphysical concept.

Kairos is a universal pattern pervading the universe, the pattern of conflict and resolution. They conceived of Kairos as signifying a sort of metaphysical duality. This echoes the manifold dualities inherent in the problem-solution structure, which is both a rhetorical structure and one of the foremost structures of human reality. In fact, it is a rhetorical structure because it is so intrinsic to the human experience. Remember this: Resolution flows out of conflict. Without conflict, there can be no resolution, and you are trying to persuade a resolution.

### THE PROBLEM, AGITATE, SOLUTION, AGITATE STRUCTURE

| STRUCTURE | "PASA" Structure | | | |
|---|---|---|---|---|
| BEHAVIORAL DUALITY | Escape | | Approach | |
| SEMANTIC DUALITY | Problem | | Solution | |
| EMOTIONAL DUALITY | Pain | | Pleasure | |
| TEMPORAL DUALITY | Now | | Later | |
| EXISTENTIAL DUALITY | Here | | There | |
| DESIRE DUALITY | Aversion | | Desire | |
| MODAL DUALITY | Chaos | | Order | |
| STATE DUALITY | Actual | | Potential | |
| KAIROS DUALITY | Conflict | | Resolution | |
| THE SEQUENCE | Problem | Agitate | Solution | Agitate |

### KEY INSIGHT:

Chaos and Order, Tension and Resolution, Problem and Solution, Pain and Pleasure, Nihilism and Meaning, Terror and Strength, Light and Dark, Yin and Yang.

## TRYING TO SOLVE PAIN PEOPLE DON'T FEEL

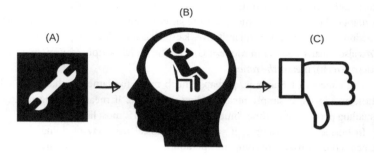

FIGURE 110: Trying to sell a solution (A) when to the audience it appears as if the reality of the world is telling them to "relax" (B) is more likely to result in failure (C).

## OFFERING A DROWNING PERSON A LIFEJACKET

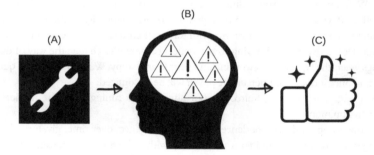

FIGURE 111: Trying to sell a solution (A) when to the audience it appears as if the reality of the world is shouting "DANGER, PROBLEM, FIX IT, DANGER, PROBLEM, FIX IT; PAIN, FAILURE, STRUGGLE, DESPERATION" (B) is more likely to result in success (C).

Correctly timing your communication is one of the biggest credibility boosters. I promised brevity, but Kairos is so important that I want to explain it in as many ways as possible. I want to make sure that your understanding of Kairos is so fluent and innate that you never miss an opportunity to employ it in your favor.

So, to that end, here's how I described Kairos in my first book, *How to Master Public Speaking:* "This is the dictionary entrance for Kairos: 'Kairos (**καιρός**) is an Ancient Greek word meaning the right, critical, or opportune moment. The ancient Greeks had two words for time: chronos (χρόνος) and kairos. The former refers to chronological or sequential time, while the latter signifies a proper or opportune time for action. While chronos is quantitative, kairos has a qualitative, permanent nature. *Kairos* also means *weather* in Modern Greek. The plural, καιροί (*kairoi* (Ancient and Modern Greek)) means *the times.*'

The concept of Kairos is, perhaps, much more fundamental than even ethos, pathos, and logos. It simply means biding your time. It means waiting to attempt persuading people until a time comes when persuasion is most likely to work.

In business, for example, if you have a radical new way of doing things that challenges the status quo of company operations, then Kairos is your friend. Unless you are sure of your ability to persuade the organization to adopt the change you want to see, then simply bide your time. Wait, and while you wait, keep developing your idea as well as a plan for implementing it. Keep it at the ready, but keep it concealed.

Eventually, there will be a time of crisis. Investors will get cold feet, manufacturing will fail, a public relations scandal will occur, etc. As Kairos suggests, the time of crisis will be the time to attempt to persuade the company to change its operations. That is because, during this time of crisis, people are especially persuadable and willing to try new things. The status quo is not working, and thus they will be much more malleable and open to your ideas.

Wait for the opportune time, and use your persuasion when it will be most effective. If you can combine ethos, pathos, logos, reciprocity, authority, scarcity, likeability, consensus, and consistency with Kairos, then you maximize your persuasive power. Don't give a speech trying to persuade a company to change the way of doing things when the status quo is working and people are happy. Wait for the status quo to fail, and once it does, your persuasive power will be maximized.

A huge part of using Kairos to your advantage is tuning in to the motions of collective opinion.

Any group tends to experience opinion-convergence: over time, given no drastic changes, many common opinions will develop within the group. Be sensitive to these collective opinions, especially when they might be in flux. That will help you find the right time, and as you may have heard, timing is everything."

Talk of environmental regulation goes up when there is a major climate change-related natural disaster. That's Kairos. Talk of border security goes up when an undocumented immigrant commits a crime that makes it into the news. That's Kairos. Talk of military improvements goes up when North Korea launches its latest missile test (unless, of course, it happens to abruptly return to Earth ten seconds after it launches, like many of their missiles have). That's Kairos.

Bernie Sanders gave a seven-hour speech on the floor of the Senate – a filibuster, though a substantive one (unlike Ted Cruz reading Dr. Seuss' *Green Eggs and Ham*) – which centered on matters of wealth inequality, corporate domination of American life, and the like. Congress was just about to pass massive bailout bills for the very institutions that caused the 2008 recession, which is what Bernie was filibustering. It was that act by Congress which gave Bernie the mandate for this speech. That's Kairos.

JFK would not have had the mandate to say, "Let every nation know, whether it wishes us well or ill, that we shall pay any price, bear any burden, meet any hardship, support any friend, oppose any foe, in order to assure the survival and the success of liberty," in the absence of a major threat to liberty.

Reagan would not have had the mandate to say "Mr. Gorbachev, tear down this wall!" in the absence of records of the poverty and squalor in Soviet-controlled East Berlin.

FDR would not have had the mandate to promise massive expansion of the federal government in his inaugural address – the one we previously analyzed – had the Great Depression not ravaged America for far too long.

Kairos, Kairos, and more Kairos.

(It's a cool word, isn't it?)

And there's another powerful tool that, combined with Kairos, is yet another case of one plus one equals three. Or, rather, one plus one equals one hundred. It's that powerful. This tool?

Fear-based persuasion.

It's true: many things can trigger Kairos. But the most compelling Kairos-triggers are those which create fear. And the more fear, the more strength is given to the Kairos.

In other words, JFK not only had the mandate to say what he said because the threat to liberty created Kairos, but because that threat scared the hell out of everyone. Same with Reagan, and FDR; they all had some scary real-world scenario that gave their words force through Kairos.

And so, Kairos triggered by fear is the most compelling kind. This is when people are willing to, more than any other time, expand the power of their leaders. So, this motivates the following question.

"What kind of fear is most scary?"

Reading Win Bigly by Scott Adams, I came across the following analysis of which type of fear is most powerful (to which I've added some rows).

A big fear is more compelling and Kairos-activating than a small fear.

It is a small fear if it does not trigger the amygdala.

A personal fear is more compelling and Kairos-activating than a generic fear.

It is a generic fear if it does not trigger mental movies someone themselves personally faced with the fear, or if they cannot possibly believe that it will impact them, though it may impact others.

A top-of-mind fear is more compelling and Kairos-activating than a buried fear.

It is a buried fear if it is not frequently thought of, or if people are not constantly seeing reminders of it everywhere they look.

A visual fear is more compelling and Kairos-activating than a non-visual fear.

It is a non-visual fear if there is no visual component or mental movie attached to it.

An experienced fear is more compelling and Kairos-activating than a non-experienced fear.

It is a non-experienced fear if someone has never dealt with the fear-inducing agent.

A specific fear is more compelling and Kairos-activating than a non-specific fear.

It is a non-specific fear if the absence of associated details makes it less plausible.

A desire-associated fear is more compelling and Kairos-activating than a non-desire-associated fear.

It is a non-desire-associated fear if it is not tied to the loss of a core human desire, or the dissatisfaction of a core human need.

A believable fear is more compelling and Kairos-activating than an unbelievable fear.

It is an unbelievable fear if, while fearsome, it seems very unlikely.

A loss-based fear is more compelling than non-loss-based fear.

It is a non-loss-based fear if it is not associated with any loss.

An urgent fear is more compelling than a distant fear.

It is a distant fear if there is ample time before the fear is supposed to manifest itself in reality.

An uncontrollable fear is more compelling and Kairos-activating than a controllable fear.

It is a controllable fear if something can be done to prevent it.

A new fear is more compelling than an old fear.

It is an old fear if it has habituated to the point of psychological impotency.

A preventable fear is more compelling than a non-preventable one.

It is a non-preventable fear if nothing can be done to fight the fear-inducing agent. This last one is interesting.

Why is a preventable fear more compelling?

Because it leaves room for hope, and action only occurs in the presence of a hope that the action can produce a positive outcome. An unpreventable fear makes us go "eh, whatever... we can't do anything anyway... so let's not even bother with it."

Why do these things work? In a word: psychology. And if you're wondering what type of fear to use, the fear of not satisfying one of the basic human desires is very strong."

## STRUCTURED CONCLUSIONS

There are three salient components of communication that compels intentional action from people.

The first: the bulk of the speech, and how persuasive you were leading up to the call to action.

The second: the elements drawing the speech to a close, leading to the policy statement.

The third: the policy statement(s).

We've discussed the first and the third. Now, we turn to the second step and close the gap. Think of it as a funnel. It starts broad. It persuades. It sets the context. It validates the need for action. That's the first step. It narrows toward the end. It grows more specific. It narrows its scope. It includes action-driven language, though vague, without a policy statement. That's the second step. It gets incredibly narrow. It centers on a set of specific policies. It directs the audience toward a set of specific, intentional actions. It includes only action-driven language. That's the third step.

It's always getting narrower, drawing its focus on the policy statements. Much of what precedes serves to empower those policy statements. Much of what goes in – steps one and two – are designed to empower that which comes out, a set of specific policy statements, so that attached to them is the impact and persuasive power of steps one and two. So, how do we accomplish the second step?

How do we begin to narrow down the scope of our communication, and begin bringing it to a compelling, clear, and confident conclusion?

That's the question we focus on in this section. In my analysis of the conclusions of the world's most lauded pieces of communication – specifically of the conclusions, the parts that began to usher in policies – I've discovered a set of repetitively used ingredients. And these ingredients can be organized into a set of compelling concluding structures. It is these structures that I present to you in this section. These are proven strategies for how to end your persuasive communication with efficacy and style. They are going to instantly take the confusion and anxiety out of ending your persuasive communication. They will give you easy and reliable guidelines to follow that are specifically designed to meet the correct goals of conclusions. They are ten easy, step-by-step ending formulas that are yet another set of persuasive templates and patterns that you can simply fill in with your specific content.

Great, right? Not only do these make you infinitely more persuasive and compelling, but they also give you the benefit of ease: instead of confusion, you have a clear set of choices to choose from. This should reduce your anxiety about your presentation, your writing, your speech, or whatever form your persuasive communication takes.

## KEY INSIGHT:

# Rhetorical Structures Focus You. They Offer You a Precise Path to a Precise Presentation. Precision Persuades. Clarity Compels.

## DON'T MISS THIS CRUCIAL MOMENT TO ASK FOR ACTION

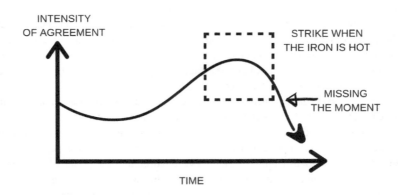

FIGURE 112: Call for action or make your big persuasive request when the intensity of the audience's agreement peaks. Don't miss the moment. Strike when the iron is hot.

Benefits, Ease, Certainty, Soft Call to Action, Hard Call to Action: Benefits: "We will [insert benefit one], [insert benefit two], and [insert benefit three]." Ease: "We will do it with a process that only costs [insert dollar amount if applicable] and takes only [insert time commitment] to implement." Certainty: "This process is proven, tested, and guaranteed to get us [insert benefits] for just [insert resources necessary]." Soft call to action: "My work here will be complete if you recognize this as the immense opportunity that it is." Hard call to action: "But it's up to you to seize it by [insert first step]."

Hope, Unity, Empowerment, Outcome: Hope: "The future can be better: [insert how]." Unity: "Together, we can create a future that [insert positive characteristics]. Divided, we are resigned to a future that [insert negative characteristics]." Empowerment: "But I know we can come together and create incredible outcomes for everyone. We've done this before: [insert example one], [insert example two], and [insert example three]." Outcome: "And if we do it again, we can [insert positive vision of the future]."

Review Outcome, Summary, Remember This, Sentential, Triggers, Confirmation Bias: Review outcome: "If we take [insert action], we can [insert outcome]." Summary: "[insert sub-point one], [insert sub-point two], and [insert sub-point three]." Remember this: "I want you to remember [insert core message]." Sentential (a rhetorically charged sentence summarizing the preceding material): "I want you to remember [insert sentential]." Triggers: "Every time you see [insert situation one], [insert situation two], and [insert situation three], I want you to remember what it really is." Confirmation bias: "I want you to remember that it is an example of [insert what it is an example of]."

We Know, We Know, We Know, Question: We know: "We know that [insert agreed-upon fact]." We know: "We know that [insert second agreed-upon fact]." We know: "We know that [insert third agree-upon fact]." Question: "But what we don't know is this: will we [insert action] to create [insert positive outcome]?"

Before, After, Means, Future: Before: "When I first started speaking, you were [insert characteristics of insufficiency]." After: "Now, you are [insert characteristics of sufficiency]." Means: "This is because you are equipped with the knowledge of [insert subject]." Future: "This knowledge will allow you to [insert benefit one], [insert benefit two], and [insert benefit three]."

Review, Use, Soft Call to Action: Review: "Today, you learned [insert subject]." Use: "I want you to rely on this knowledge every time [insert situation] happens." Soft call to action: "I want you to feel [insert positive emotions], knowing that what you learned about [insert subject] will equip you to succeed every time [insert situation] happens."

Not This, But That, Intensifying Repetition: Not this: "[insert situation] is not [insert archetypal situation]..." But that: "...but [insert other archetypal situation]." Intensifying repetition: "not [insert another more intense archetypal situation], but [another more intense archetypal situation]. Not [insert another even more intense archetypal situation], but [another more intense archetypal situation]." (By archetypal situation, I mean a common situation that reoccurs throughout history in the abstract. For example: "a situation of the strong oppressing the weak.")

Trigger, Confirmation Bias, Not This, But That: Trigger: "I want you to keep what I told you in mind every time you see [insert common occurrence]." Confirmation bias: "I want you to remember that [insert common occurrence] is an example of [insert your main point]." Not this: "I want you to remember that it is not a [insert archetypal situation]." But that: "I want you to remember that it is, in truth, a [insert the archetypal situation you said something is]."

What's Done, What's Next: What's done: "We've come a long way. We have [insert example one], [insert example two], and [insert example three]." What's next: "But there's much more that must still be done. We must [insert goal one], [insert goal two], and [insert goal three], by [insert means], because [insert reasons]."

Main Point, Evidence, Logic, Emotion: Main point: "The truth is that [insert your main point]." Evidence: "And we know this is true because [insert evidence]." Logic: "[insert evidence] means [insert main point] because [logical connections between evidence and claim]." Emotion: "[insert emotional agitators]."

**KEY INSIGHT:**

# A Rhetorical Structure Should Act As a Guardrail Not a Straightjacket

## HOW TO VIRTUALLY GUARANTEE PERSUASIVE SUCCESS

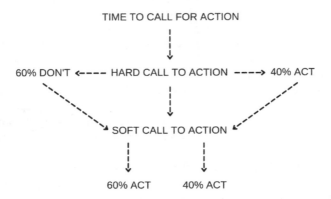

FIGURE 113: Hard calls to action request concrete actions in the real world. Soft calls to action request subtle internal changes, like "thinking a certain way about this" or "remembering this about that." By introducing both, you almost guarantee that you will persuade nearly everyone in the audience to follow one or both of the calls to action.

---

**KEY INSIGHT:**

## A Hard Call to Action Is Tangible, Visible, and Concrete. It Is to Act. It Is Real.

## A Soft Call to Action Is Intangible, Invisible, and Mental. It Is to Believe. It Is No Less Real.

---

# UNSTRUCTURED CONCLUSIONS

If you want a less structured, simpler, and more fluid approach to your conclusion, I suggest these.

Unscripted Passion: This was one of my favorite strategies. By the end of my competitive debate rounds (each one was one hour long, and there were five or six rounds per competition), I was not in the mood to write down my main ideas in the one-minute prep for closing statements, meticulously plan it all out, and deliver according to a prepared structure. I just cleared my head in that one minute, and let the passionate words flow out of me uninhibited when the time came. And I found that this was much better, in some cases, than going according to a planned structure. I always planned my openings, but by the end of the round, I was so warmed-up that it was no problem winging it, and not only was it just not a problem, it was actually the best strategy.

Hope: If you're talking about a problem, and you want people to solve it, then ending on hope is a very powerful strategy. Why? Because if a problem is hopeless, why even try to solve it? By ending on hope, you increase the chance that your audience will take an action to solve a problem, because they now believe the problem is actually solvable. Don't fall into the doom-and-gloom trap: fear and loss are powerful motivators, but they have to be coupled with a true hope that the fear and loss can be prevented. If not? People won't do anything.

Review Outcome: This one is simple: all you have to do is review the outcome of your speech. It's good for casual informational speeches. "Today, you learned exactly how to do [insert action]. You learned how to avoid beginner mistakes, like [insert beginner mistakes]. And you learned how you can use [insert action] to get [insert benefits]."

Remember This: This one is easy: it uses direct requests, and is simple to formulate. All you have to do is this: identify the one idea you want your audience to remember, and tell them you want them to remember it. "But the crucial truth about [insert subject] that any informed citizen must remember, and that I want you to remember, is [insert what you want them to remember]."

Moral: This one depends on your speech: are you speaking about a set of themes? Perhaps speaking in terms of a narrative or chronology? Are you telling stories or reciting history? If so, do this: identify the one moral lesson about life that can be drawn from your stories, and introduce it by specifically enumerating it in your closing: "So what can we learn from this story? What does it mean? Here's the moral: [insert moral]."

Matter of Fact: This one is fun: all you have to do is introduce a summary, review, central moral, or anything you want your audience to remember, with the assertive "matter-of-fact" phrases: "The fact of the matter is that..." "The fact is that..." "The truth about this is..."

Empowerment: This one is perhaps the best: close your speech by empowering your audience. Leave them with whatever gift your speech gave them, plus some inspiration that they can use the gift, and have the personal power to take positive action.

Fork in the Road: This one is captivating: present two possible paths forward, and the position your audience is in right now as that moment when a challenging fork in the road is ahead. It adds a sense of serious sentiment to the moment. It makes them think "This is real. We have to make a choice. The time to decide who we are going to be is now."

## "THE CHOICE IS YOURS" FRAMEWORK PART TWO

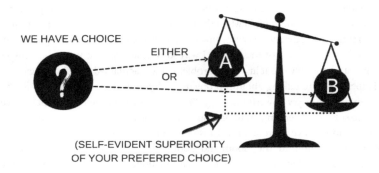

FIGURE 114: You can also use this type of framework, which we discussed earlier, to contrast two different future paths.

Summary: summarize your speech; the main takeaways, the big ideas, some evidence, and what it means for your audience. Take the most important sentence from each section of your speech, reword it, and repeat it at the end.

## YOU COMPLETED STEP THREE OF FIVE

FIGURE 115: In this chapter, you learned how to complete the third step: backing attention with intentional action.

...............................Chapter Summary................................

- The human mind clings to questions. Asking questions can facilitate patterns of long-term favorable actions.
- There are various subtleties concerning calls to action; different words producing slightly different subtexts.
- Present policies: statements of "who should do what, and how" to achieve the goals you advocate.
- Kairos is when the reality of the world acts as your partner in persuasion. Speak at the opportune time to achieve Kairos.
- Structured conclusions follow step-by-step processes to tie up the speech in a compelling manner.
- Unstructured conclusions are more free-flowing, instead achieving a broad directive for tying together the speech.

---

**KEY INSIGHT:**

# Attention Aimed at a Definite Purpose Backed by Action Acts as the Tripartite Foundation of the Communication of Leadership

## The Next Two Parts, Correct Thinking and Powerful Motive, Both Strengthen and Are Strengthened By This Foundation.

---

## THE FIVE-STEP FRAMEWORK (PART THREE)

| 1 | Controlling Attention |
|---|---|
| 1.1 | Portray Empathy |
| 1.2 | Portray Authority |
| 1.3 | Set High Expectations |
| 1.4 | Expose a Hidden Miracle |
| 1.5 | Speak to the People's Pain |
| 1.6 | Build a Coalition |
| 1.7 | Make Bold Promises |
| 1.8 | Divulge the Brutal Truth |
| 1.9 | Shift the Perspective |
| 1.10 | Speak to Broken Justice Problems |
| 1.11 | Present a Moment of Decision |
| 1.12 | Tell a Story |
| 1.13 | Future Significance Today |
| 1.14 | Difficulty-Confidence Matrix |
| 1.15 | Declaratory Cascade |
| 1.16 | Superabundance |
| 1.17 | Speak to the Moment |
| 2 | Directing Attention to a Definite Purpose |
| 2.1 | Achieve Singularity |
| 2.2 | Organize a Pyramid |
| 2.3 | Create Visualization |

| 2.4 | Promise Benefits |
|------|------|
| 2.5 | Promise Loss-Minimization |
| 2.6 | Appeal to Needs |
| 2.7 | Promise Means |
| 2.8 | Present Solvency |
| 2.9 | Promise Rectification |
| **3** | **Backing the Attention with Intentional Action** |
| 3.1 | Ask Questions |
| 3.2 | Interrogative Cascade |
| 3.3 | "Let's" Statements |
| 3.4 | "We Will" Statements |
| 3.5 | "We Must" Statements |
| 3.6 | "We Say" Statements |
| 3.7 | "We Should" Statements |
| 3.8 | "Let" Statements |
| 3.9 | Action Words |
| 3.10 | Present Policies |
| 3.11 | Achieve Kairos |
| 3.12 | Structured Conclusions |
| 3.13 | Unstructured Conclusions |
| **4** | **Backing the Intentional Action with Correct Thinking** |
| **5** | **Backing the Entire Process with a Powerful Motive** |

**Claim These Free Resources that Will Help You Unleash the Power of Your Words and Speak with Confidence. Visit www.speakforsuccesshub.com/toolkit for Access.**

### 18 Free PDF Resources

*12 Iron Rules for Captivating Story, 21 Speeches that Changed the World, 341-Point Influence Checklist, 143 Persuasive Cognitive Biases, 17 Ways to Think On Your Feet, 18 Lies About Speaking Well, 137 Deadly Logical Fallacies, 12 Iron Rules For Captivating Slides, 371 Words that Persuade, 63 Truths of Speaking Well, 27 Laws of Empathy, 21 Secrets of Legendary Speeches, 19 Scripts that Persuade, 12 Iron Rules For Captivating Speech, 33 Laws of Charisma, 11 Influence Formulas, 219-Point Speech-Writing Checklist, 21 Eloquence Formulas*

**Claim These Free Resources that Will Help You Unleash the Power of Your Words and Speak with Confidence. Visit www.speakforsuccesshub.com/toolkit for Access.**

**30 Free Video Lessons**

We'll send you one free video lesson every day for 30 days, written and recorded by Peter D. Andrei. Days 1-10 cover authenticity, the prerequisite to confidence and persuasive power. Days 11-20 cover building self-belief and defeating communication anxiety. Days 21-30 cover how to speak with impact and influence, ensuring your words change minds instead of falling flat. Authenticity, self-belief, and impact – this course helps you master three components of confidence, turning even the most high-stakes presentations from obstacles into opportunities.

# SPEAK FOR SUCCESS COLLECTION BOOK

# III

# HOW LEGENDARY LEADERS SPEAK CHAPTER

# V

# STEP FOUR:

# 11 Ways to Back the Intentional Action with Correct Thinking

## EXPLAIN *LOGOS*

A BOUT 2,000 YEARS AGO, ARISTOTLE, brilliant as he was, gifted us a conception of rhetoric and persuasion that exists to this day.

He argued that all persuasion could be broken down into three categories of rhetoric.

Pathos: using emotion.

Ethos: using expertise, evidence, and portraying your genuine interest in your audience's well-being.

Logos: using logic.

And in this section on how to back intentional action with correct thinking, we focus on logos. But first, let's talk about that goal in the first place; the goal of backing intentional action with correct thinking. Why does it matter? Why do it at all? Why not skip straight to step five, backing the entire process with a powerful motive?

Good question. The answer? That people's actions are the direct products of their thoughts, and there is a set of correct thoughts – in other words, a pristine mental climate – that will produce the best possible actions. Get it?

That's where people's actions come from.

And every single set of actions has its specific mental climate, uniquely suited to it, that can alone produce the best follow-through. So, the question I have to ask myself is this: given the fact that all my readers are probably in a situation motivating them to inspire a unique set of actions from their subordinates, am I completely hamstrung in trying to aid that pursuit by teaching you how to create correct thinking, simply because each set of actions has its unique set of correct thoughts?

I thought so, at first. But then I realized, not at all. Why not? Because every single ideal mental climate for each unique set of desired actions – no matter how different to one another they may be – are empowered by the same set of fundamental principles.

And that's what we're going to get into next, after covering Logos. Anyway – back to logos.

What is logos?

It's not just logic. The best definition of Logos, even for our modern leadership purposes, is found in the year 500 B.C. A man named Heraclitus defined it as "that universal principle which animates and rules the world." And that's exactly what it is for those of us who strive to achieve the communication of leadership.

**KEY INSIGHT:**

# Your Logos Constitutes Your Nonnegotiable Moral Foundation.

## HOW TO PRESENT YOUR ARGUMENT PERFECTLY

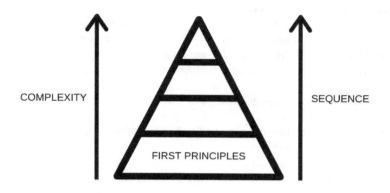

FIGURE 116: Structure your argument by first presenting undeniable, axiomatic first principles, and building everything else on the basis of these first principles.

That definition is also the foundation of the rest of this chapter. Why? Because your logos is more than just your dry logic connecting evidence to claims (though that's part of it). Your logos is that universal set of principles that animate and rule your organization, movement, coalition, etc.

Express it, until ignorance of it is wiped out. Articulate it, beyond the point of the slightest ambiguity. Clarify it, until it stands self-evident. When we expand our definition of logos, we find that the vast majority of examples of the communication of leadership were saturated with Logos. Why? Because those legendary leaders knew that correct thinking – that a universal set of animating and ruling principles – is not only empowering for intentional action but necessary for intentional action.

It's simple. Thoughts create actions, and legendary leaders seek to place the correct thoughts in people's minds, so that those correct thoughts may empower the intentional actions.

Now, let's break down the phrase "principles."

What do we find contained in it?

Values.

Rights.

Values and rights hierarchies.

Beliefs.

Goals.

Conceptions of how the world works.

An understanding of what is sanctioned in the pursuit of goals.

A principled leader is a leader who articulates the principles – the fundamental, foundational Logos – of his or her movement.

I recall a movement expert who coached famous boxer Connor McGregor saying something interesting in a social media video. Sadly, this coach's name escapes my memory, even after trying to track down his account for hours to give him proper credit.

He said that he teaches the principles of movement, not the techniques of boxing, because – and this is the interesting part – the principles create the techniques instantly, in the moment. In other words, the principles, and the depth and fluency of understanding they represent, create whatever technique the situation calls for, right there in the moment.

Interesting. And exactly right. When a legendary leader expresses their Logos, they express the principles – the pieces of a deep and fluent understanding – which allows them to create the techniques, or the intentional actions, effortlessly out of thin air.

Principles create techniques.

Logos creates intentional actions.

Same thing. And that's the secret of every legendary leader who created a movement of people who, time and time again, acted intentionally in response to situations just as the leader wanted them to. Why did they do that?

The leader didn't tell them to specifically act in those ways, so why did they?

Because the leader articulated the principles which created those intentional actions.

### CONVEYING LOGOS VERSUS CONVEYING POLICIES

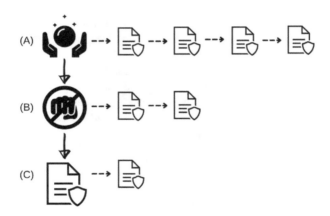

FIGURE 117: Values (A) create beliefs (B) which create policies (C). If you target policies with your persuasive attempts, you may inspire the execution of one policy. If you target beliefs – where policies come from – you may inspire the execution of twice as many policies. If you target values – where beliefs and policies come from – you inspire a sequence of policy-like actions over a long period of time, in a similar manner as to how questions create a sequence of conscious thoughts over a long period of time.

Get it? It's much like a broad policy statement. Some examples of logos? Let's draw them from Ronald Reagan. Today, and certainly in his day, a man of potentially divisive politics, much of his appeal came from the unparalleled degree to which he exposed the fundamental logos of his movement. Before I show you the examples, I ought to give you a formal definition of logos in regards to communication. So, here: the fundamental, core principles ruling and animating the movement defined by the goals the speaker wants to advance. Ronald Reagan spoke these Logos-driven words in a speech supporting the Republican presidential candidate Barry Goldwater (who lost in a massive landslide).

"And this idea that government is beholden to the people, that it has no other source of power except the sovereign people, is still the newest and the most unique idea in all the long history of man's relation to man. This is the issue of this election: whether we believe in our capacity for self-government or whether we abandon the American revolution and confess that a little intellectual elite in a far-distant capitol can plan our lives for us better than we can plan them ourselves."

In just this short excerpt, he advanced two tremendously important principles ruling and animating his conservative cause and coalition. First, that government is beholden to the people. Second, that we ought to govern ourselves as much as possible. These can't be broken down any further; their moral appeal is seemingly self-evident. They are his Logos.

## THE AXIOMATIC NATURE OF YOUR LOGOS AND PRINCIPLES

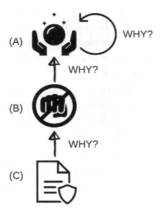

FIGURE 118: While values (A) create beliefs (B) which create policies (C), asking "why?" of a policy yields the belief as an answer, and asking "why?" of the belief yields the value as the answer. This is not a hard-and-fast rule. There may be some exceptions. Finally, asking "why?" of the value yields the value. It is "self-contained."

Another example, from someone who couldn't be further from Reagan's political inclinations? Let's look at FDR's first State of the Union address. "If I read the temper of our people correctly, we now realize as we have never realized before our interdependence on each other; that we cannot merely take but we must give as well; that if we are to go forward, we must move as a trained and loyal army willing to sacrifice for the good of a common discipline, because without such discipline no progress is made, no leadership becomes effective. We are, I know, ready and willing to submit our lives and property to such discipline, because it makes possible a leadership which aims at a larger good. This I propose to offer, pledging that the larger purposes will bind upon us all as a sacred obligation with a unity of duty hitherto evoked only in time of armed strife."

He, like Reagan, also advanced two ruling, animating principles of his movement in this excerpt. First, that we are interdependent on one another. Second, that we ought to sacrifice for the common good (he repeated this three times).

Let's apply an equation in a form familiar to you.

Logos = [1*(fundamental animating and ruling principles presented) + 0.5*(first repetition of a principle) / (number of statements)]*100.

Logos-driven communication yields a higher value when plugged into this equation. Another example? Let's take the transcript of Pete Buttigieg's 2020 announcement of his presidential race. "Because there is a myth being sold to industrial and rural communities: the myth that we can stop the clock and turn it back *(principle)*. It comes from people who think the only way to reach communities like ours is through resentment and nostalgia, selling an impossible promise of returning to a bygone era that was never as great as advertised to begin with *(principle repeated once)*. The problem is, they're telling us to look for greatness in all the wrong places *(principle repeated twice)*. Because if there is one thing the city of South Bend has shown, it's that there is no such thing as an honest politics that revolves around the word 'again *(principle two)*.' It's time to walk away from the politics of the past, and toward something totally different *(principle two repeated once)*."

In 7 statements, he advanced two main principles and some repetitious statements of previously presented principles. First, the principle that we can't always look backward for our answers; that the answers to the problems of the present and the future lie in innovation, not restoration. Second, that we ought to leave the politics of the past behind. The equation? 1 + 1 (the two principles advanced) plus 0.5 + 0.5 (they were each repeated once) / 7 = 4 / 7 = ~57%. Let's compare that to a segment with a much higher Logos score later on in the transcript. I bolded each principle – each animating, ruling idea – he advanced.

"Change is coming, ready or not (statement one). The question of our time is whether families and workers will be defeated by the changes beneath us or whether we will master them and make them work toward a better everyday life for us all (statement two). Such a moment calls for hopeful and audacious voices from communities like ours (statement three). And yes, it calls for a new generation of leadership (statement four). The principles that will guide my campaign are simple enough to fit on a bumper sticker (statement five): freedom, security, and democracy (statement six)."

In this more Logos-driven section, he advanced 6 principles in 6 statements. 100% Logos-driven language.

And you can see how powerful that made it, right? Just read it again. Now, this doesn't mean that each statement presents a principle; some statements present more than one (the last one presents six).

Another brilliant example of this strategy? Tulsi Gabbard, another 2020 Democratic primary candidate, said the following in her announcement speech. "Our nation was founded on the principle that our government should be of the people, by the people, and for the people – where all people are treated equally, and with respect, in these United States of America."

This example expresses the simplicity of the strategy: simply enumerate your core animating principles. And that concludes our discussion of Logos. Let's move on to what I promised at the start of this section: the core elements that will empower any set of intentional actions, whether it is expanding a business, passing a bill, or winning a war.

## GUARANTEED VICTORY

There's an incredibly compelling strategy that can empower any set of intentional actions you desire, by making victory appear guaranteed.

Now, why does that matter in the first place? Because humans are risk-averse. And because we perform counterfactual simulation – the production of predictive mental movies – to judge whether or not we should do something.

So, let me give you an example. Let's say your audience performs a counterfactual simulation of throwing their all in your favor, of expending their reservoirs of energy, and fully and faithfully pursuing your presented purpose, and the result of this mental movie is that victory remains unlikely. That introduces an action-paralyzing agent by activating our risk-averse, loss-averse tendencies.

What happens after that mental movie? People simulate the single most paralyzing terror possible in such a situation; people simulate the pain of the future regret they will feel when they put all that energy into the goal, and it failed. That prevents people from taking intentional action. Maybe not all of them, but enough of them to hurt your cause, and hurt it badly. So, that's why the guaranteed victory approach is so important.

People do not act in the presence of doubt.

The guaranteed-victory mindset is a form of correct thinking designed to quiet down the risk-averse mental tendencies that paralyze people against action.

It ensures that when your audience performs the mental movie, they have an overwhelmingly positive vision of what will happen because there won't be any future regret of putting mountains of energy toward something that might go nowhere.

## POSITIVE COUNTERFACTUAL SIMULATION PRECEDES ACTION

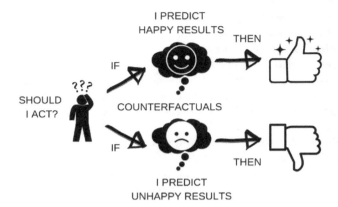

FIGURE 119: When people are considering if they should take an action, if they predict the action leading to positive results, then they do. If they predict the action leading to negative results, then they don't. These predictive mental movies are called counterfactual simulations.

So, what exactly does it mean to present guaranteed victory? Well, it's a little more sophisticated than saying, "this is guaranteed to work."

It's doing three things designed to create the correct thoughts; the thoughts that resist paralyzing risk-averse and loss-averse tendencies.

Thing one: presenting the very high chances of victory. This one is very simple and is the first level of this strategy. And you know how to do it. We won't be focusing on this one in this section.

Thing two: presenting the possible outcomes as two ways to win, and no ways to lose. In other words, "if [possible outcome one] happens, we win, because [reasons]; and if [possible outcome two] happens, we still win, because [reasons]. In short, this is two ways to win, and no ways to lose, which is why we should act."

Thing three: presenting multiple "fail-safes," presenting multiple ways that the cause can survive temporary defeat, presenting multiple layers to the conflict, which raises your chances of victory.

To be truthful, I couldn't find an example of a legendary leader doing thing two. So, rather than precariously finding an example and tenuously stretching it to fit the strategy, I'll just give you a contrived example of two ways to win, no ways to lose.

Let's say you propose that your company buys stock in your biggest competitor. How would you achieve the two ways to win, no ways to lose strategy?

"There are two things that can happen if we buy stock in this competitor, and both of them are good. The first one is that the stock goes up in value. If that happens, since we own stock in the company, obviously that's good for us. The second one, however, is that the stock goes down in value. What then? Well, even if that happens, we still win, because while we did lose money directly on the stock, it is our competitor's stock value dropping after all, and we can expedite that fall by selling off our shares right as it drops, pushing it down yet further. And since it is our competitor, our stock value, as an economic substitute, will rise. So, no matter which of the two possibilities happens here, we win. That's why I propose this strategy."

Alright. What about thing three? What about presenting multiple fail-safes, multiple lines of defense, multiple layers to the conflict?

Well, for that, I do have an example. And it is an incredibly compelling example, from one of the recurring characters in this book: Churchill. In fact, this is the very end of the same "we shall never surrender" speech we analyzed multiple times already through the lens of many other strategies. Think about it: what he is doing is trying to create intentional action, and this final section represents him backing the intentional action with correct thinking; thinking designed to empower that action by making it seem like a guaranteed victory, which will push people to act instead of falling victim to risk-averse paralysis.

Let's bring forth the transcript. Here is the entirety of that final, concluding paragraph containing the declaratory cascade we analyzed previously. "I have, myself, full confidence that if all do their duty, if nothing is neglected, and if the best arrangements are made, as they are being made, we shall prove ourselves once again able to defend our Island home, to ride out the storm of war, and to outlive the menace of tyranny, if necessary for years, if necessary alone. At any rate, that is what we are going to try to do. That is the resolve of His Majesty's Government – every man of them. That is the will of Parliament and the nation. The British Empire and the French Republic, linked together in their cause and in their need, will defend to the death their native soil, aiding each other like good comrades to the utmost of their strength. Even though large tracts of Europe and many old and famous States have fallen or may fall into the grip of the Gestapo and all the odious apparatus of Nazi rule, we shall not flag or fail. We shall go on to the end, we shall fight in France, we shall fight on the seas and oceans, we shall fight with growing confidence and growing strength in the air, we shall defend our Island, whatever the cost may be, we shall fight on the beaches, we shall fight on the landing grounds, we shall fight in the fields and in the streets, we shall fight in the hills; we shall never surrender, *and even if, which I do not for a moment believe, this Island or a large part of it were subjugated and starving, then our Empire beyond the seas, armed and guarded by the British Fleet, would carry on the struggle, until, in God's good time, the New World, with all its power and might, steps forth to the rescue and the liberation of the old.*"

Did you catch that? Did you capture how he added another layer to the conflict, thus drastically increasing the perceived chances of victory, which is a form of correct thinking backing intentional action because it makes intentional action much more likely by quieting the paralyzing influence of our risk-averse tendencies? Simple, but effective. He said that even if we lose on this layer of the conflict – "which I do not for a moment believe" – there is another layer of the conflict, which is our massive global armada defending our colonies, and the armies of the colonies themselves. Thus, while victory is not guaranteed, it is very likely, because even if they take the island, we can carry on the conflict globally.

Get it? See how this strategy raised the perceived chances of victory, adding a fail-safe, which quiets the risk-averse tendencies that tell us not to throw our all into unlikely bets? See how this strategy quiets those tendencies by making the bets seem drastically less unlikely and much more guaranteed? Wonderful. Let's move on.

## VIRTUOUS THINKING

Virtuous thinking produces results. Virtuous thinking advances causes where negative thinking fails to do so. If we drown in our cynicism, there will be no progress, because cynics are beyond hoping that the future can be better, and hope is the foundation of action.

Why act if you believe – in fact, if you know (or think you know) – that nothing good can come of acting? And what is a common element of cynicism? The abandonment of virtue. And we are moral creatures, though flawed ones.

We respect morality. We respect movements that do not yield to hatred, or give in to the variety of vicious vices that threaten to tear the cooperative fabric of humanity apart, splitting us asunder, sowing the seeds of dark division where unity once reigned supreme. We respect movements that cling to virtue, especially when doing so appears nearly impossible; especially when doing so means turning the other cheek, and fighting hatred not by fueling it with more hatred, but by dousing it with love.

The finest example of a leader backing intentional action with positive thinking is Mahatma Gandhi's world-changing communication of leadership.

People yearn for freedom.

And Gandhi's people had it torn from them by an oppressive colonial power. Sage-like, ascetic in his ways, noble in his appearance, and transcendent in his speech, Gandhi was able to bring people together under a banner of a fundamentally virtuous Logos.

When the minds of men were motivated by hatred, Gandhi inspired love. When the minds of men were motivated toward violence, Gandhi inspired peace. When the minds of men were motivated to abandon virtue in favor of vice, Gandhi inspired the human proclivity to manifest virtue. This is why his followers called him "the great-souled one."

Ultimately, it was this virtue that prevailed in the noble fight. Ultimately, it was the non-violent protest that won where violence was most tempting, but also the precise path to suffering and failure. And ultimately, it was the communication of leadership that inspired the virtue and non-violence; virtue and non-violence that converted the improbable hope of an unlikely victory into the undeniable reality of a sweeping success.

Gandhi empowered the intentional actions associated with peaceful protest by backing them with correct thinking centered around virtue. Here is the transcript of his "Quit India" speech. I have numbered all the virtues. And note this: the virtues are often implicit, though still powerful. "Before you discuss the resolution, let me place before you one or two things, I want you to understand two things very clearly and to consider them from the same point of view from which I am placing them before you *(virtue #1)*. I ask you to consider it from my point of view, because if you approve of it, you will be enjoined to carry out all I say. It will be a great responsibility *(virtue #2)*. There are people who ask me whether I am the same man that I was in 1920, or whether there has been any change in me. You are right in asking that question. Let me, however, hasten to assure that I am the same Gandhi as I was in 1920. I have not changed in any fundamental respect *(virtue #3)*. I attach the same importance to non-violence that I did then *(virtue #4)*. If at all, my emphasis on it has grown stronger *(virtue #5)*. There is no real contradiction between the present resolution and my previous writings and utterances *(virtue #6)*. Occasions like the present do not occur in everybody's and but rarely in anybody's life. I want you to know and feel that there is nothing but purest Ahimsa in all that I am saying and doing today *(virtue #7)*. The draft resolution of the Working Committee is based on Ahimsa *(virtue #8)*, the contemplated struggle similarly has its roots in Ahimsa *(virtue #9)*. If, therefore, there is any among you who has lost faith in Ahimsa or is wearied of it, let him not vote for this resolution *(virtue #10)*. Let me explain my position clearly *(virtue #11)*. God has vouchsafed to me a priceless gift in the weapon of Ahimsa *(virtue #12)*. I and my Ahimsa are on our trail today *(virtue #13)*. If in the present crisis, when the earth is being scorched by the flames of Himsa and crying for deliverance, I failed to make use of the God given talent, God will not forgive me and I shall be judged un-wrongly of the great gift *(virtue #14)*. I must act now *(virtue #15)*. I may not hesitate and merely look on, when Russia and China are threatened *(virtue #16)*. Ours is not a drive for power *(virtue #17)*, but purely a non-violent fight for India's independence *(virtue #18)*. In a violent struggle, a successful general has been often known to effect a military coup and to set up a dictatorship *(virtue #19)*. But under the Congress scheme of things, essentially non-violent as it is *(virtue #20)*, there can be no room for dictatorship *(virtue #21)*. A non-violent soldier of freedom will covet nothing for himself *(virtue #22)*, he fights only for the freedom of his country *(virtue #23)*. The Congress is unconcerned as to who will rule *(virtue #24)*, when freedom is attained *(virtue #25)*. The power, when it comes, will belong to the people of India *(virtue #26)*, and it will be for them to decide to whom it placed in the entrusted *(virtue #27)*. May be that the reins will be placed in the hands of the Parsis, for instance – as I would love to see happen – or they may be handed to some others whose names are not heard in the Congress today *(virtue #28)*. It will not be for you then to object saying, "This community is microscopic. That party did not play its due part in the freedom's struggle; why should it have all the power *(virtue #29)*?" Ever since its inception the Congress has kept itself meticulously free of the communal taint *(virtue #30)*. It has thought always in terms of the whole nation and has acted accordingly *(virtue #31)*. I know how imperfect our Ahimsa is and how far away we are still from the ideal *(virtue #32)*, but in Ahimsa there is no final failure or defeat *(virtue #33)*. I have faith *(virtue #34)*, therefore, that if, in spite of our shortcomings *(virtue #35)*, the big thing does happen, it will be because God wanted to help us by crowning with success our silent *(virtue #36)*, unremitting *(virtue #37)* Sadhana *(virtue #38)* for the last twenty-two years *(virtue #39)*. I believe that in the history of the world, there has not been a more genuinely democratic struggle for freedom than ours *(virtue #40)*. I read Carlyle's French Resolution while I was in prison, and Pandit Jawaharlal has told me something about the Russian revolution. But it is my conviction that inasmuch as these struggles were fought with the weapon of violence they failed to realize the democratic ideal *(virtue #41)*. In the democracy which I have envisaged *(virtue #42)*, a democracy established by non-violence, *(virtue #43)* there will be equal freedom for all *(virtue #44)*. Everybody will be his own master *(virtue #45)*. It is to join a struggle for such democracy that I invite you today *(virtue #46)*. Once you realize this you will forget the differences between the Hindus and Muslims *(virtue #47)*, and think of yourselves as Indians only *(virtue #48)*, engaged in the common struggle *(virtue #49)* for independence *(virtue #50)*. Then, there is the question of your attitude toward the British. I have noticed that there is hatred toward the British among the people. The people say they are disgusted with their behavior. The people make no distinction between British imperialism and the British people. To them, the two are one. This hatred would even make them welcome the Japanese. It is most dangerous. It means that they will exchange one slavery for another. We must get rid of this feeling *(virtue #51)*. Our quarrel is not with the British people *(virtue #52)*, we fight their imperialism *(virtue #53)*. The proposal for the withdrawal of British power did not come out of anger *(virtue #54)*. It came to enable India to play its due part at the present critical juncture *(virtue #55)*. It is not a happy position for a big country like India to be merely helping with money and material obtained willy-nilly from her while the United Nations are conducting the war *(virtue #56)*. We cannot evoke the true spirit of sacrifice and valor *(virtue #57)*, so long as we are not free. I know the British Government will not be able to withhold freedom from us, when we have made enough self-sacrifice *(virtue #58)*. We must, therefore, purge ourselves of hatred *(virtue #59)*. Speaking for myself, I can say that I have never felt any hatred *(virtue #60)*. As a matter of fact, I feel myself to be a greater friend of the British now than ever before *(virtue #61)*. One reason is that they are today in distress. My very friendship, therefore, demands that I should try to save them from their mistakes *(virtue #62)*. As I view the situation, they are on the brink of an abyss. It, therefore, becomes my duty to warn them of their danger even though it may, for the time being, anger them to the point of cutting off the friendly hand that is stretched out to help them *(virtue #63)*. People may laugh, nevertheless that is my claim. At a time when I may have to launch the biggest struggle of my life, I may not harbor hatred against anybody *(virtue #64)*."

(Ahimsa is defined as respect for all living things and an avoidance of violence).

## HOPEFUL THINKING

I alluded to this previously. And it is deeply significant. If people are beyond hoping that their actions can produce a better future, they will not act. And why should they, if it is true that their actions can't do much good?

People do not act in the absence of hope.

The truth is this: one of the most critical roles of a leader during a time of crisis it to acknowledge the crisis and be forthcoming about the associated difficulties, but simultaneously inspire a sense of hope. Let's talk about FDR's accomplishments again. Let's break down the essence of many of his specific policies. What were they? What did they do? How did they work? They were supposed to stave off the Great Depression, an economic downturn the likes of which the country – in fact, the world – has never before seen. So, how did he do it?

He pulled a variety of economic levers, but nearly all of them hinged on one critical component: getting people to act as if it was guaranteed that the plans would work.

In fact, it was only guaranteed that the plans would work if people acted like it; if people put their money back into banks; if people began buying again; if employers began employing again; if people bought into his New Deal era Keynesian strategies, in all their measures. In other words, he needed to back intentional action with hopeful thinking.

Why? Because in desperate, depressing, dark, and difficult situations like the Great Depression, people will only act if they can find hope in themselves that their actions will produce a positive outcome.

Thus, in desperate situations, in crisis moments, and in nearly all moments of difficulty, no matter how large or small, hopeful thinking is not a supplement to creating intentional action, but a prerequisite.

It's the same story with nearly all of these examples of the communication of leadership. It's true. They are all saturated with hopeful language. Language that says we can do it. Language that says it is possible. Language that presents an improbable hope as a guaranteed victory.

## VISUALIZING THE FUNDAMENTAL NATURE OF WHAT HOPE IS

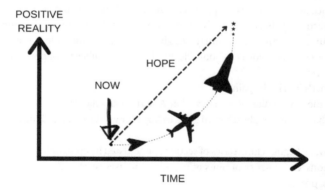

FIGURE 120: Hope is looking forward to a more positive reality and daring to believe it will happen.

Do you recall Barack Obama's slogan when he ran for president? Do you recall his message of an overwhelmingly positive hope? Do you recall his tremendous ability to rally massive crowds of both demographic and ideological diversity? If you're wondering how he did those things, the answer is this: presenting hope. We're going to analyze some of the most compelling sections of his victory speech. First, he opened by acknowledging this critical ingredient: hope. And yet, when I first heard this, just like so many other people, I didn't even realize how blatantly obvious he made it. I had chalked up his victory to a variety of factors but overlooked the most obvious one, so obvious that it is boldly featured in the beginning of his speech: hope.

"If there is anyone out there who still doubts that America is a place where all things are possible, who still wonders if the dream of our founders is alive in our time, who still questions the power of our democracy, tonight is your answer. It's the answer told by lines that stretched around schools and churches in numbers this nation has never seen, by people who waited three hours and four hours, many for the first time in their lives, because they *believed* that this time must be different, that their voices could be that difference."

Belief is hope, for one must have hope to believe. He continues. I skip to the most representative parts, leaving out things like pleasantries to his opponent.

"We are, and always will be, the United States of America. It's the answer that led those who've been told for so long by so many to be *cynical and fearful and doubtful* about what we can achieve to put their hands on the arc of history and bend it once more toward the *hope* of a better day."

See what I mean? It's a construction of hope clearing the dark thickets of cynicism, fear, and doubt. And it's not only explicitly presented, but the actual truth of his campaign; his movement was a coalition built on a foundation of hope.

"The road ahead will be long. Our climb will be steep. We may not get there in one year or even in one term. But, America, I have never been more *hopeful* than I am tonight that we will get there."

"To those – to those who would tear the world down: we will defeat you. To those who seek peace and security: we support you. And to all those who have wondered if America's beacon still burns as bright: tonight we proved once more that the true strength of our nation comes not from the might of our arms or the scale of our wealth, but from the enduring power of our ideals: democracy, liberty, opportunity and *unyielding hope.*"

Think that's it? Think again.

"That's the true genius of America: that America can change. Our union can be perfected. What we've already achieved gives us hope for what we can and must achieve tomorrow."

And now, he begins a long series of sections punctuated by epistrophe: the strategy of ending a consecutive series of units of meaning (phrases, sentences, or paragraphs) with the same phrase.

The phrase?

"Yes, we can."

His campaign slogan, and the single most hopeful set of words I've heard in my lifetime, seemingly embodying the essence of what it means to have hope.

"And tonight, I think about all that she's seen throughout her century in America – the heartache and the *hope*; the struggle and the progress; the times we were told that we can't, and the people who pressed on with that American creed: *Yes, we can.*

At a time when women's voices were silenced and their hopes dismissed, she lived to see them stand up and speak out and reach for the ballot. *Yes, we can.*

When there was despair in the dust bowl and depression across the land, she saw a nation conquer fear itself with a New Deal, new jobs, a new sense of common purpose. *Yes, we can.*

When the bombs fell on our harbor and tyranny threatened the world, she was there to witness a generation rise to greatness and a democracy was saved. *Yes, we can.*

She was there for the buses in Montgomery, the hoses in Birmingham, a bridge in Selma, and a preacher from Atlanta who told a people that 'We Shall Overcome.' *Yes, we can.*

A man touched down on the moon, a wall came down in Berlin, a world was connected by our own science and imagination.

And this year, in this election, she touched her finger to a screen, and cast her vote, because after 106 years in America, through the best of times and the darkest of hours, she knows how America can change. *Yes, we can.*

America, we have come so far. We have seen so much. But there is so much more to do. So tonight, let us ask ourselves – if our children should live to see the next century; if my daughters should be so lucky to live as long as Ann Nixon Cooper, what change will they see? What progress will we have made?

This is our chance to answer that call. This is our moment. This is our time, to put our people back to work and open doors of opportunity for our kids; to restore prosperity and promote the cause of peace; to reclaim the American dream and reaffirm that fundamental truth, that, out of many, we are one; that while we breathe, *we hope.* And where we are met with cynicism and doubts and those who tell us that we can't, we will respond with that timeless creed that sums up the spirit of a people: *Yes, we can.* Thank you. God bless you. And may God bless the United States of America."

Another example? Let's draw one from Maya Angelou. Who was she? She was the second poet, the first woman, and the first African American in American history to read a poem at the inauguration of an American president. Whose inauguration? Bill Clinton's 1993 inauguration. The poem?

"Here on the pulse of this new day
You may have the grace to look up and out
And into your sister's eyes,
Into your brother's face, your country
And say simply
Very simply
*With hope*
Good morning."

What is another critical function of hope?

It lightens an unbearable burden. A set of difficulties plus hope is significantly less difficult to bear than those struggles alone, though they remain identical in reality. Why? Because hope lets us see the light at the end of the tunnel, and that makes us keep going.

## WHY HOPE IS A PREREQUISITE FOR DOING HARD THINGS

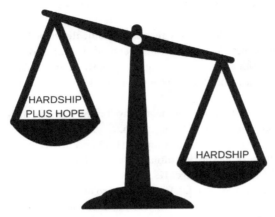

FIGURE 121: Hardship plus hope is a significantly lighter burden to carry than hardship alone.

It makes us keep struggling. It makes us keep pushing, no matter the obstacles in our way. It makes us stare straight ahead, see the coming challenges, and instead of shrinking from them, holster our guns, steel our spirits, ask "can we overcome it?" answer "yes, we can," and begin a regimen of intentional action: a regimen of one small step followed by another and another, a regimen of one clawing grasp forward at a time, despite our aching souls and the doubts fluttering in our minds. Why? Because hope is on our side.

## OPPORTUNISTIC THINKING

What is Mayor Pete Buttigieg (ironically, a man criticized for his rhetorical imitation of Obama), really doing when he says the following in a Democratic 2020 primary debate? Pay close attention.

"I think there's a better way. It's true, the American people are ready. There's a historic majority right now, even broader than what was available to President Obama a decade ago. There is now a majority ready to act to make sure there is no such thing as an uninsured American and no such thing as an unaffordable prescription. Just so long as we don't command people to accept a public plan if they don't want to. That's the idea of Medicare for All Who Want It. My point is, what I am offering is campaigning for all of these things that America wants. Yes, higher wages, doubling the rate of unionization in this country, making corporations and the wealthy pay their fair share, delivering healthcare and college affordability. But also offering a way to do these game changing transformations that will actually galvanize and energize, not polarize the American people. That is not only what we need in order to win, it's what we need in order to govern and actually get these things done."

Did you find it? Did you find how Mayor Pete used opportunistic thinking to back intentional action with conducive thoughts? It's quite compelling. "I think there's a better way. It's true, the American people are ready. There's a historic majority right now, even broader than what was available to President Obama a decade ago. There is now a majority ready to act to make sure there is no such thing as an uninsured American and no such thing as an unaffordable prescription."

It goes like this: there's a historic majority right now that wants to do what we want to do, and I'm the candidate up here who won't squander this historic majority. In other words, we have a massive, historically unprecedented opportunity before us, and I won't mess it up by trying to command people to do something they don't want to do. Get it? Opportunistic thinking backs intentional action in the pursuit of a definite goal. Why? Because of a common agent of our shared psychological tendencies: loss aversion. Counterfactual simulation plays a role here as well.

People hear opportunistic language – "we have a historic majority... let's not waste this opportunity" – and they feel loss aversion; they are compelled to throw their lot in with that leader because they fear the loss of the opportunity, and because they perform counterfactual simulation and simulate the pain of their future regret at losing the opportunity.

Simple, but effective. Loss aversion and counterfactual simulation. Two incredibly powerful agents of human psychology, especially when acting in tandem with one another. Pete also used unified thinking in this excerpt. And it is this to which we turn now.

## UNIFIED THINKING

There's a special sentiment enshrined in the words "historic majority," at least in Pete's context. The sentiment? Unity.

Why is unity a form of correct thinking that backs intentional action? A few reasons.

Our tribal tendencies drive us to throw our lot in with a tribe; a group of people united around common goals, common symbols, and common beliefs; and when we adopt a group identity, we act with increased vigor in striving for the group's shared objectives.

### KEY INSIGHT:

# The Psychological Basis of Unity is Also the Psychological Basis of Division. But We Can Dull One Edge of the Sword and Sharpen the Other.

## WHY INTELLECTUAL CONFLICT REALLY IS VERBAL COMBAT

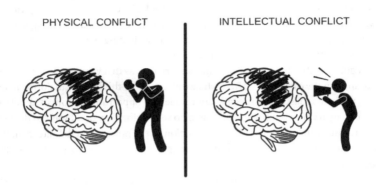

FIGURE 122: The same parts of the brain that light up during physical conflict light up during intellectual conflict.

## HOW COMFORT-MAXIMIZATION PRODUCES ECHO CHAMBERS

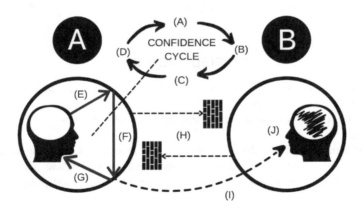

FIGURE 123: There are two intellectual coalitions here: A and B. As a review, the confidence cycle is the cyclical relationship between pride (A), conviction (B), confirmation bias (C), and validation (D). In the echo chambers, members send out messages (E) that bounce around for a while (F) and return, in some form or another, back to the source (G). This step is the "echo." This cycle in the echo chamber produces the confidence cycle. Meanwhile, messages the A and B coalitions send to each other get blocked as people seek to avoid the pain of intellectual conflict (H). However, if a message from one coalition reaches the other (I), it often causes psychological pain and cognitive dissonance (J), making them feel "attacked." This may then

contribute to a strengthening of the barriers as a means to protect against further "attacks."

The second reason? The principle of social proof.

It's also called the principle of persuasive consensus. We follow the crowd. We follow the big gathering of people doing the same thing. We follow the majority, especially the historic majority. Our views are validated by a majority on our side. Our actions are confirmed by the crowd around us, acting the same ways we are. Our lifestyles, identities, beliefs; our manners of speech and thought; everything about us falls into the purview of the social proof tendency. And that's not always a bad thing.

We have a finite budget of mental energy. We cannot make every single decision in a rational, objective, crowd-ignoring way, because we would run out of mental energy and have an incredibly difficult time trying to resolve the important questions.

So, we outsource our judgment to the crowd. But the point of telling you this is not to cast judgment on whether it's good or bad but to explain why unified thinking is so important. If people perceive unity, our social-proof crowd-following tendency kicks in, our group-identifying fervor kicks in, and we subscribe to that unity, acting with confidence because our actions are confirmed by the crowd. There is unity, after all.

## THE SOCIAL-PROOF TENDENCY VISUALIZED

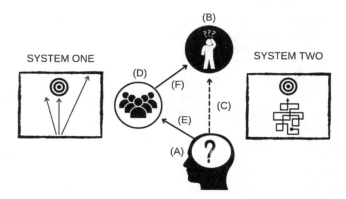

FIGURE 124: Prompted by a question (A), we seek to evaluate the target question of "what we should do" (B). However, this evaluation (C) is difficult. So, we substitute the heuristic question "what other people are doing" (D), evaluate this (E), and transfer the answer to the target question (F).

See where I'm going with this? See how unified thinking can back intentional action in the pursuit of a defined goal? See how unified thinking can create confident, intentional action? Now, how many times do you recall seeing words like "common purpose" in these excerpts of legendary examples of the communication of leadership?

Maybe you don't recall, but these words come up over and over again. Why? Because they achieve that special sentiment that can push people to pursue a goal with confident, intentional action, and unrestrained vigor; that unique quality which activates our social-proof crowd-following tendencies and our group-identifying tendencies: unity.

### THE POWERFUL COALITION PRINCIPLE VISUALIZED

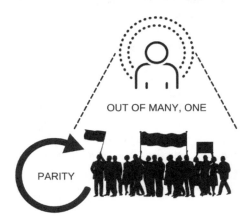

FIGURE 125: Present parity between the members of a coalition. Show the members what they have in common with one another. This strengthens the group.

Emmeline Pankhurst used this strategy too. Who was she? The woman who organized the right to vote movements in the United Kingdom, forcing the country to follow through on the mandate of its title as one of the world's oldest democracies. What did she say about her movement? "We wear no mark; we belong to every class; we permeate every class of the community from the highest to the lowest; and so you see in the woman's civil war the dear men of my country are discovering it is absolutely impossible to deal with it: you cannot locate it, and you cannot stop it." See the unity?

And now you know why that's so powerful; why unity is a form of correct thinking that can back intentional action for tremendously successful results.

## HIGHER-PURPOSE THINKING

Which of the following goals do you think people will throw more energy in the form of intentional action behind?

Goal one: a common, everyday pursuit, with low stakes, of little consequence?

Goal two: a pursuit emanating from an elevated existential plane; the clarion call of a higher purpose, coaxing us to pursue a viciously worthwhile goal of incredible impact, significant stakes, and surpassing historical importance? Goal two.

So, the goal of higher-purpose-driven language is to create higher-purpose-driven thinking, which sees your definite purpose as a goal two, not a goal one.

## DOES YOUR GOAL DRAG THEM DOWN OR RAISE THEM UP?

GOAL ONE

THEIR BASELINE

GOAL TWO

FIGURE 126: Higher-purpose thinking occurs when your goal pulls them up instead of dragging them down.

Understand? This is everywhere in history's examples of the communication of leadership. FDR did it. MLK did it. JFK did it. LBJ did it. Why? Why did they all do it? They all created higher-purpose thinking because they all understood that it is one of the best forms of correct thinking that backs intentional action, empowering it with effortless ease.

But how did they do it? I'll give you three strategies. With elevated language. With enumerated impact. With raised stakes.

What is elevated language? Elevated language is evocative, eloquent, and compelling; it makes us feel something; it gives us goosebumps. It's the stuff we can listen to over and over again in our favorite songs without getting bored. Why? Because we feel something every single time.

What is enumerated impact? Enumerated impact is clearly and concisely explaining what is at stake. It is telling everyone how the subject has an impact. And what did I tell you about impact? Impact is about how a subject hurts or helps people. Keep that in mind. It all comes back to people and their stories.

What are raised stakes? Raised stakes are explaining the impact of something, and then elevating that impact to a more extreme position. It's saying "here's what will happen as a result of this subject – this is the impact of this, and why we need to make things happen now... but it gets yet more extreme – it gets yet more compelling, because [insert raised stakes] will also happen." The art of raising the stakes is the art of making it seem like so much is riding on the outcome of a pursuit, and that it is of utmost, unparalleled importance to everyone.

Want an example of these principles in action? Let's draw one from the birth of this country. At the start, I bolded the examples of elevated language. I challenge you to find them further. I italicized markers of the enumerated impact and raised stakes.

"No man thinks more highly than I do of the **patriotism**, as well as abilities, of the very **worthy** gentlemen who have just addressed the House. But different men often see the same subject in different lights; and, therefore, I hope it will not be thought disrespectful to those gentlemen if, entertaining as I do opinions of a character very opposite to theirs, I shall speak forth my sentiments freely and without reserve. This is no time for ceremony. The question before the House is one of **awful** moment to this country *(enumerated impact)*. For my own part, I consider it as nothing less than a question of **freedom** or **slavery** *(enumerated impact)*; and in proportion to the magnitude of the subject ought to be the **freedom** of the debate *(enumerated impact)*. It is only in this way that we can hope to arrive at **truth**, and fulfill the **great responsibility** which we hold to **God** and our **country**. Should I keep back my opinions at such a time, through fear of giving offense, I should consider myself as **guilty of treason** toward my country, and of an **act of disloyalty** toward the **Majesty of Heaven**, which I **revere** above all **earthly kings**.

Mr. President, it is natural to man to indulge in the **illusions of hope**. We are apt to **shut our eyes** against a **painful truth**, and listen to the **song of that siren** till she transforms us into **beasts**. Is this the part of **wise** men, engaged in a **great and arduous struggle for liberty**? Are we disposed to be of the number of those who, **having eyes, see not, and, having ears, hear not**, the things which so nearly concern their **temporal salvation**? For my part, whatever **anguish of spirit** it may cost, I am willing to know the whole **truth**; to know the worst, and to provide for it.

I have but one lamp by which my feet are guided, and that is the lamp of experience. I know of no way of judging of the future but by the past. And judging by the past, I wish to know what there has been in the conduct of the British ministry for the last ten years to justify those hopes with which gentlemen have been pleased to solace themselves and the House. Is it that insidious smile with which our petition has been lately received *(enumerated impact)*? Trust it not, sir; it will prove a snare to your feet *(enumerated impact)*. Suffer not yourselves to be betrayed with a kiss. Ask yourselves how this gracious reception of our petition comports with those warlike preparations which cover our waters and darken our land *(enumerated impact)*. Are fleets and armies necessary to a work of love and reconciliation *(enumerated impact)*? Have we shown ourselves so unwilling to be reconciled that force must be called in to win back our love *(enumerated impact)*? Let us not deceive ourselves, sir. These are the implements of war and subjugation *(enumerated impact)*; the last arguments to which kings resort. I ask gentlemen, sir, what means this martial array, if its purpose be not to force us to submission *(enumerated impact)*? Can gentlemen assign any other possible motive for it? Has Great Britain any enemy, in this quarter of the world, to call for all this accumulation of navies and armies? No, sir, she has none. They are meant for us *(enumerated impact)*: they can be meant for no other. They are sent over to bind and rivet upon us those chains which the British ministry have been so long forging *(enumerated impact)*. And what have we to oppose to them? Shall we try argument? Sir, we have been trying that for the last ten years. Have we anything new to offer upon the subject? Nothing *(enumerated impact)*. We have held the subject up in every light of which it is capable; but it has been all in vain. Shall we resort to entreaty and humble supplication? What terms shall we find which have not been already exhausted? Let us not, I beseech you, sir, deceive ourselves. Sir, we have done everything that could be done to avert the storm which is now coming on *(enumerated impact)*. We have petitioned; we have remonstrated; we have supplicated; we have prostrated ourselves before the throne, and have implored its interposition to arrest the tyrannical hands of the ministry and Parliament *(enumerated impact)*. Our petitions have been slighted (*enumerated impact);* our remonstrances have produced additional violence and insult (*enumerated impact);* our supplications have been disregarded (*enumerated impact);* and we have been spurned (*enumerated impact)*, with contempt, from the foot of the throne *(enumerated impact)!* In vain, after these things, may we indulge the fond hope of peace and reconciliation. There is no longer any room for hope. If we wish to be free *(raised stakes)* – if we mean to preserve inviolate those inestimable privileges for which we have been so long contending *(raised stakes)* – if we mean not basely to abandon the noble struggle in which we have been so long engaged (raised stakes), and which we have pledged ourselves never to abandon until the glorious object of our contest shall be obtained *(raised stakes)* – we must fight *(raised stakes)!* I repeat it, sir, we must fight! An appeal to arms and to the God of hosts is all that is left us *(raised stakes)!*

They tell us, sir, that we are weak; unable to cope with so formidable an adversary. But when shall we be stronger? Will it be the next week, or the next year? Will it be when we are totally disarmed, and when a British guard shall be stationed in every house *(raised stakes)?* Shall we gather strength by irresolution and inaction? Shall we acquire the means of effectual resistance by lying supinely on our backs and hugging the delusive phantom of hope, until our enemies shall have bound us hand and foot *(raised stakes)?* Sir, we are not weak if we make a proper use of those means which the God of nature hath placed in our power. The millions of people, armed in the holy cause of liberty, and in such a country as that which we possess, are invincible by any force which our enemy can send against us *(raised stakes)*. Besides, sir, we shall not fight our battles alone. There is a just God who presides over the destinies of nations, and who will raise up friends to fight our battles for us *(raised stakes)*. The battle, sir, is not to the strong alone; it is to the vigilant, the active, the brave. Besides, sir, we have no election. If we were base enough to desire it, it is now too late to retire from the contest. There is no retreat but in submission and slavery *(raised stakes)!* Our chains are forged *(raised stakes)!* Their clanking may be heard on the plains of Boston (raised s*takes)!* The war is inevitable – and let it come *(raised stakes)!* I repeat it, sir, let it come *(raised stakes)*.

It is in vain, sir, to extenuate the matter. Gentlemen may cry, Peace, Peace – but there is no peace. The war is actually begun *(raised stakes)!* The next gale that sweeps from the north will bring to our ears the clash of resounding arms *(raised stakes)!* Our brethren are already in the field *(raised stakes)!* Why stand we here idle? What is it that gentlemen wish? What would they have? Is life so dear, or peace so sweet, as to be purchased at the price of chains and slavery *(raised stakes)?* Forbid it, Almighty God! I know not what course others may take; but as for me, give me liberty or give me death (*raised stakes)!"*

Is there anyone who can listen to these immortal words and not feel called to ambitious action and to account and to audacity by a higher purpose?

Now you know why.

Elevated language.

Enumerated impact.

Raised stakes.

The triad of higher-purpose-driven language.

But now, we turn to another strategy, one that is yet more versatile and compelling, playing upon yet another hidden psychological tendency.

We turn to mirroring.

---

**KEY INSIGHT:**

Elevated Language: "This Matters So Much I Revere It."

Enumerated Impact: "This Might Hurt Us Badly, Or Save Us."

Raised Stakes: "This Might Hurt *Everyone* Badly, Or Save Them."

---

### ACHIEVE MIRRORING

What do these quotes all have in common?

"I believe that I interpret the will of the Congress and of the people when I assert that we will not only defend ourselves to the uttermost, but will make it very certain that this form of treachery shall never again endanger us. With confidence in our armed forces, with the unbounding determination of our people, we will gain the inevitable triumph – so help us God." FDR's address to the nation after the pearl harbor attack.

"I am delighted to be here and I'm particularly delighted to be here on this occasion." JFK's speech at Rice University, advancing the goal of landing a man on the moon.

"I have, myself, full confidence that if all do their duty, if nothing is neglected, and if the best arrangements are made, as they are being made, we shall prove ourselves once again able to defend our Island home, to ride out the storm of war, and to outlive the menace of tyranny, if necessary for years, if necessary alone." Winston Churchill's "We Shall Never Surrender" speech.

"You and I, as individuals, can, by borrowing, live beyond our means, but for only a limited period of time. Why, then, should we think that collectively, as a nation, we are not bound by that same limitation?" Ronald Reagan's first inaugural address.

"Speaking for myself, I can say that I have never felt any hatred. As a matter of fact, I feel myself to be a greater friend of the British now than ever before." Mahatma Gandhi's "Quit India" speech.

"I know I have the body of a weak, feeble woman; but I have the heart and stomach of a king, and of a king of England too, and think foul scorn that Parma or Spain, or any prince of Europe, should dare to invade the borders of my realm; to which rather than any dishonour shall grow by me, I myself will take up arms, I myself will be your general, judge, and rewarder of every one of your virtues in the field." Queen Elizabeth I's speech to her army in 1588.

Did you figure it out? Did you find their commonality? It's the principle of mirroring.

It's not "we ought to have this quality," but "I have this quality."

What's mirroring?

We discussed it previously in a different context. To redefine it, leader-mirroring is when people look to their leader and subconsciously mirror his or her sentiments.

And so, these quotes all represent the same strategy: the legendary leaders presented their own correct thinking because they knew that listeners would mirror it. Leader-mirroring is the essence of leading by example.

I'm a big fan of military history, and I was reading through some World War Two manuals of German squad tactics for squad leaders. It said something along the lines of "as squad leader, if there is a cowardly, discomposed, or crying soldier in your squad, do not try to forcefully reorient him; instead, behave courageously yourself, for he will then *mirror your courage.*"

### KEY INSIGHT:

# I Once Said We Have Four Languages: Words, Voice, Body, and Visuals. I Forgot the Language of Action.

## THE LEADER-MIRRORING PRINCIPLE VISUALIZED

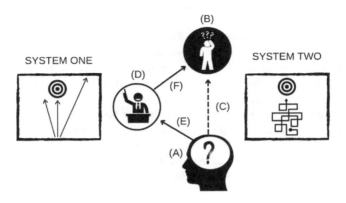

FIGURE 127: Prompted by a question (A), we seek to evaluate the target question of "how should I think and feel" (B). However, this evaluation (C) is difficult. So, we substitute the heuristic question "what is my leader doing" (D), evaluate this (E), and transfer the answer to the target question (F).

That's the same principle at play. Let's revisit the six examples that opened this chapter.

The first example? FDR presented his interpretation of the will of Congress and of the people, as well as his confidence, because he wanted people to mirror that interpretation and confidence in a positive outcome to the conflict.

The second example? JFK presented his excitement and personal delight to be there on that occasion because he wanted people to mirror that excitement and delight.

The third example? Winston Churchill presented his confidence in Great Britain's ability to succeed because he wanted people to mirror that confidence.

The fourth example? Ronald Reagan presented his intuitive personal understanding of limitations on financial borrowing because he wanted people to mirror that intuitive understanding.

The fifth example? Gandhi presented his love and peaceful sentiment toward the British people because he wanted people to mirror that love and peace in their hearts and minds.

The sixth example? Queen Elizabeth I presented her iron will and determination to defend her country no matter the cost because she wanted her army to mirror that selfless devotion.

## WHAT TO TELL PEOPLE TO INSPIRE THEM TO BELIEVE

SET OF POSSIBLE CHARACTER TRAITS

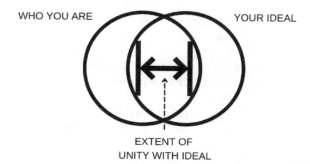

FIGURE 128: To get people to believe in themselves, tell them that they already are who they need to be to do what they want to do.

## WHAT TO TELL PEOPLE TO GIVE THEM SELF-CONFIDENCE

SET OF CONCIEVABLE ACCOMPLISHMENTS

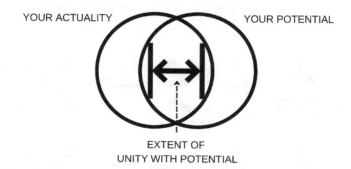

FIGURE 129: To get people to believe in themselves, tell them that they already are who they need to be to do what they want to do; show them how much of their potential they have already actualized.

Mirroring is a compelling, effective, and powerful tool for backing intentional action with correct thinking. But the best part? It's easy. :)

## ALL-IN THINKING

When I first read *Think and Grow Rich*, by Napoleon Hill, five years ago, something stuck with me in particular.

The second time I read it two years ago, the importance of this story was reinforced. And the third time I read it earlier this year, it was reinforced yet more. The story? I'll break it down to its bare essentials.

Ferdinand Magellan (a man whose pursuits we find immoral today) took a bunch of boats with soldiers to the distant shores of a foreign land. There, he encountered natives; natives he had to defeat in battle to claim this new, lucrative land for his home country, and collect the metallic riches hidden in its caves.

Just one problem. These natives were particularly fierce, fearsome, and brave in battle; they were more than capable of defeating his cadre of combatants, well equipped with guns, pikes, and steel armor as his invading troop may have been.

So, what did he do? He landed on shore, unloaded his ships, set up camp on the beach, and then did something very, very stupid. Or maybe brilliant. What did he do? He set fire to his boats.

Why? Because, once he did that, there was no going back. Beat them in battle, or die trying. No retreat. No surrender. Not because he said so, but because it would be impossible, what with the fact that he burned their ships.

The only option was to win.

### REVEALING THE IMMENSE POWER OF ALL-IN THINKING

FIGURE 130: When you cut off all routs of escape, people give 100% of themselves. This is why the common adage to "never back an enemy into a corner" holds true. When he has no chance but to attack, he will attack, and attack with an unparalleled vigor and strength.

He bound them, chained them, to their goal; he staked the lives of his entire cadre – including his own life – on achieving their goal (though it was a dishonorable goal by contemporary standards).

How does this relate to the topic of this section? I'll tell you. He backed intentional action with all-in thinking. What's that? A type of thinking that produces particularly forceful and effective intentional action; the type of thinking and the resulting action that come from betting a massive amount of one's wellbeing (in this example, one's own life) on achieving a goal; the type of thinking that creates the rare vigor that comes from staking everything on success.

Let's grab another example from World War Two. When Stalin issued order number 227 during the battle of Stalingrad, amidst siege-style warfare to beat back the death and dark destruction wrought by the German army, an order also known as the "not one step back order," which threatened capital punishment on retreating soldiers, the vigor of his armies became animalistic in its force and extremity.

It's the same principle. And these are just illustrations. I'm not an advocate for Stalin's leadership style...

Leaders we can look up to apply the same strategy. Leaders we can appreciate as moral inspire all-in thinking too. Leaders we can (somewhat) agree pursue laudable goals use this method frequently. Though it is not as extreme as burning boats, or issuing order 227, leaders like FDR and Reagan inspired all-in thinking with grand efficacy. Some examples? Let's start with Reagan. Let's examine exactly how he inspired all-in thinking to back intentional action in pursuit of his definite goal of reducing the size of government.

"We are at war with the most dangerous enemy that has ever faced mankind in his long climb from the swamp to the stars, and it has been said if we lose that war, and in doing so lose this way of freedom of ours, history will record with the greatest astonishment that those who had the most to lose did the least to prevent its happening. Not too long ago, two friends of mine were talking to a Cuban refugee, a businessman who had escaped from Castro, and in the midst of his story one of my friends turned to the other and said, *'We don't know how lucky we are.' And the Cuban stopped and said, 'How lucky you are? I had someplace to escape to.' And in that sentence, he told us the entire story. If we lose freedom here, there's no place to escape to. This is the last stand on Earth.* And this idea that government is beholden to the people, that it has no other source of power except to sovereign people, is still the newest and most unique idea in all the long history of man's relation to man."

And now, let's examine exactly how FDR inspired all-in thinking to back intentional action in pursuit of his definite goal of increasing the size of government. This increase was in response to the Great Depression, and was defined by his "New Deal." (This New Deal is the increase in size Reagan sought to reverse).

"But in the event that the Congress shall fail to take one of these two courses, and in the event that the national emergency is still critical, I shall not evade the clear course of duty that will then confront me. I shall ask the Congress for the one remaining instrument to meet the crisis – broad Executive power to wage a war against the emergency, as great as the power that would be given to me if we were in fact invaded by a foreign foe."

What do these two examples from pure political opposites have in common?

They both represent the leaders creating all-in thinking, though in two different ways. Reagan created all-in thinking by way of burning boats; or rather, not by burning boats, but by drawing attention to the fact that there are no boats to turn to if the tragedy of freedom's death happens in the United States; by expressing that there is no untainted island to sail to if freedom falls in America.

That's the first form of all-in thinking: "we have no salvation if we fail here."

FDR created all-in thinking by committing a massive amount of resources to his definite purpose; by expressing that his absolute goal commanded his energy absolutely; by publicly pledging extreme, energetic action to ease the emergency, such as the expansion of executive power if Congress fails to pursue his agenda.

That's the second form of all-in thinking: "we are going to commit a massive amount of our resources to this goal."

Both are effective, and yes, you can use both. Great. We are almost finished with part four. After this, we turn to part five: how to back the entire process with a powerful motive. But for now, we turn to another form of correct thinking, and the final one we discuss in this book: loving thinking.

## LOVING THINKING

Humans love love. But not only love of the romantic brand. Love of community. Love of country. Love of family. Love of self. Love of cause. Love of friends. Love of journey. Love of humanity. We are enamored by these things. For all the sins recorded in our history – which some might say is just a record of our mistakes, and an embarrassing one at that – there is still a lot of love to be found in the story of our time on this Earth. A lot of sacrifice. A lot of virtue. A lot of goodness.

I will not belabor this topic. All legendary leaders communicate in a way that creates loving thinking. In fact, that's what you've seen this entire chapter, in nearly every single example we've discussed. In nearly every single example, you've seen the elevation of love; the elevation of our highest virtue, our virtue from which all values flow, such that, in its absence, we can find ourselves nowhere but in the vicious grip of vice.

One of the finest examples of a legendary leader creating loving thinking is found in the immortal words of Aung San Suu Kyi. Who is she? The leader of Myanmar's National League for Democracy Party. She won a Nobel Prize, and drew inspiration for how to peacefully conduct her movement from Gandhi and the American Civil Rights Movement. And here are some of her immortal words. "Of the sweets of adversity, and let me say that these are not numerous, I have found the sweetest, the most precious of all, is the lesson I learnt on the value of kindness. Every kindness I received, small or big, convinced me that there could never be enough of it in our world. To be kind is to respond with sensitivity and human warmth to the hopes and needs of others. Even the briefest touch of kindness can lighten a heavy heart. Kindness can change the lives of people."

Loving thinking is not a supplement, but a prerequisite.

## DESCRIBE LEADERSHIP

A seemingly elementary but secretly effective strategy is describing the qualities of your own leadership. It seems fairly basic, right? Correct. This is basic. And yet, why do so many of our examples of legendary leaders producing legendary communication flock to this strategy like moths to a flame? Because it works.

What does it do?

It sets the tone for your leadership.

It sets the context through which your proposals will be viewed.

It sets the mutual understanding of what you are going to do, and how you see your role.

It sets expectations. Some examples? Let's draw our first from FDR's inaugural address. "I am certain that my fellow Americans expect that on my induction into the Presidency *I will address them with a candor and a decision which the present situation of our Nation impels.* This is preeminently the time to speak the truth, the whole truth, frankly and boldly. Nor need we shrink from honestly facing conditions in our country today. This great Nation will endure as it has endured, will revive and will prosper. So, first of all, let me assert my firm belief that the only thing we have to fear is fear itself – nameless, unreasoning, unjustified terror which paralyzes needed efforts to convert retreat into advance. *In every dark hour of our national life a leadership of frankness and vigor has met with that understanding and support of the people themselves which is essential to victory. I am convinced that you will again give that support to leadership in these critical days.*"

He characterizes his own leadership as one with candor, decisiveness, frankness, vigor, and one that he expects will receive the understanding and support of the people.

### KEY INSIGHT:

# Framing Your Leadership Is Necessary, Unavoidable, and Establishes the Expectations that Shape the Future.

## WHEN IT'S OKAY TO TELL YOUR AUDIENCE ABOUT YOURSELF

FIGURE 131: While it may seem like leaders often talk about themselves, they are often talking about the audience through the lens of their own lives. There's a crucial difference between this and self-aggrandizing talk.

Another example? Let's draw our second example from Pete Buttigieg's 2020 announcement speech for his ultimately unsuccessful, but very impressive, presidential run. I cut some segments in between these portions of the speech that represent this strategy to make it clearer and more concise, and I italicized the leadership-characterizing language.

"So that's why I'm here today, joining you to make a little news. My name is Pete Buttigieg. They call me Mayor Pete. *I am a proud son of South Bend, Indiana.* And I am running for president of the United States.

I recognize the *audacity* of doing this as a *Midwestern millennial mayor. More than a little bold – at age 37 –* to seek the highest office in the land.

*I take the long view because I have to. I come from the generation that grew up with school shootings as the norm, the generation that produced the bulk of the troops in the post-9/11 conflicts, the generation that is going to be on the business end of climate change for as long as we live.*

A generation that stands to be the first ever in America to come out worse off economically than our parents if we don't do something truly different.

This is one of those rare moments between whole eras in the life of our nation. I was born in another such moment, in the early 1980s, when a half-century of New Deal liberalism gave way to forty years of Reagan supply-side conservatism that created the terms for how Democrats as well as Republicans made policy. And that era, too, is now over.

Such a moment calls for *hopeful and audacious voices from communities like ours. And yes, it calls for a new generation of leadership.*"

Now, what does this do?

Why is this a compelling strategy?

Because it sets up the framework of values – and the personal background that created this value-framework – which will govern the relation of leader to follower as a binding social contract. It tells people that "this is who I am, this is where I come from, and this is what you can expect from me."

It also produces trust, and trust is an essential element not only of all effective leadership but all worthwhile communication. Without trust, communication (and leadership) fail. With trust, they both flourish, even in the absence of much else, like basic competency. Trust is that important. But this strategy goes a little deeper. The New York Times annotated this announcement speech. Here's what they had to say about the excerpts I presented.

The first annotation, that "Mr. Buttigieg's fans often liken him to Barack Obama, because of his youth and persona as a cerebral outsider. This line is an almost explicit invocation of Mr. Obama's 2007 announcement speech, when he said, 'I recognize there is a certain presumptuousness, a certain audacity' to a junior senator like him seeking the presidency. Mr. Buttigieg uses Obama-esque flourishes throughout, including more than half a dozen references each to 'hope' and 'change.'"

The second annotation, that "This is the big idea behind Mr. Buttigieg's campaign, that there is an intellectual and social cohesion to the population of voters under 40, and that only a person who shares their experiences and mind-set can address the problems common to this group. Climate change, which he deals with at greater length later in the speech, may be the most important example – the best case study, as Mr. Buttigieg tells it, in how people who will have to feel the longest-term consequences of a social problem are best equipped to deal with it."

What does this all come down to?

That through self-characterization, staying within the fine line that marks the boundary of the territory of braggadocios self-centeredness, Buttigieg represented that his leadership has a compelling set of qualities to the average voter, at least of his party.

Quality #1: son of a small, recently economically downtrodden middle-America town.

Quality #2: Midwestern.

Quality #3: millennial.

Quality #4: Mayor.

Quality #5: more than a little bold.

Quality #6: 37 years old.

Quality #7: takes the long view.

Quality #8: comes from the generation that grew up with school shootings as the norm.

Quality #9: comes from the generation that produced the bulk of troops for post-9/11 conflicts.

Quality #10: comes from the generation that is going to deal with the aftereffects of climate change for their entire lives.

Quality #11: comes from the first generation in American history to potentially be worse off economically than their parents.

Quality #12: born in a confusing, ethos-less "blank-page" moment between distinct eras.

Quality #13: hopeful.

Quality #14: audacious.

Quality #15: representative of a new generation of leadership.

This set of qualities tells us something.

What does it tell us? It tells us that this strategy is about reading the room; it is about being in-tune with the flux of opinion, knowing where it diverges and converges, and subtly but decisively representing your leadership as capable of mending – or at least not aggravating – the divergence, while expertly satisfying the convergence.

This strategy – done right – calls upon a massive amount of clairvoyance; it demands an immense quantity of awareness. And there's an even better way to represent this. I'd like to advance the idea of an ideal leadership formula.

What's an ideal leadership formula?

The set of qualities of what most people in a group – or as an inferior alternative, a sub-group or sub-coalition – would agree define their ideal leader. So, characterize your leadership as one that fits this ideal leadership formula.

That's what FDR tried to do, and Pete as well; they both asked themselves, "what do people want to see in their leader right now?" and "how can I represent myself as satisfying those desires?"

## PRESENTING YOURSELF AS THE LEADER THEY WANT

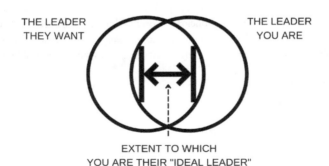

SET OF POSSIBLE QUALITIES

THE LEADER THEY WANT

THE LEADER YOU ARE

EXTENT TO WHICH
YOU ARE THEIR "IDEAL LEADER"

FIGURE 132: Satisfying the ideal leadership formula is a matter of presenting to people that you have the qualities they are looking for in a leader right now.

Simple, but effective. And now, we turn to our final and shortest step in the process. The four steps thus far covered are the core of the process of the communication of leadership, but by no means does that render the final step – which we cover now, in part five – unimportant. It's just that it has inadvertently been satisfied in the process of achieving these first four steps, leaving us three remaining strategies that fall under its umbrella.

They are three critical strategies, however, not to be brushed aside as peripheral to your goals but to be understood as deeply powerful strategies for empowering your people, your communication, and thus, your leadership.

## YOU COMPLETED STEP FOUR OF FIVE

FIGURE 133: In this chapter, you learned how to complete the fourth step: back intentional action with correct thinking.

.................................Chapter Summary.................................

- Explain your Logos, or the axiomatic moral principles animating your cause and your coalition.
- Empower virtuous, hopeful, opportunistic, unified, all-in, loving, and higher-purpose thinking.
- Inspiring the correct habits of thought produces much more powerful and sustained impact in the real world.
- Describe your leadership to establish a clear-cut hierarchy of expectations, beliefs, and values.
- Present guaranteed victory and strive to attain some level of certainty to inspire massive enthusiasm.
- Achieve mirroring by presenting the qualities you want your audience to adopt in yourself. They will mirror them.

**KEY INSIGHT:**

Presenting Yourself as the Leader They Want Does Not Mean Hiding Your True Character, Deceiving, or Manipulating.

Rather, It Means Shaping Your Character to Develop the Virtues the Moment Demands, And It Means Communicating Your Commitment to Those Virtues.

In Part, the Public and Verbal Commitment Serves as a Forcing Function, a Crucial Step to Accountability.

## THE FIVE-STEP FRAMEWORK (PART FOUR)

| 1 | Controlling Attention |
|------|------------------------------|
| 1.1 | Portray Empathy |
| 1.2 | Portray Authority |
| 1.3 | Set High Expectations |
| 1.4 | Expose a Hidden Miracle |
| 1.5 | Speak to the People's Pain |
| 1.6 | Build a Coalition |
| 1.7 | Make Bold Promises |
| 1.8 | Divulge the Brutal Truth |
| 1.9 | Shift the Perspective |
| 1.10 | Speak to Broken Justice Problems |
| 1.11 | Present a Moment of Decision |
| 1.12 | Tell a Story |
| 1.13 | Future Significance Today |
| 1.14 | Difficulty-Confidence Matrix |
| 1.15 | Declaratory Cascade |
| 1.16 | Superabundance |
| 1.17 | Speak to the Moment |
| 2 | Directing Attention to a Definite Purpose |
| 2.1 | Achieve Singularity |
| 2.2 | Organize a Pyramid |
| 2.3 | Create Visualization |

| 4.3 | Virtuous Thinking |
|---|---|
| 4.4 | Hopeful Thinking |
| 4.5 | Opportunistic Thinking |
| 4.6 | Unified Thinking |
| 4.7 | Higher-Purpose Thinking |
| 4.8 | Achieve Mirroring |
| 4.9 | All-In Thinking |
| 4.10 | Loving Thinking |
| 4.11 | Describe Leadership |
| 5 | Backing the Entire Process with a Powerful Motive |

**KEY INSIGHT:**

# The Three Strategies in Our Next and Final Section Are Not Afterthoughts. They Are Powerful Principles that Should Permeate and Inform Your Entire Message.

# YOUR LOGOS IS THE HEART OF EVERYTHING

SUSTAINED (HONEST) INQUIRY OF ANY ASPECT
OF YOUR MOVEMENT ENDS AT YOUR LOGOS,
YOUR MORAL "FIRST PRINCIPLES"

**Claim These Free Resources that Will Help You Unleash the Power of Your Words and Speak with Confidence. Visit www.speakforsuccesshub.com/toolkit for Access.**

**2 Free Workbooks**

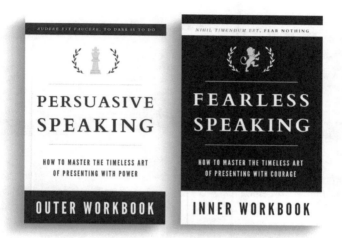

We'll send you two free workbooks, including long-lost excerpts by Dale Carnegie, the mega-bestselling author of *How to Win Friends and Influence People* (5,000,000 copies sold). *Fearless Speaking* guides you in the proven principles of mastering your inner game as a speaker. *Persuasive Speaking* guides you in the time-tested tactics of mastering your outer game by maximizing the power of your words. All of these resources complement the Speak for Success collection.

**Claim These Free Resources that Will Help You Unleash the Power of Your Words and Speak with Confidence. Visit www.speakforsuccesshub.com/toolkit for Access.**

**18 Free PDF Resources**

*12 Iron Rules for Captivating Story, 21 Speeches that Changed the World, 341-Point Influence Checklist, 143 Persuasive Cognitive Biases, 17 Ways to Think On Your Feet, 18 Lies About Speaking Well, 137 Deadly Logical Fallacies, 12 Iron Rules For Captivating Slides, 371 Words that Persuade, 63 Truths of Speaking Well, 27 Laws of Empathy, 21 Secrets of Legendary Speeches, 19 Scripts that Persuade, 12 Iron Rules For Captivating Speech, 33 Laws of Charisma, 11 Influence Formulas, 219-Point Speech-Writing Checklist, 21 Eloquence Formulas*

**Claim These Free Resources that Will Help You Unleash the Power of Your Words and Speak with Confidence. Visit www.speakforsuccesshub.com/toolkit for Access.**

### 30 Free Video Lessons

We'll send you one free video lesson every day for 30 days, written and recorded by Peter D. Andrei. Days 1-10 cover authenticity, the prerequisite to confidence and persuasive power. Days 11-20 cover building self-belief and defeating communication anxiety. Days 21-30 cover how to speak with impact and influence, ensuring your words change minds instead of falling flat. Authenticity, self-belief, and impact – this course helps you master three components of confidence, turning even the most high-stakes presentations from obstacles into opportunities.

# SPEAK FOR SUCCESS COLLECTION BOOK

# III

# HOW LEGENDARY LEADERS SPEAK CHAPTER

# VI

# STEP FIVE:

## Three Ways to Back the Entire Process with a Powerful Motive

## ACHIEVE ALIGNMENT

I FIND MYSELF WRITING THE SAME EIGHT MAGIC WORDS over and over again in all my books on communication.

The eight magic words?

"Alignment is the foundation of influence and impact."

What is alignment?

It is the tool you use to guarantee that what your audience wants connects to your communication. Or rather, that your communication connects to what your audience wants. Alignment is taking your subject – which your audience might not care about – and connecting it to something that they do care about.

If your subject is block-chain information aggregation in the healthcare industry, do not assume people share your passion for block-chain information aggregation in the healthcare industry. Instead, align this arcane, highly niched subject to something you know with certainty they care about: saving lives.

Alignment is asking yourself the question, "At the end of the day, what are the impacts on these people's lives that result as a consequence of my subject?" and then making those impacts a core element of your communication. Alignment is connecting what you care about to what people care about because this will make them care about what you care about.

Get it? Now, how do you determine what people care about? Apply analysis based on three qualities: saliency, intensity, and stability. This following excerpt first appeared in my first book, *How to Master Public Speaking*, and it will appear in every single publication I produce on the subject of communication theory for the rest of my life.

"Every single statement has three qualities: saliency, intensity, and stability. Every statement has these qualities in varying amounts, and the most compelling statements have the most of all of them.

Saliency refers to how many people care about a given subject, or in other words, how important a given subject is. It is the portion of the population that cares about something.

Intensity is a measure of how strongly people care about a subject. It is a measure of how much energy people are willing to devote to one topic.

Stability is how long people are willing to continue caring about a given subject, or how easy it is to switch the opinions of those who do care about a given subject.

In summary, saliency is how many people care, intensity is how much they care, and stability is for how long they will care.

Because saliency, intensity, and stability are not intuitive concepts, here's another helpful way to think about them: saliency is how important a topic is, intensity is how important it is to those who think it's important, and stability is for how long it will be important to those who think it's important.

Every compelling subject or statement is salient, intense, and stable: by combining these three qualities, you can maximize the chance that what you're saying will have an impact on your audience and that they will tune in. In many cases, however, your topic might not be salient, intense, or stable. In this case, the best strategy is to find the most salient, intense, and stable consequences of what you're speaking about and deliberately connect them to your subject.

Everything of impact occurring in the real world has consequences and is connected to other occurrences. Many topics are part of an interconnected consequence web of second, third, and fourth order effects, in which everything impacts everything else in one way or another.

## THIS IS HOW YOU DRAW PEOPLE INTO YOUR ORBIT

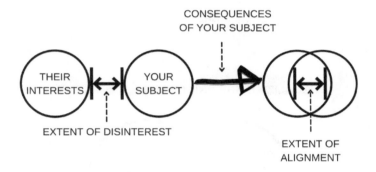

FIGURE 134: Connect your subject to their interest by discussing the consequences of your subject that connect to their interests.

By tapping into and connecting your subject to another one which is more salient, intense, and stable, you gain the very useful benefit of speaking in terms of something which most people in your audience will care about, which they will care about strongly, and which they will continue caring about long after you finish your speech. Stability is particularly important: stability is essentially the longevity of concern, interest, or relevance your ideas have to your audience. If they only care about what you're saying when you're saying it, and not after or even before you've said it, that's obviously not a good situation. Avoid this by connecting your idea to something you know your audience will care about in the long run.

As any career politician will vehemently assert, the economy is the most salient, intense, and stable issue. People will vote for a candidate who has a disappointing personal track record if they believe that he or she will lower their taxes. People love money. It's that simple. In order for our climatologist to tap into the salient, intense, and stable nature of how the general population thinks about the economy, money, and personal finance, they can say something like this: 'To my understanding, people usually don't realize how expensive climate change will be. It's not their fault, of course, but let me illuminate some numbers. The federal government, as well as state governments across the country, will have to increase taxes in order to deal with the consequences of climate change, so the average increase in taxes per person can be up to $1,000 annually.

Similarly, if you live close to a coast, lake, or major river, you might have to pay up to $10,000 to protect your house from flooding caused by climate change.'

It might make you cynical to think that money is high on the list of what people care about, but it shouldn't. It makes sense that it is, so use it to your advantage.

Think of these three qualities as a three-way Venn diagram. In other words, think of them as three circles that each overlap each other. Something can be in only one circle, in two circles, or in the center where they all overlap, and it is enclosed by all three circles. The more circles your subject and theme are enclosed by, the more interested in your speech your audience will be. If your subject either ends up in the middle of that diagram, or you can find a logical connection that brings it there, then your persuasive power will be maximized."

This strategy of aligning your subject to something your audience cares about – something salient, intense, and stable to them – is the essence of backing the entire process with a powerful motive.

**VISUALIZING THE PRINCIPLE OF ALIGNMENT**

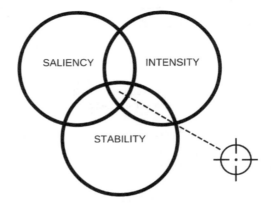

FIGURE 135: Conceive of saliency, intensity, and stability as a three-way Venn-diagram. Ensure your message is salient, intense, and stable; ensure it occupies the central position of the diagram.

**KEY INSIGHT:**

Cared For. Cared For Widely.
Cared For Widely and Intensely.

## UNDERSTANDING WHAT REALLY MOTIVATES PEOPLE

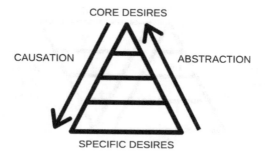

FIGURE 136: Desires higher on the human desire pyramid are more abstract and universal. Lower on the pyramid, they are more concrete and individualized.

## HOW YOUR MESSAGE CAN APPEAL TO ALMOST ANYONE

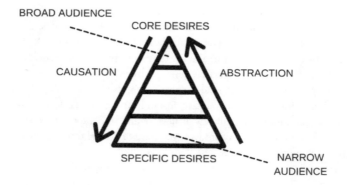

FIGURE 137: To address a broad audience, speak in terms of the core desires almost every human shares. If you are speaking to a narrow, uniformed audience of people who share specific desires, address both specific desires and the core desires at the top of the pyramid.

## WHAT HUMAN DESIRES ARE MOST COMMON?

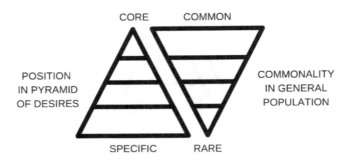

FIGURE 138: This is another way to view the relationship between the tier of a desire and the commonality of that desire in a population.

## RESONATE EMOTIONALLY

What does all communication backed by a powerful motive accomplish? It resonates emotionally. What is the essence of manipulating affect? Raising people from a one to a ten on perception of one of the most common heuristic attributes: affect; feeling; emotion. People substitute the heuristic attribute of "my feelings about X" for the target attribute "the truth of X." We can also say they substitute the heuristic question "how do I feel about X?" with the target question "is X true?"

When people say emotion is key to persuasion, they're right. But why? Because of emotional substitution. If you want to instantly make people love your ideas and proposal, if you want to immediately achieve significantly more influence, and if you want to alter any situation in your favor, you have to do one thing: make people feel a certain way about your proposal.

But how do you make people feel? How do you make people resonate emotionally with your idea? Think of persuasion as invading a castle; the castle of your audience's bias to disconfirm; the castle of your audience's skepticism; the castle of your audience's pain from being lied to over and over again by people who look, sound, and talk just like you.

Logic is just the moat: the channel of water around the castle, designed to keep invaders away from the walls. But emotional resonance will break down the walls and allow your persuasion to penetrate their minds until they are as much on your side as you are.

You have to pass the moat to get to the castle. You have to satisfy their logical "check-box" before they even allow the possibility of emotional resonance working its magic and breaking down their walls. You have to present some evidence, some logic-driven language, and some ethos-building information about your authority and how you have their interests at heart.

But once you do, you need to pull out your emotional resonance. If persuasion-resistance is a tree, emotional resonance is a chainsaw. The thicker the trunk of the tree, the longer you need to keep that chainsaw buzzing.

I took an effective speaking class in college. I was certainly an effective speaker at the time (perhaps one of the most effective in the state of Massachusetts, according to the Massachusetts Speech and Debate League). I just wanted an easy A, and to further immerse myself in the subject I love, while helping some fellow students who needed it. But I'm not going to pretend I didn't learn anything. One of my most vivid memories from the class was the teacher saying something along these lines: "If I want to persuade someone to stop smoking, I should not just hammer them with statistic after statistic about the risks and dangers associated with smoking. I should tell them a story; an emotional one; a personal one. I should say, 'I've heard all the statistics, but I couldn't stop smoking. I learned the habit from my Grandma. What really pushed me to quit was seeing her in her later years; seeing the sparkle slowly extinguish from her eyes as she lacked the lung capacity to join the family in our favorite activities, like hiking; seeing the emotional toll evident in the way she carried herself, and in her saddened face, the toll of knowing what she had sacrificed due to the habit she nurtured for most of her life; seeing the regret on her face and hearing it in her words, when she told me with tear-rimmed eyes, even as she lit yet another cigarette, that if she could do it all over again, she would never have started, though it was too late for her now." Matched with his expert emotional delivery, this story hooked and persuaded us all. Why? Because of emotional resonance.

## THE PROVEN TWO-PRONGED PERSUASIVE ATTACK

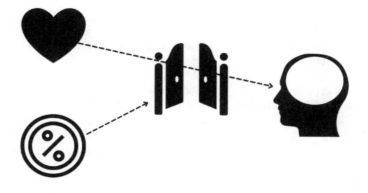

FIGURE 139: Logical argumentation and quantitative evidence opens the gate. It makes people feel safe letting you persuade them. Then, emotional influence goes through that gate to achieve

impact and influence. Of course, this is not a perfect model. Both elements do both tasks, but this is the general division of labor.

All effective communication connects the speaker to the receiver(s), the receiver(s) to the subject, and the subject to the speaker. The communicator creates this three-way connection (the communication triad) by applying words, body language, and vocal tonalities.

The communication toolbox is your words, body language, and vocal tonalities – the tools you have at your disposal to get the job done.

Emotionally resonating stories accomplish the communication triad. The personal story connects the speaker to the receivers. The subject of the story becomes intriguing to the receivers, thus connecting them to it in a compelling way. Finally, the personal story connects the speaker to the subject by expressing the speaker's relationship to it.

## THE FOUNDATION OF ALL EFFECTIVE COMMUNICATION

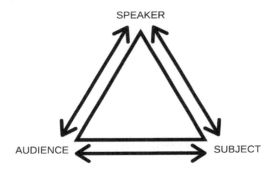

FIGURE 140: Successful communication connects speaker with subject, audience with subject, and speaker with audience, in no particular order.

This is all perfected with emotionally charged words.

Accompany those words with emotionally charged body language (principally facial expressions, which people emotionally mirror the most).

And layer on emotionally charged vocal tonalities.

Remember: You can only achieve emotional impact in the presence of this effective paralanguage; in the presence of impactful vocal modulation and body language.

Tell a personal, emotional story with emotional words, emotional body language, and emotional vocal modulation, completing the three connections in the triad for massive emotional resonance.

## THE FOUNDATION OF ALL EMOTIONAL PARALANGUAGE

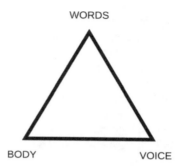

FIGURE 141: Your "public speaking toolbox" or "communication toolbox" consists of the three components of your communication: your words, body language, and vocal tonalities. Nearly every piece of communication advice relates to improving one of these three tools.

## EMOTIONAL PARALANGUAGE AND THE THREE CONNECTIONS

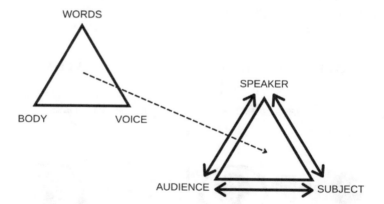

FIGURE 142: You form the three connections in the public speaking triad by using your three languages. You interconnect the speaker, audience, and subject by using your words, body language, and voice. Emotional paralanguage delivering an emotional story forms these connections around pathos.

I just handed you a chainsaw.

I just gave you a Trojan Horse.

I was talking to a friend who was involved in operating the apparatus of a national political campaign devoted to whipping up votes, support, and donations from my state.

He told me something interesting. He said that when canvassing (going door-to-door to help undecided voters come to the obviously correct conclusion that they should vote for your candidate), you have to use a particular strategy – and it's not what anyone thinks.

I was fascinated, and this confirmed a long-term hunch of mine. It also evoked an image of a Trojan Horse. The Trojan Horse (a personal story) was how the Greek military (your persuasive ideas) invaded the impervious walls of Troy (your audience's persuasion resistance); they built a giant wooden horse, and stuck a small squadron of Greek soldiers in it, before offering it as an olive-branch to Troy.

The Trojans took it in without realizing what it contained. As a result, the Greek soldiers managed to take the city from within after years of brutal and unsuccessful siege combat from outside the walls.

Let me explain the canvassing strategy. What do you not do? Go in there and say, "Here's why you should vote for this candidate." That's the intuitive image of persuasion we assume goes down in these door-to-door meetings. It's jumping straight to leading. And that's what the Greeks were doing for years before they got the Trojan Horse idea.

The better strategy is to do something entirely different. Something that embeds the elements of persuasion in the sneaky, subtle facade of a personal story. So, instead of saying, "here's why you should vote for this candidate," you're supposed to say, "I was once undecided myself. The reason I am now a supporter of this candidate is that…" and tell the story of your conversion from undecided to decided.

## TELLING STORIES THAT WIN HEARTS AND CHANGE MINDS

ATTACKING DIRECTLY

THE TROJAN HORSE TECHNIQUE

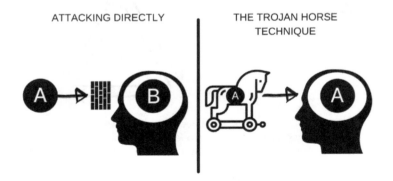

FIGURE 143: Instead of approaching your persuasive prospects by flatly stating the core persuasive epiphany you would like them

> to adopt, embed this persuasive epiphany in a story that will give
> them the ingredients to experience the belief-shift themselves.

It is a form of pacing and leading. More accurately, it is pacing and leading layered under a story of your conversion.

It activates the intuitive bias. It activates countless functions of human psychology that we discussed, all in your favor.

It is gentle, and gentle persuasion builds credibility while overt and aggressive persuasion destroys it.

It fosters likeability, and people find those they like much more credible.

It is conversational and promotes two-way communication, which is attention-grabbing. Attention is a prerequisite for credibility because it is a prerequisite for communication and communication is a prerequisite for credibility. In short, the strategy is this: Embedding persuasive elements in a personal story or the story of someone similar to your audience.

Maybe like this: "I used to believe X because… and now I believe Y, because…"

Or like this: "I used to believe X. One time I [insert personal story]. This was when I realized that [insert what you want them to believe]."

And even this: "I used to be a fervent opponent of X, but after I experienced a particular moment that I will never forget, I realized that maybe it wasn't so bad all along. What happened was [insert personal story]."

The stories should be personal and should foster a connection between you and your audience. This is always true: First connect, then persuade. That is not merely a better way. It is the only way.

But that's just one way of achieving emotional resonance and manipulating affect. The other is with empathy. How do you achieve emotional resonance by way of empathy? By describing in vivid detail your audience's emotional state; expressing their struggle as a shared struggle; presenting body language and vocal tonality that imply the following: "I feel what you feel."

### KEY INSIGHT:

## Connection is the First Step to Persuasion. To Change What They Believe, Know Why They Believe It. To Open Others Up to Being Persuaded, Open Yourself Up to Being Persuaded.

## CONNOTATION IS ANOTHER WAY TO RESONATE

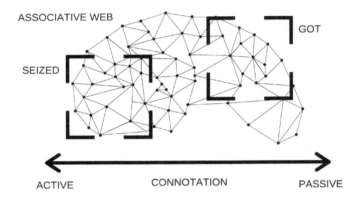

FIGURE 144: Resonating with your audience is expressing how your range of relevant emotions mirrors theirs. One way to do this is with connotation. Seemingly synonymous words carry different tones and implications; they connote different emotional textures in addition to their similar meanings. Compare the emotional implications surrounding the word "got" and those surrounding the word "seized."

## UNDERSTAND IMPACT

Impact. I've said it before, and I'll say it again: impact is about people. If it's not about people, nobody will care. Bill Clinton's campaign had a special slogan repeated by members of his political apparatus to keep them on message. It was designed to guarantee that they never forgot the key component of their message; a component so persuasive, impactful, and motivating that I believe (as a proponent of communication theory) it won him the election. The slogan?

"It's the economy, stupid."

It was this often-single-minded focus on the economy, matched with his authority and empathy (as we discussed at the very start of the book), that made Clinton one of the most compelling communicators in American political history. And it was this slogan that reminded Clinton of this foundational Logos of his campaign. People will realize this eventually.

But I believe that even this drastically, dramatically effective slogan was a step behind the truth, reflecting only the second most compelling focus possible, not the most powerful. I believe that this internal slogan, to a particularly perceptive observer, may imply – and only imply – the truth about the most compelling focus possible, to which the economy is only second best (or, as some might say, first loser). What is that truth? What would have surpassed "it's the economy, stupid" in its efficacy as a reminder to stay on message – and as a focus for the message?

What would a more compelling internal slogan have been?

This: "it's peop*le*, stupid." Why is the economy important? *Because it impacts people.* The economy is not inherently impactful; it is only impactful because it massively impacts people. So, I close this section, the final one in this book, with this slogan.

**IT'S PEOPLE, STUPID**

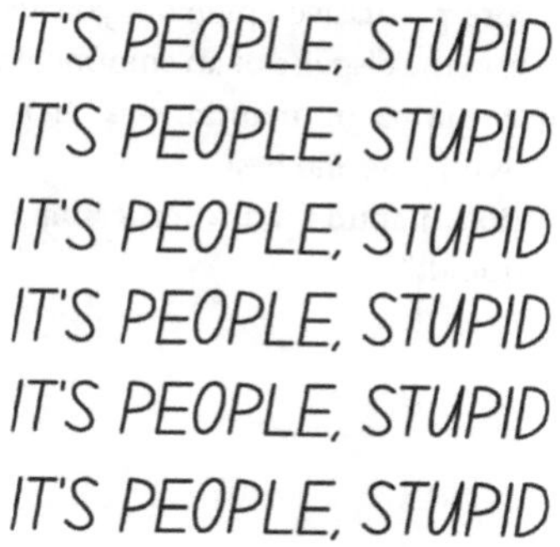

*IT'S PEOPLE, STUPID*

*IT'S PEOPLE, STUPID*

*IT'S PEOPLE, STUPID*

*IT'S PEOPLE, STUPID*

*IT'S PEOPLE, STUPID*

*IT'S PEOPLE, STUPID*

FIGURE 145: It's people, stupid.

**YOU COMPLETED STEP FIVE OF FIVE**

FIGURE 146: In this chapter, you learned how to complete the fifth step: back the entire process with a powerful motive.

...............................Chapter Summary...............................

- Align your interests to the interests of your audience. If they are not the same, find a way to connect them.
- Resonate emotionally by presenting emotionally resonating stories with emotional paralanguage.
- Speak about subjects and consequences salient, intense, and stable to your audience.
- Embed the core persuasive epiphany you seek to inspire in your audience in the disguise of an emotional story.
- Bill Clinton's campaign mantra was "it's the economy, stupid." This is only second best.
- The best possible mantra for any leadership endeavor is this: "it's people, stupid."

## KEY INSIGHT:

# It's People, Stupid.

## THE FIVE-STEP FRAMEWORK (PART FIVE)

| 1 | Controlling Attention |
|---|---|
| 1.1 | Portray Empathy |
| 1.2 | Portray Authority |
| 1.3 | Set High Expectations |
| 1.4 | Expose a Hidden Miracle |
| 1.5 | Speak to the People's Pain |
| 1.6 | Build a Coalition |
| 1.7 | Make Bold Promises |
| 1.8 | Divulge the Brutal Truth |
| 1.9 | Shift the Perspective |
| 1.10 | Speak to Broken Justice Problems |
| 1.11 | Present a Moment of Decision |
| 1.12 | Tell a Story |
| 1.13 | Future Significance Today |
| 1.14 | Difficulty-Confidence Matrix |
| 1.15 | Declaratory Cascade |
| 1.16 | Superabundance |
| 1.17 | Speak to the Moment |
| 2 | Directing Attention to a Definite Purpose |
| 2.1 | Achieve Singularity |
| 2.2 | Organize a Pyramid |
| 2.3 | Create Visualization |

**KEY INSIGHT:**

# It's People…

## SOMETHING WAS MISSING. THIS IS IT.

D ECEMBER OF 2021, I COMPLETED the new editions of the 15 books in the Speak for Success collection, after months of work, and many 16-hour-long writing marathons. The collection is over 1,000,000 words long and includes over 1,700 handcrafted diagrams. It is *the* complete communication encyclopedia. But instead of feeling relieved and excited, I felt uneasy and anxious. Why? Well, I know now. After writing over 1,000,000 words on communication across 15 books, it slowly dawned on me that I had missed the most important set of ideas about good communication. What does it *really* mean to be a good speaker? This is my answer.

### THERE ARE THREE DIMENSIONS OF SUCCESS

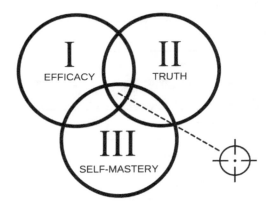

FIGURE I: A good speaker is not only rhetorically effective. They speak the truth, and they are students of self-mastery who experience peace, calm, and deep equanimity as they speak. These three domains are mutually reinforcing.

### THE THREE AXES, IN DIFFERENT WORDS

| Domain One | Domain Two | Domain Three |
|---|---|---|
| Efficacy | Truth | Self-Mastery |
| Rhetoric | Research | Inner-Peace |
| Master of Words | Seeker of Truth | Captain of Your Soul |
| Aristotle's "Pathos" | Aristotle's "Logos" | Aristotle's "Ethos" |
| Impact | Insight | Integrity |
| Presence of Power | Proper Perspective | Power of Presence |
| Inter-Subjective | Objective | Subjective |
| Competency | Credibility | Character |
| External-Internal | External | Internal |
| Verbal Mastery | Subject Mastery | Mental Mastery |
| Behavioral | Cognitive | Emotional |

I realized I left out much about truth and self-mastery, focusing instead on the first domain. On page 27, the practical guide is devoted to domain I. On page 34, the ethical guide is devoted to domain II. We will shortly turn to domain III with an internal guide.

## WHAT A GOOD SPEAKER LOOKS LIKE

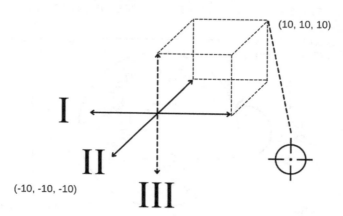

FIGURE II: We can conceptualize the three domains of success as an (X, Y, Z) coordinate plane, with each axis extending between -10 and 10. Your job is to become a (10, 10, 10). A (-10, 10, 10) speaks the truth and has attained self-mastery, but is deeply ineffective. A (10, -10, 10), speaks brilliantly and is at peace, but is somehow severely misleading others. A (10, 10, -10), speaks the truth well, but lives in an extremely negative inner state.

## THE THREE AXES VIEWED DIFFERENTLY

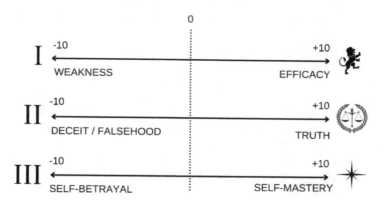

FIGURE III: We can also untangle the dimensions of improvement from representation as a coordinate plane, and instead lay them out flat, as spectrums of progress. A (+10, -10, -10) is a true monster, eloquent but evil. A (10, 10, 10) is a Martin Luther King. A more realistic example is (4, -3, 0): This person is moderately persuasive, bends truth a little too much for comfort (but not horribly), and is mildly anxious about speaking but far from falling apart. Every speaker exists at some point along these axes.

## THE EXTERNAL MASTERY PROCESS IS INTERNAL TOO

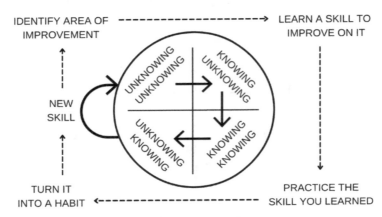

FIGURE IV: The same process presented earlier as a way to achieve rhetorical mastery will also help you achieve self-mastery. Just replace the word "skill" with "thought" or "thought-pattern," and the same cyclical method works.

# THE POWER OF LANGUAGE

Language has generative power. This is why many creation stories include language as a primordial agent playing a crucial role in crafting reality. "In the beginning was the Word, and the Word was with God (John 1:1)."

Every problem we face has a story written about its future, whether explicit or implicit, conscious or subconscious. Generative language can rewrite a story that leads downward, turning it into one that aims us toward heaven, and then it can inspire us to realize this story. It can remove the cloud of ignorance from noble possibilities.

And this is good. You can orient your own future upward. That's certainly good for you. You can orient the future upward for yourself and for your family. That's better. And for your friends. That's better. And for your organization, your community, your city, and your country. That's better still. And for your enemies, and for people yet unborn; for all people, at all times, from now until the end of time.

And it doesn't get better than that.

Sound daunting? It is. It is the burden of human life. It is also the mechanism of moral progress. But start wherever you can, wherever you are. Start by acing your upcoming presentation.

But above all, remember this: all progress begins with truth.

Convey truth beautifully. And know thyself, so you can guard against your own proclivity for malevolence, and so you can strive toward self-mastery. Without self-mastery, it's hard, if not nearly impossible, to do the first part; to convey truth beautifully.

Truth, so you do good, not bad; impact, so people believe you; and self-mastery, as an essential precondition for truth and impact. Imagine what the world would be like if everyone were a triple-ten on our three axes. Imagine what good, what beauty, what bliss would define our existence. Imagine what good, what beauty, what bliss *could* define our existence, here and now.

It's up to you.

# THE INNER GAME OF SPEAKING

R EFER BACK TO THIS INTERNAL GUIDE as needed. These humble suggestions have helped me deliver high-stakes speeches with inner peace, calm, and equanimity. They are foundational, and the most important words I ever put to paper. I hope these ideas help you as much as they helped me.

**MASTER BOTH GAMES.** Seek to master the outer game, but also the inner game. The self-mastery game comes before the word-mastery game, and even the world-mastery game. In fact, if you treat *any* game as a way to further your self-mastery, setting this as your "game above all games," you can never lose.

**ADOPT THREE FOUNDATIONS.** Humility: "The other people here probably know something I don't. They could probably teach me something. I could be overlooking something. I could be wrong. They have something to contribute" Passion: "Conveying truth accurately and convincingly is one of the most important things I'll ever do." Objectivity: "If I'm wrong, I change course. I am open to reason. I want to *be* right; I don't just want to seem right or convince others I am."

**STRIVE FOR THESE SUPERLATIVES.** Be the kindest, most compassionate, most honest, most attentive, most well-researched, and most confident in the room. Be the one who cares most, who most seeks to uplift others, who is most prepared, and who is most thoughtful about the reason and logic and evidence behind the claims.

**START BY CULTIVATING THE HIGHEST VIRTUES IN YOURSELF:** love for your audience, love for truth, humility, a deep and abiding desire to make the world a better place, the desire to both be heard and to hear, and the desire to both teach and learn. You will find peace, purpose, clarity, confidence, and persuasive power.

**START BY AVOIDING THESE TEMPTING MOTIVES.** Avoid the desire to "outsmart" people, to overwhelm and dominate with your rhetorical strength, to embarrass your detractors, to win on the basis of cleverness alone, and to use words to attain power for its own sake. Don't set personal victory as your goal. Strive to achieve a victory for truth. And if you discover you are wrong, change course.

**LISTEN TO YOURSELF TALK.** (Peterson, 2018). See if what you are saying makes you feel stronger, physically, or weaker. If it makes you feel weaker, stop saying it. Reformulate your speech until you feel the ground under you solidifying.

**SPEAK FROM A PLACE OF LOVE.** It beats speaking from a desire to dominate. Our motivation and purpose in persuasion must be love. It's ethical *and* effective.

**LOVE YOUR ENEMIES (OR HAVE NONE).** If people stand against you, do not inflame the situation with resentment or anger. It does no good, least of all for you.

**AVOID THESE CORRUPTING EMOTIONS:** resistance, resentment, and anger. Against them, set acceptance, forgiveness, and love for all, even your enemies.

**PLACE YOUR ATTENTION HERE, NOW.** Be where you are. Attend to the moment. Forget the past. Forget the future. Nothing is more important than this.

**FOCUS ON YOURSELF, BUT NOW.** Speaking gurus will tell you to focus solely on your audience. Yes, that works. But so does focusing on yourself, as long as you focus on yourself *now*. Let this focus root you in the present. Don't pursue a mental commentary on what you see. Instead, just watch. Here. Now. No judgment.

**ACCEPT YOUR FEAR.** Everyone fears something. If you fear speaking, don't fear your fear of speaking too. Don't reprimand yourself for it. Accept it. Embrace it, even. Courage isn't action without fear. Courage is action despite fear.

**STARE DOWN YOUR FEAR.** To diminish your fear, stare at the object of your fear (and the fear itself), the way a boxer faces off with his opponent before the fight. Hold it in your mind, signaling to your own psyche that you can face your fear.

**CHIP AWAY AT YOUR FEAR.** The path out of fear is to take small, voluntary steps toward what you fear. Gradual exposure dissolves fear as rain carves stone.

**LET THE OUTER SHAPE THE INNER.** Your thoughts impact your actions. But your actions also impact your thoughts. To control fear, seek to manage its outward manifestations, and your calm exterior will shape your interior accordingly.

**KNOW THAT EGO IS THE ENEMY.** Ego is a black storm cloud blocking the warm sunlight of your true self. Ego is the creation of a false self that masquerades as your true self and demands gratification (which often manifests as the destruction of something good). The allure of arrogance is the siren-song of every good speaker. With it comes pride and the pursuit of power; a placing of the outer game before the inner. Don't fall for the empty promises of ego-gratification. Humility is power.

**DON'T IDENTIFY WITH YOUR POSITIONS.** Don't turn your positions into your psychological possessions. Don't imbue them with a sense of self.

**NOTICE TOXIC AVATARS.** When person A speaks to person B, they often craft a false idea, a false avatar, of both themselves and their interlocuter: A1 and B1. So does person B: B2 and A2. The resulting communication is a dance of false avatars; A1, B1, B2, and A2 communicate, but not person A and B. A false idea of one's self speaks to a false idea of someone else, who then does the same. This may be why George Bernard Shaw said "the greatest problem in communication is the illusion that it has been accomplished." How do you avoid this dance of false avatars? This conversation between concepts but not people?

Be present. Don't prematurely judge. Let go of your *sense* of self, for just a moment, so your real self can shine forth.

**MINE THE RICHES OF YOUR MIND.** Look for what you need within yourself; your strengths and virtues. But also acknowledge and make peace with your own capacity for malevolence. Don't zealously assume the purity of your own motives.

**RISE ABOVE YOUR MIND.** The ability to think critically, reason, self-analyze, and self-criticize is far more important than being able to communicate, write, and speak. Introspect before you extrospect. Do not identify as your mind, but as the awareness eternally watching your mind. Do not be in your mind, but above it.

**CLEAR THE FOG FROM YOUR PSYCHE.** Know what you believe. Know your failures. Know your successes. Know your weaknesses. Know your strengths. Know what you fear. Know what you seek. Know your mind. Know yourself. Know your capacity for malevolence and evil. Know your capacity for goodness and greatness. Don't hide any part of yourself from yourself. Don't even try.

**KNOW YOUR LOGOS.** In 500 B.C. Heraclitus defined Logos as "that universal principle which animates and rules the world." What is your Logos? Meditate on it. Sit with it. Hold it up to the light, as a jeweler does with a gem, examining all angles.

**KNOW YOUR LIMITS.** The more you delineate and define the actions you consider unethical, the more likely you are to resist when they seem expedient.

**REMEMBER THAT EVERYTHING MATTERS.** There is no insignificant job, duty, role, mission, or speech. Everything matters. Everything seeks to beat back chaos in some way and create order. A laundromat doesn't deal in clean clothes, nor a trash disposal contractor in clean streets. They deal in order. In civilization. In human dignity. Don't ignore the reservoir of meaning and mattering upon which you stand. And remember that it is there, no matter where you stand.

**GIVE THE GIFT OF MEANING.** The greatest gift you can give to an audience is the gift of meaning; the knowledge that they matter, that they are irreplaceable.

**HONOR YOUR INHERITANCE.** You are the heir to thousands of years of human moralizing. Our world is shaped by the words of long-dead philosophers, and the gifts they gave us: gems of wisdom, which strengthen us against the dread and chaos of the world. We stand atop the pillars of 4,000 years of myth and meaning. Our arguments and moral compasses are not like planks of driftwood in a raging sea, but branches nourished by an inestimably old tree. Don't forget it.

**BE THE PERSON YOU WANT TO BE SEEN AS.** How do you want to be seen by your audience? How can you actually be that way, rather than just seeming to be?

**HAVE TRUE ETHOS.** Ethos is the audience's perception that the speaker has their best interests at heart. It's your job to make sure this perception is accurate.

**CHANGE PLACES WITH YOUR AUDIENCE.** Put yourself in their shoes, and then be the speaker you would want to listen to, the speaker worthy of your trust.

**ACT AS THOUGH THE WHOLE WORLD IS WATCHING.** Or as though a newspaper will publish a record of your actions. Or as though you're writing your autobiography with every action, every word, and even every thought. (You are).

ACT WITH AUDACIOUS HONOR. As did John McCain when he called Obama, his political opponent, "a decent family man, [and] citizen, that I just happen to have disagreements with." As did Socrates and Galileo when they refused to betray truth.

ADOPT A MECHANIC'S MENTALITY. Face your challenges the way a mechanic faces a broken engine; not drowning in emotion, but with objectivity and clarity. Identify the problem. Analyze the problem. Determine the solution. Execute the solution. If it works, celebrate. If not, repeat the cycle. This is true for both your inner and outer worlds: your fear of speaking, for example, is a specific problem with a specific fix, as are your destructive external rhetorical habits.

APPLY THE MASTERY PROCESS INTERNALLY. The four-step mastery process is not only for mastering your rhetoric, but also for striving toward internal mastery.

MARSHAL YOURSELF ALONG THE THREE AXES. To marshal means to place in proper rank or position – as in marshaling the troops – and to bring together and order in the most effective way. It is a sort of preparation. It begins with taking complete stock of what is available. Then, you order it. So, marshal yourself along three axes: the rhetorical axis (your points, arguments, rhetorical techniques, key phrases, etc.), the internal axis (your peace of mind, your internal principles, your mental climate, etc.), and the truth axis (your research, your facts, your logic, etc.).

PRACTICE ONE PUNCH 10,000 TIMES. As the martial arts adage says, "I fear not the man who practiced 10,000 punches once, but the man who practiced one punch 10,000 times." So it is with speaking skills and rhetorical techniques.

MULTIPLY YOUR PREPARATION BY TEN. Do you need to read a manuscript ten times to memorize it? Aim to read it 100 times. Do you need to research for one hour to grasp the subject of your speech? Aim to research for ten.

REMEMBER THE HIGHEST PRINCIPLE OF COMMUNICATION: the connection between speaker and audience – here, now – in this moment, in this place.

KNOW THERE'S NO SUCH THING AS A "SPEECH." All good communication is just conversation, with varying degrees of formality heaped on top. It's all just connection between consciousnesses. Every "difference" is merely superficial.

SEE YOURSELF IN OTHERS. What are you, truly? Rene Descartes came close to an answer in 1637, when he said "cogito, ego sum," I think therefore I am. The answer this seems to suggest is that your thoughts are most truly you. But your thoughts (and your character) change all the time. Something that never changes, arguably even during deep sleep, is awareness. Awareness is also the precondition for thought. A computer performs operations on information, but we don't say the computer "thinks." Why? Because it lacks awareness. So, I believe what makes you "you," most fundamentally, is your awareness, your consciousness. And if you accept this claim – which is by no means a mystical or religious one – then you must also see yourself in others. Because while the contents of everyone's consciousness is different, the consciousness itself is identical. How could it be otherwise?

FORGIVE. Yourself. Your mistakes. Your detractors. The past. The future. All.

FREE YOUR MIND. Many of the most challenging obstacles we face are thoughts living in our own minds. Identify these thoughts, and treat them like weeds in a garden. Restore the pristine poise of your mind, and return to equanimity.

**LET.** Let what has been be and what will be be. Most importantly, let what is be what is. Work to do what good you can do, and accept the outcome.

**FLOW.** Wikipedia defines a flow state as such: "a flow state, also known colloquially as being in the zone, is the mental state in which a person performing some activity is fully immersed in a feeling of energized focus, full involvement, and enjoyment in the process of the activity. In essence, flow is characterized by the complete absorption in what one does, and a resulting transformation in one's sense of time." Speaking in a flow state transports you and your audience outside of space and time. When I entered deep flow states during my speeches and debates, audience members would tell me that "it felt like time stopped." It felt that way for me too. Speaking in a flow state is a form of meditation. And it both leads to and results from these guidelines. Adhering to them leads to flow, and flow helps you adhere to them.

**MEDITATE.** Meditation brings your attention to the "here and now." It creates flow. Practice silence meditation, sitting in still silence and focusing on the motions of your mind, but knowing yourself as the entity watching the mind, not the mind itself. Practice aiming meditation, centering your noble aim in your mind, and focusing on the resulting feelings. (Also, speaking in flow is its own meditation).

**EMBARK ON THE GRAND ADVENTURE.** Take a place wherever you are. Develop influence and impact. Improve your status. Take on responsibility. Develop capacity and ability. Do scary things. Dare to leap into a high-stakes speech with no preparation if you must. Dare to trust your instincts. Dare to strive. Dare to lead. Dare to speak the truth freely, no matter how brutal it is. Be bold. Risk failure. Throw out your notes. The greatest human actions – those that capture our hearts and minds – occur on the border between chaos and order, where someone is daring to act and taking a chance when they know they could fall off the tightrope with no net below. Training wheels kill the sense of adventure. Use them if you need to, but only to lose them as soon as you can. Speak from the heart and trust yourself. Put yourself out there. Let people see the gears turning in your mind, let them see you grappling with your message in real time, taking an exploration in the moment. This is not an automaton doing a routine. It's not robotic or mechanical. That's too much order. It's also not unstructured nonsense. That's too much chaos. There is a risk of failure, mitigated not by training wheels, but by preparation. It is not a perfectly practiced routine, but someone pushing themselves just beyond their comfort zone, right at the cutting-edge of what they are capable of. It's not prescriptive. It's not safe either. The possibility that you could falter and fall in real-time calls out the best from you, and is gripping for the audience. It is also a thrilling adventure. Have faith in yourself, faith that you will say the right words when you need to. Don't think ahead, or backward. Simply experience the moment.

**BREAK THE SEVEN LAWS OF WEAKNESS.** If your goal is weakness, follow these rules. Seek to control what you can't control. Seek praise and admiration from others. Bend the truth to achieve your goals. Treat people as instruments in your game. Only commit to outer goals, not inner goals. Seek power for its own sake. Let anger and dissatisfaction fuel you in your pursuits, and pursue them frantically.

FAIL. Losses lead to lessons. Lessons lead to wins. If there's no chance of failure in your present task, you aren't challenging yourself. And if you aren't challenging yourself, you aren't growing. And that's the deepest and most enduring failure.

DON'T BETRAY YOURSELF. To know the truth and not say the truth is to betray the truth and to betray yourself. To know the truth, seek the truth, love the truth, and to speak the truth and speak it well, with poise and precision and power… this is to honor the truth, and to honor yourself. The choice is yours.

FOLLOW YOUR INNER LIGHT. As the Roman emperor and stoic philosopher Marcus Aurelius wrote in his private journal, "If thou findest in human life anything better than justice, truth, temperance, fortitude, and, in a word, anything better than thy own mind's self-satisfaction in the things which it enables thee to do according to right reason, and in the condition that is assigned to thee without thy own choice; if, I say, thou seest anything better than this, turn to it with all thy soul, and enjoy that which thou hast found to be the best. But if nothing appears to be better than [this], give place to nothing else." And as Kant said, treat humans as ends, not means.

JUDGE THEIR JUDGMENT. People *are* thinking of you. They *are* judging you. But what is their judgment to you? Nothing. (Compared to your self-judgment).

BREAK LESSER RULES IN THE NAME OF HIGHER RULES. Our values and moral priorities nest in a hierarchy, where they exist in relation to one another. Some are more important than others. If life compels a tradeoff between two moral principles, as it often does, this means there is a right choice. Let go the lesser of the two.

DON'T AVOID CONFLICT. Necessary conflict avoided is an impending conflict exacerbated. Slay the hydra when it has two heads, not twenty.

SEE THE WHOLE BOARD. Become wise in the ways of the world, and learned in the games of power and privilege people have been playing for tens of thousands of years. See the status-struggles and dominance-shuffling around you. See the chess board. But then opt to play a different game; a more noble game. The game of self-mastery. The game that transcends all other games. The worthiest game.

SERVE SOMETHING. Everyone has a master. Everyone serves something. Freedom is not the absence of service. Freedom is the ability to choose your service. What, to you, is worth serving? With your work and with your words?

TAKE RESPONSIBILITY FOR YOUR RIPPLE EFFECT. If you interact with 1,000 people, and they each interact with 1,000 more who also do the same, you are three degrees away from one billion people. Remember that compassion is contagious.

ONLY SPEAK WHEN YOUR WORDS ARE BETTER THAN SILENCE. And only write when your words are better than a blank page.

KNOW THERE IS THAT WHICH YOU DON'T KNOW YOU DON'T KNOW. Of course, there's that you know you don't know too. Recognize the existence of both of these domains of knowledge, which are inaccessible to you in your present state.

REMEMBER THAT AS WITHIN, SO (IT APPEARS) WITHOUT. If you orient your aim toward goals fueled by emotions like insecurity, jealousy, or vengeance, the world manifests itself as a difficult warzone. If you orient your aim toward goals fueled by emotions like universal compassion and positive ambition, the beneficence of the world manifests itself to you. Your aim and your values alter your perception.

ORIENT YOUR AIM PROPERLY. Actions flow from thought. Actions flow from *motives*. If you orient your aim properly – if you aim at the greatest good for the greatest number, at acting forthrightly and honorably – then this motive will fuel right actions, subconsciously, automatically, and without any forethought.

STOP TRYING TO USE SPEECH TO GET WHAT YOU WANT. Try to articulate what you believe to be true as carefully as possible, and then accept the outcome.

USE THE MOST POWERFUL "RHETORICAL" TACTIC. There is no rhetorical tool more powerful than the overwhelming moral force of the unvarnished truth.

INJECT YOUR EXPERIENCE INTO YOUR SPEECH. Speak of what you know and testify of what you have seen. Attach your philosophizing and persuading and arguing to something real, some story you lived through, something you've seen.

DETACH FROM OUTCOME. As Stoic philosopher Epictetus said: "There is only one way to happiness and that is to cease worrying about things which are beyond the power of our will. Make the best use of what is in your power, and take the rest as it happens. The essence of philosophy is that a man should so live that his happiness shall depend as little as possible on external things. Remember to conduct yourself in life as if at a banquet. As something being passed around comes to you, reach out your hand and take a moderate helping. Does it pass you? Don't stop it. It hasn't yet come? Don't burn in desire for it, but wait until it arrives in front of you."

FOCUS ON WHAT YOU CONTROL. As Epictetus said, "It's not what happens to you, but how you react to it that matters. You may be always victorious if you will never enter into any contest where the issue does not wholly depend upon yourself. Some things are in our control and others not. Things in our control are opinion, pursuit, desire, aversion, and, in a word, whatever are our own actions. Things not in our control are body, property, reputation, command, and, in one word, whatever are not our own actions. Men are disturbed not by things, but by the view which they take of them. God has entrusted me with myself. Do not with that all things will go well with you, but that you will go well with all things." Before a high-stakes speech or event, I always tell myself this: "All I want from this, all I aim at, is to conduct what I control, my thoughts and actions, to the best of my ability. Any external benefit I earn is merely a bonus."

VIEW YOURSELF AS A VESSEL. Conduct yourself as something through which truth, brilliantly articulated, flows into the world; not as a self-serving entity, but a conduit for something higher. Speak not for your glory, but for the glory of good.

Email Peter D. Andrei, the author of the Speak for Success collection
and the President of Speak Truth Well LLC directly.

pandreibusiness@gmail.com

Made in United States
Troutdale, OR
10/18/2023

13799875R00179